City Schools/Suburban Schools

A History of Fiscal Conflict

EDUCATION IN LARGE CITIES SERIES
Alan K. Campbell, *Series Editor*

The Education in Large Cities Series
ALAN K. CAMPBELL, *editor*

City Schools/Suburban Schools

A History of Fiscal Conflict

SEYMOUR SACKS

with DAVID RANNEY *and*
RALPH ANDREW

SYRACUSE UNIVERSITY PRESS 1972

Library of Congress Cataloging in Publication Data

Sacks, Seymour.
   City schools/suburban schools.

   (Education in large cities series, 4)
   Bibliography: p.
   1. Education—U. S.—Finance. 2. Urban schools
—U. S. 3. Suburban schools—U. S. I. Title.
II. Series
LB2825.S25   379'.1'0973   70-39585
ISBN 0-8156-2156-6
ISBN 0-8156-2158-2 (pbk.)

Manufactured in the United States of America

Foreword

Over a decade ago, faculty and graduate students of The Maxwell School of Syracuse University began to study the economics, finance, and governance of public education. Most of the studies produced by their work emerge from two major undertakings, both financed by the Carnegie Corporation.

The first such project, the Economics and Politics of Education, was directed by Jesse V. Burkhead; the Education in Large Cities Study followed. Together these studies have produced to date 15 volumes and numerous articles.

The present volume, the fourth in the Education in Large Cities Series, by Seymour Sacks and his colleagues is the most comprehensive yet published. Its historical perspective offers a most useful framework for analyzing the current fiscal crises of American education, particularly the tangle of difficulties that complicates the provision of educational services in 37 of the largest American cities.

Although the severity and characteristics of the fiscal dilemma vary from state to state and from city to city, underlying commonalities appear. These include such issues as the equity of distribution of resources between city and suburb, the impact of state and federal aid, and the influence of differential assignments of fiscal responsibility between state and local levels of government.

For some years, problems created by these behavioral characteristics of education finance have preoccupied many students, from several disciplines. Today, these issues have moved out of the study, the classroom, and the library and into the political limelight. Courtrooms and legislative chambers alike debate the best way to finance public education.

Legislators faced with mounting taxpayer resistance to increased governmental expenditure and school boards whose constituents have repeatedly voted down school finance proposals are near desperation in their search for new ways to pay for education. Legislative committees and commissions, school board associations and citizens' groups are studying (or hiring others to study) the problem.

Meanwhile the state and federal courts have begun to apply the "equal protection of the laws" test to how we pay for education. Against this principle, the present system has been found wanting by at least four courts. Justice Sullivan's opinion for the 6–1 majority of the prestigious California Supreme Court argues that California's school finance system "invidiously discriminate(s) against the poor [by making] the quality of a child's education a function of the wealth of his parents and neighbors."

A federal district court in Minnesota makes the same argument against that state's system of school finance.

> The issue posed by the children . . . is whether pupils in publicly financed elementary and secondary schools enjoy a right under the equal protection guarantee of the 14th Amendment to have the level of spending for their education unaffected by variations in the taxable wealth of their school district or their parents. This Court concludes that such a right indeed exists and that the principle announced in *Serrano* v. *Priest* is correct. Plainly put, the rule is that the level of spending for a child's education may not be a function of wealth other than the wealth of the state as a whole.

The findings and analyses presented in Professor Sacks' book speak directly to these urgent issues of public policy. By examining the patterns produced by our present system of financing education, their historical roots and underlying determinants, Sacks provides a base for reaching future public policy decisions.

This book, like others in the Education in Large Cities Series, thus employs the techniques and tools of the social scientist to examine issues that bear direct and immediate policy implications. All of this research is motivated by the belief that better public education in America's large cities is one of this country's critical needs. Until this need is met, most other problems bound up in what is called the "urban crisis" will remain unsolved.

The observations and views expressed in these studies are solely the authors' responsibility, but any research effort of this magnitude involves literally hundreds of people. Besides members of the research staff, these include many others whose cooperation was crucial to the project's success. The author's preface to each volume acknowledges particular help toward that volume, but it is necessary to mention here a few individuals and institutions vital to the entire undertaking.

Without the financial support of the Carnegie Corporation of New York, the Large City Education Systems study would not have been possible. Equally crucial was the cooperation of the five city school systems who hosted a representative of the Large City Study for nearly two years. In every case, the personnel of each system fully cooperated and made every effort to assist the Study representatives to carry out their assignments.

November, 1971   ALAN K. CAMPBELL
                        Editor, *Education in Large Cities Series*
                        Dean, Maxwell Graduate School of Citizenship
                        and Public Affairs, Syracuse University

Preface

The fiscal and educational difficulties of large city school systems emerged as particularly vexing national problems during the 1960s. In recognition of these problems, a large literature developed which was the product of many different disciplines. This succeeded an immediately prior body of literature which emphasized the particular problems of the rapidly growing suburban school systems. In each case the emphasis precluded a recognition of the metropolitan nature of the educational problem and the relationship between city and suburban schools, which took the form of conflict and adaptation over a very considerable period. One reflection of this problem has been a whole series of cases involving the busing of children and the financing of schools. In *Bradley* v. *Milliken*, a 1971 case in Detroit, the judge specifically mentioned the problem of crossing numerous school district and even county boundaries to achieve a social end of constitutional merit. Recent rulings in east Texas (1971) and Richmond, Virginia (1972), have included court orders for the merging of rural, suburban, and city school districts to create large metropolitan school districts. It would be difficult to overstate the future impact of such a decision if it withstands further court challenges.

The considerable literature on educational finance has tended to emphasize the problems of the small rural districts and has been limited to consideration of the issues as of a specific point in time. The educational primacy of the city was followed by the educational primacy of the suburb, and the subsequent problems were often overlooked. The historical accident which made the suburban school systems appear to have the same problems as their rural counterparts made for a state policy which was conducive to their primacy. The fiscal positions of the large city school systems were treated in a manner which emphasized special circumstances rather than the common elements. But the problem ran deeper than educational finance and the metropolitan context of education. The isolation and insulation of educational finance from other aspects of public finance tended to obliterate one of the prime concerns of large cities—their local noneducational fiscal requirements. The fundamental changes which have occurred in the last few years are completely consistent with their earlier developments with one exception:

the entrance of the Federal government into the picture. While the policy has by no means been consistent, there have been fiscal consequences which include the targeting of resources on large city school systems, especially in the North.

The conflict between large city school systems and their suburban counterparts continues. The particular role of the states, the metropolitan contexts, and the noneducational requirements have been recognized but their interaction behavior has been ignored. The effect of past history on contemporary patterns of behavior has also been ignored. The forces set in motion many years ago when cities occupied a position of relative affluence and great power have not been reversed, even though the realities no longer conform to that image. This study attempts to bring all these factors to bear in an analysis which focuses on the educational finances of the 37 largest cities and their suburbs.

As is very evident in this study, the analysis depends on the quality of the basic data. Comprehensive comparative data have been very difficult to assemble. As in other studies requiring such data, the basic source has been the Bureau of the Census, particularly its Governments Division. Without the aid and quality of data they provide, comprehensive studies of public finance in the United States would be without foundation. Use has also been made of the data which the Office of Education has assembled over a considerable period of time.

Inasmuch as this study is the product of a larger effort, it is necessary to acknowledge the contribution of my co-authors. Most importantly, Chapter VI, which is devoted to the politics of large city education, and the basic data set was the work of David C. Ranney. Ralph Andrew contributed to the over-all study by his incisive reading of the problems of the large city and suburban school fiscal problems.

Others who contributed to the statistical analysis over the years were Robert Firestine, Douglas Montgomery, and Ronald Webber. John Callahan, Richard Lehne, William Wilken, and Donald Phares contributed to the broader analysis of city/suburban fiscal problems. The Syracuse University Computing Center was most generous in extending time and facilities for the processing of the data on which this study relies so heavily.

A number of colleagues, past and present, aided in the development of this study. These included Jesse Burkhead, Jerry Miner, Roy Bahl, Joel Berke, Harold Pellish, and Donna Shalala.

Dean Alan K. Campbell provided the general direction and specific advice as the Director of the Carnegie study of Large City Education, of which this volume is part. In addition, as an active participant in the drive to apply greater intelligence to the solution of school fiscal problems of both city and suburb, his advice and counsel have been major. Virginia Halsey went far beyond the call of duty in providing final typed copy.

Finally, and not at all least, I would like to thank my wife Barbara, for bearing with me during this very long venture.

November, 1971   SEYMOUR SACKS

Contents

Tables

City Schools/Suburban Schools

A History of Fiscal Conflict

I. Introduction

The most striking facts I have gathered are these:

1. That the people of the United States spend a marvelous amount of money on their public schools, endowing education more lavishly than any other people in the world.

2. They do not spend enough. The salaries to teachers are not sufficient for the service the country desires and should have.

. . . .

One especially notable manifestation of enthusiasm (for education) I found in New York, Boston and other large cities.[1]

Among the largest enterprises in our nation are the local educational systems, both independent and dependent, which provide elementary and secondary education to those attending public schools in New York, Boston, and those "other large cities" already in existence or yet to be born in 1904. The amount expended today, no matter how measured, far exceeds the "marvelous amount of money" noted above. The local school budget for New York City now far exceeds that of the nation as a whole in 1904 and those of all but a small number of major nations of the world for all levels of education both public and private.

Even with such huge expenditures, large cities in the United States have been under continuous attack for not fulfilling their own as well as the nation's educational functions and objectives. These attacks are not new either in form or content, as an enormous volume of "domestic" literature going back to the nineteenth century attests. "They do not spend enough" has also been a continuous theme reflecting the desires and basic tenets of the American educational credo. The attacks now, unlike earlier attacks, clearly reflect the absence of that "notable manifestation of enthusiasm" which characterized large city school systems until World War II. In retrospect, it appears that the large cities certainly provided the most comprehensive and probably the best education in the nation at that time; in fact, there were no major alternatives. Very few

[1] Alfred Moseley, "A British View of American Schools," *The World's Work,* VII, No. 4 (February 1904).

good school systems existed outside of large cities. As we move into the 1970s, suburban alternatives to large city education not only exist but are flourishing. And the now accepted superiority of suburban education has had a ricochet effect on the cost, if not the quality, of large city education.

The development of alternative public elementary and secondary educational systems outside of the large cities is the product of a long-term trend. The economic and educational strength of the large city in the past was used as a basis for improving the positions of the educational systems outside of their borders. The "free," "public," "compulsory," "comprehensive," educational systems of Horace Mann and Henry Barnard were exported beyond the borders of the large cities to the suburbs and rural areas of their states. The economic-educational pendulum has swung to suburbia, but, unfortunately, unlike earlier years, there has been no compensatory state policy to help most of the economically and socially deprived areas now too frequently found in the cities.

While it is not easy to compare the elementary and secondary schools of the large cities with those of the nation as a whole in terms of their historical accomplishments, an attempt to do so is instructive. By international quantitative human resource standards, such as those used in manpower planning, the school systems in the larger cities in the United States would have to be evaluated as incredibly successful. However, as a long list of domestic critics and more recent foreign visitors have indicated, detailed analysis of the qualitative achievement has not been viewed as favorably. And in terms of the goals set, large systems of elementary and secondary education have rarely approximated success.

If comparisons were made on an intranational basis, the large cities would fall between the more affluent suburbs and the less affluent urban and rural areas which comprise most of the area in the United States. Recent literature on large city education has reduced their status even further. Today, unlike the past, it is quite clear that when the opportunity presents itself, both whites and blacks abandon the large city school system in favor of suburban and private alternatives. Relative to the past, the inferior position of the large city school systems in this era of literary overkill is certainly exaggerated, especially if one is aware of the past criticisms of these systems. But the presence of accessible alternatives and the vast expansion of the responsibilities which have been assigned to our public elementary and secondary school systems make these criticisms more telling and appropriate today.[2]

The extension of the educational domain during a period in which

[2] For a very insightful evaluation of large city education at the beginning of the Twentieth Century, see Colin Greer, "Immigrants, Negroes, and the Public Schools," *Urban Review* No. 3 (January 1969), 9–12.

are structural differences within states, but these are minor compared to the interstate differences. The state determines which units of local government, including both independent and dependent agencies, will have direct responsibility for elementary and secondary education—or "Local Schools" in Census terminology. In addition to determining the governmental units involved in educational expenditures, the state in many cases specifies the categories in which the money is to be spent. States have also had prime responsibility for the proliferation of financial obligations in recent years, as a host of nongovernmental agencies using public or comingled public and private monies have provided local schooling at preschool and other levels. Finally, the states have provided the framework as school systems have expanded their earlier educational opportunities, often undertaking the provision of adult basic education and junior or community college education. Difficulties of interpretation arise when the range of education varies between school systems and there is no common denominator.

The problem of state involvement is further complicated by the fact that while public elementary and secondary education is provided by a variety of local educational agencies (except in the case of Hawaii), the financing is carried on by other governmental agencies in addition to the government responsible for the major direct expenditure. This is true whether the local educational agency is fiscally independent or not. In the case of fiscally dependent school systems there are, however, further questions of allocating costs to local schools or to other expenditure categories. This problem also exists when other governmental units make direct expenditures in behalf of local educational agencies. This may be the case of related local governments or of state governments, and in all cases it is the distribution of revenue responsibilities among governments with different tax bases and taxpayers which determines the over-all financial status of local school systems. The crucial question that emerges is whether the distribution of revenue responsibility has varying effects on the level of local school finances, either adding to, reducing, or keeping constant the total volume of funds available for local schools in any given area.

Much more basic than the differences in the assignment of direct responsibility for expenditures between and within states are the differences in state aid and in the state designation of the local property tax base. As in the case of the diffused responsibility for direct expenditures, the central question is whether, and to what extent, state grants-in-aid reduce local effort. The differences in state aid are major, but once again it should be noted that there are important differences within states, and in many cases the major differences involve the large cities as compared to almost all other school systems. The state also prescribes the nature and the extent to which local school districts and other governments can utilize various tax bases. Among these regulations, state control of the use of the property tax base and usage of nonproperty taxes stand out, the former by its presence, the latter by its absence. The property tax provides over 95 percent of local school district tax revenues in the United States.

COTERMINALITY

There are basic differences in the local governmental environments in which school expenditures are made. The school system when it is dependent is usually, but not invariably, coterminous with the government of which it is a part, that is, the boundaries are identical. Occasionally, a dependent school system provides local school services outside of its borders, or another school district or system may provide services within its city area; this latter occurs most often in the case of specialized education. Coterminality not only occurs on the municipal level, but it also occurs on the county level as well. The extent to which systems are coterminous with central city or other boundaries depends on state practices.[5] The differences between city coterminality and county coterminality reflect the extent to which there is a sharing of the benefits and burdens of nonschool finance as well. The question of coterminality is quite central to a proper understanding of the problems of large city school finance.

The existence or absence of coterminality helps make explicit the relationship between school and nonschool finances in the large city area and the relationship between the central cities and their outlying metropolitan areas. At one extreme is what may be called simple coterminality; that is, the school system is of exactly the same territorial extent and services the same total population as the central city or other community. The school system is much more likely to be coterminous if it is dependent than if it is independent. Of all the central cities of metropolitan areas in the United States in 1967, fewer were coterminous (165) than were noncoterminous (344). Among the independent school districts, the ratio was less than one to three (89:324), while in the case of the dependent school systems the ratio of coterminality to noncoterminality was almost four to one (76:20). Dependence and coterminality generally go together, as do independence and noncoterminality.

In addition to simple coterminality, there may be a complex coterminality when more than one school system provides education for a

[5] See *Government Organization,* Vol. I, 1967, *Census of Governments* (Washington, D.C.: Government Printing Office, 1967).

large city. Generally, this takes place when there are school systems with different grade coverages—elementary, secondary, or special schools for vocational education or education for the handicapped—and these school districts are not unified or consolidated. This situation does not generally exist in large cities except in the case of junior or community colleges, which are excluded from consideration in this study. In these cases, more than one school system is involved, and it is necessary to consider them as a group in order to determine the school finances of an individual area. However, there is no problem in determining total school finances of the large city, as is the case when there is an absence of coterminality. Unfortunately, from an analytical point of view, where more than one school system provides education in the central city, there are some financial aspects which are obscured when they are aggregated and dealt with as a simple decision-making area. The existence of a specially circumstanced high-income area or industrial enclave within a city could pose rather difficult problems for the rest of the city which do not exist where there is a single system. These problems emerge when there is more than one district with fiscal decision-making capabilities—which can reflect differences in need and/or resources—providing education in the central city area. These would become important issues in the presence of *de facto* decentralization of large city school systems.

Simple and complex coterminality exist not only for cities but for the counties as well. In this instance, the county provides education for all the jurisdictions within its borders, the central city as well as the outlying areas. Under this circumstance, there is no possibility of having any observed differences in the educational finances of the central city and the remainder of the county in which it is located. This situation exists in only a limited number of cities in Florida included in this study, but it exists in other large city areas which are not under consideration. Hawaii is the only instance of state–school district coterminality, since education is a state function.

The problem of noncoterminality emerges both as an omnipresent data problem and a substantive issue. It is sufficiently widespread in the case of the large cities outside of the Northeast and the specially circumstanced city-county entities, to warrant special comment at this point. The absence of coterminality is usually dealt with analytically by taking the municipal boundaries as the unit of analysis or by taking the principal school system servicing the large city as the unit. When the school system is not coterminous with the city there are difficulties of interpretation if one tries to understand large city behavior, because it is no longer a clearly defined category. Relative to the large city, the first approach is analytically much neater, the second much easier. What is absolutely necessary is a conscious recognition of the approach used and its implication from a large city standpoint.

As in the case of coterminality, there are different kinds of noncoterminality. One relatively simple kind is when a large city school system encompasses the entire city plus some outside area. This is basically the situation in such diverse cases as Los Angeles, Cleveland, and Rochester. In the Los Angeles case, a considerable portion of the school system goes beyond the boundaries of the central city. This is indicated by the size of the school district—711 squares miles, as opposed to 464 square miles for the city. Thus, a comparison with the Los Angeles School District—which covers 23 suburban cities and its surrounding area—would have to be very carefully analyzed and interpreted, for it is quite clear that neither all the expenditures nor all the revenues can be even approximately attributed to the central cities when there is this kind of noncoterminality.

Another kind of noncoterminality involves one or more school districts that are entirely located within the central city area with one or more school districts which are only partly located within the central city area. The number of school districts involved may be very large, especially if the city has undergone recent municipal annexations or there are forces which condone the existence of many small school districts within the central city. The situation in Kansas City and San Antonio—with 17 and 15 school districts, respectively, wholly or in part within the city—represents extremes of this kind of complexity. In a number of cases there are inner city school systems exhibiting the most extreme ethnic and economic problems which are entirely separate local governmental entities from the dominant large city system.

The absence of detailed information makes it very difficult to make comparisons between coterminous and noncoterminous cities, and between each of these cities and their surrounding areas. The absence of coterminality also raises the question as to the best way of dealing with the problems involved. As in many other cases, the answer depends upon the object of the analysis and has no universally appropriate answer. Before attempting to answer the question, it is necessary to know something about the large city itself.

Throughout this study the large city is placed in its metropolitan context. This reflects not only the complex socioeconomic integration characteristic of metropolitan areas, but also reflects the presence or absence of fiscal integration of the large city with its surrounding area. The case of the noncoterminous school district represents a kind of fiscal integration of the central city and outside area, but the allocation problem on the educational side is minor compared to those which emerge in the absence of coterminality of the noneducational portion of the local governmental system. Once again, the question is whether the observed differences are only a matter of appearance or whether there are substantive differences which arise from different structures and which have consequences for school finances. In the case of the city located within a county, the particular problem is one of allocating the financial behavior attributable to the county and any other overlying government to the central city area and, for purposes of comparison, to the outside central city areas. A city located in a county shares in the fiscal costs and fiscal benefits, depending on the assignment of expenditure and revenue responsibility to the county and other overlying governments. The movement of a function from a city to the county—such as a hospital, as was the case in Cleveland and Cuyahoga County—is reflected in a lower city responsibility but a higher county responsibility; insofar as the city has less than 100-percent responsibility, it can reduce its fiscal cost—while of course reducing its benefits defined fiscally. Where a city is not located in a county area—*i.e.,* when it is its own county—it cannot share in overlying fiscal costs or benefits except insofar as a larger government unit (such as the Port of New York Authority) also exists. Where a city is an independent county, it tends to differ from its own surrounding areas, although such cities differ very much among themselves as well. The large central city versions of these city-counties are all recognizable by the fact that they have a concentration of functional responsibilities which distinguish them from other local governments, either other central cities or suburbs, having overlying county governments.

The singling out of coterminous city-county areas is not only a matter of proper designation, but of recognizing and anticipating different fiscal consequences as well. If there is no overlying county government, then there cannot be the kind of cost and revenue sharing that exists in such a situation. Whether this is of net benefit to the large central city is a moot point, as was indicated above. Since all these city-county areas have coterminous school districts, several important questions about the size of the over-all fiscal burdens and benefits are raised, not in terms of governmental structure alone but of the economic and social integration of the metropolitan areas of which they are part. Similar questions emerge in the case of other large cities.

THE DIMENSIONS OF SCHOOL FINANCE

As will be demonstrated in more detail in Chapter II, school finances may be viewed as having two dimensions, the educational and the fiscal. The educational dimension deals with the level, nature, and distribution of educational expenditures. Standing by itself, it tells very little about the total benefit accruing to a community; usually it is measured in terms of the pupil population it is designed to serve.

This particular concept of educational finance—the educational dimension—measures the current expenditures for public elementary and secondary schools only, and primarily the expenditures attributable to full-time pupils. These in turn are divisible into instructional and non-instructional expenditures. The expenditures may be financed by the local school agency or by some other agency. The instructional share of the total will vary, depending not only on its own level but also on the extent to which the noninstructional expenditures are made by the local educational system involved. There are some other expenditures on food services and student-body activities which also enter into the totals for current expenditures.

A measurement problem emerges when more than one government provides the resources for local school expenditures. First, comparisons between school systems are rendered difficult when only part of the expenditure is reported. This problem emerges fairly frequently in the provision of health and transportation services to full-time pupils, where the expenditures may be reported by another government which does not have any educational functions. The principal difficulties are associated with the expenditures included in the fixed-charge category. The differences between systems are most pronounced in the case of expenditures made by the school systems for employees' retirement, and the case where they are made by other governments. Comparisons of per-pupil expenditures which do not recognize the magnitude of the disparities occasioned by the differential expenditure assignment between and within states are very suspect.

The fiscal dimension of school finances deals with the expenditures and revenues in terms which are comparable to other aspects of public finance. Generally speaking, these are in such units as amount per capita, or per unit of income, or in terms of rates—usually property tax rates. The fiscal and education dimensions of school finances are related, but the relationship is not constant. A high level of expenditure per pupil does not indicate very much concerning the local expenditure per capita, nor does it throw much light on the level of taxes or other revenues drawn from local sources. At one time, the fiscal and education dimensions of school finance could have been viewed as virtually interchangeable, although even in the earlier period there were some differences. The fiscal dimension deals with education relative to the entire population of the city, whereas the educational dimension deals only with the population directly benefiting from the expenditure.

The particular fiscal dimensions to be considered reflect the total amount of resources being devoted to local schools. The level of per-capita expenditure not only reflects the expenditure per pupil, but also the fraction of the total resident population attending school in the community involved. Unlike the educational dimension, there is little meaning that can be attached to the per-capita cost of instruction, for example, because its object is left undefined. The absence of such information from Census sources is due to the fact that it is impossible to develop such criteria across other expenditure categories and get meaningful results. Expenditures, when there is more than a single government involved, can be determined by the use of the Census data for the central city area and for the outside area, both in the aggregate and in detail, using classifications of expenditure which are applicable to all parts of the nation. In a dependent school district a problem remains, since only through a detailed analysis and audit can the expenditures be extricated from the larger total. The last expenditure dimension to be considered will be the relationship between educational and noneducational expenditures. This analysis is only possible when there is comprehensive and comparable data for all the local governments involved and the problems raised by overlying and noncoterminous governments are resolved.

The level of expenditures does not indicate anything about the tax burden on the local community. The break in the linkage in the case of education reflects the assignment of educational responsibilities as well as the amount of aid from other local governments, states, and the federal government. The tax burden also reflects the other demands being serviced. This is true when only the property tax is being considered and other taxes being used by local governments are ignored. The problem is further complicated in that there are basic differences between localities where taxes can be "exported" outside the area, and where they can not.[6]

FACTORS DETERMINING LARGE CITY SCHOOL FINANCES

School finances in large cities are meaningful when viewed as part of a broad process of decision-making. Some decisions were made years ago and can be altered only with the greatest of difficulty; other decisions are made by other units of government and only a residual set of decisions is made by the operating units involved. It is not only necessary to know the educational and fiscal patterns, but, much more basic, it is also necessary to determine the reasons for their being. Only with a

[6] See Donald Phares, "The Structure of State-Local Tax Burdens, 1962," unpublished doctoral dissertation, Syracuse University, 1970, for a detailed analysis of the problems of tax exporting.

knowledge of the patterns and the reasons for their existence is it possible to construct meaningful policy alternatives.

Underlying the observed patterns of school finances in large cities are a variety of factors, some of which have been already mentioned but which have not yet been integrated in their total context. In the remainder of the study, the multiple forces impinging on school finances are analyzed in terms of the specific groupings of large cities and large city school districts, which are the objects of our contemporary educational anxiety. Chapter II deals with the large school finances in detail, both in cross section and in historical perspective. Most of the basic data are laid out at this point. The long-term history indicates a shift of the large city from a position of leadership, in the sense of higher expenditures, to that of a reluctant follower. The city, which had led in the expansion of educational opportunities, first in the provision of post-elementary education and then in the quality of its offerings, found itself still in a position of advantage after World War II. This advantage began to disappear as the suburbs grew in economic power and built up more modern educational and noneducational physical plants. And while the educational demands on the city grew, its ability to cope with them became less a function of its own ability and more a function of forces over which it had little or no control.

The major emphasis of Chapter III is on the relationship between the large city and its surrounding metropolitan area. The purpose is to indicate the changing nature of this relationship. The metropolitan context of large city school finances has emerged as one of the most important determinants of the educational and fiscal dimensions of school finances measured in terms of direct and indirect effects. This aspect emerges in both detailed state-wide analyses, such as those carried on in New York and elsewhere, and it is of basic importance in explaining variations in large city school finances between states as well.

While the analysis of the set of interrelationships is left to later chapters, the partial analysis is designed to show the interaction that arises out of the metropolitan context of large city school finances. This involves the structural and substantive fiscal interrelationships (discussed in Chapter II) which assume meaning in the metropolitan context (Chapter III).

A major proposition of Chapter III is that it is not only of interest and consequence to know something of the absolute position of the large city, but that its position assumes meaning in its metropolitan context. Thus, it is noted that while small cities are poor relative to their larger counterparts, they are relatively well-off compared to their surrounding areas. The opposite is true of most large cities. This phenomenon is of exceptional consequence in explaining the difficulties of large city school systems with regard both to their own metropolitan areas and to the rest of the states of which they are part.

The placing of the large city in its metropolitan context also permits a clearer analysis of the noneducational requirements and behavior patterns than is generally available. In particular, it permits a meaningful analysis of the trade-offs between educational and noneducational finances.

Chapter IV deals with the role of state government which, in its broadest context, determines the position of local public elementary and secondary education by establishing basic rules and requirements. Additionally, since it establishes the resource bases from which educational funds are raised, via its control of the property tax, the state also establishes the general local government context of school finances.

The position of the state is not materially reduced if a narrower definition of the role of the state is considered, including the direct behavior of the state. This influence is not necessarily uniform within states, however. In certain cases, the large city school system is treated differentially, and the differential treatment is in many instances historically grounded in the presumed fiscal superiority of the large city school system. This is reflected in lower state aid, greater imposition of responsibilities, or both, and is evident in the case of educational and noneducational local finances. The problem is thus not only one which involves differentiating among states, a relatively simple problem and one which is useful as a first approximation, but also one which involves a further differentiation between the large cities and their suburbs within states.

The general aid patterns are considered in Chapter IV; their quantitative effect on school finances is considered in Chapter VII. The restriction of the analysis to the year 1962 and, to a lesser extent, 1964–65, allows one to leave out the role of the federal government insofar as most of the large cities are concerned.

Chapter V represents a serious but limited attempt to look at the noneducational counterparts of educational finances in the metropolitan context of large cities. The analysis is undertaken both in terms of large city school district bounded areas (school district basis) and in terms of large city municipally bounded areas (city basis). The two approaches are at variance with each other and, since they are drawn from different samples, the results are sometimes difficult to compare. The effects of the trade-offs and spill-overs of noneducational fiscal behavior cannot be ignored, but neither can they be measured very easily. Again there are important differences among states in the assignment of responsibilities for the raising and spending of money on the local government level. It is only in the unusual case that a single government has direct responsibility for all local noneducational expenditures within its geographical area, and there are none which have complete financial responsibility for the raising of revenues. Once again there is variety within as well as between states, with the principal differences existing between the large cities and other local governments in the state. In the case of noneducational expenditure, the most important question is whether the assignment of functional responsibilities has an effect on the level of finances other than that which would be logically attributed to them by their proportionate assignment of revenue and expenditure responsibilities.

In addition to the consideration of the nature and extent of the relationship which exists between noneducational and educational finances in the large city areas, Chapter V also includes a summary of the burgeoning literature on the determinants of noneducational expenditures in cities. The techniques used in Chapter VII will be introduced at this point, both as an explanation of the literature on determinants and as an introduction to the general problem which emerges when the various strands are brought together. It should be noted that, just as the literature on educational finances has tended to ignore the problem of noneducational finance, the literature on noneducational finances has generally tended to ignore the problem raised and associated with educational finances.

Chapter VI turns to the question of the governance of education in large cities and its effects on school finances. Several aspects have been considered in constructing the data, and their specific nature and effects are considered in Chapter VI. Most formal types of analysis have dealt with the consequences of fiscal independence. Like its predecessor analyses in the literature, the question of fiscal independence is initially analyzed in terms of the fiscal behavior of the overlying governments from which it is either independent or dependent.

The particular emphasis of Chapter VII is on bringing together the various strands of the earlier chapters in a single quantitative model. The purpose is to determine the extent to which the various forces, when viewed together, influence the pattern of large city finances as measured in both their educational and fiscal dimensions. The principal tool used to achieve such a goal is that of multivariate analysis, considering the differential effects and interrelationships. An attempt is made to state explicitly the nature of the expected relationships and expected importance of the variables at each stage of the analysis. The particular independent variables to be considered are as follows: income; aid for education; proportion of the population attending school; noneducational expenditures; and the metropolitan context.

In addition to the analysis of the factors influencing the behavior of large city school finances, the factors influencing the behavor of the areas surrounding the large cities are also considered. The purpose of this is to determine, in as quantitative a manner as is possible, the extent to which the factors influencing cities differ from or are similar to the factors influencing behavior patterns of the suburban areas to which they are most integrally related, socioeconomically as well as governmentally. This is done for both large cities and suburbs, using identical models, thus providing a better perspective on large city school finances than can be obtained from one dealing only with cities.

Chapter VIII serves a dual capacity. In it the results of the statistical analysis of Chapter VII are combined with the earlier analyses of Chapters I–VI, as well as presenting the general conclusions of the study.

II. The Nature of Large City School Finances

As has been noted, school finances have two dimensions, the educational and the fiscal. The first dimension of school finances represents an aspect of the expenditure side of the picture; the second measures the amount of public resources devoted to local schools as well as the cost to the jurisdiction making the direct expenditure, and to the overlying governments, including the federal, state, and any intermediary governments which provide revenues in terms of fiscal units.

While the two dimensions are related, the relationships are complex and vary among areas and over time. It is easier to measure the total amount expended for public elementary and secondary education for the entire United States than to do so for an individual state, and, in the same manner, it is easier to measure the state totals than to measure local totals.

In an earlier era of school finance in the United States there was a closer relationship between the two dimensions of school finance than there is today. This was especially true of the individual school districts; where the educational dimension was high, as measured by the expenditure per pupil, the fiscal dimension, as measured by the expenditure per capita, was also high. And, generally speaking, the local tax cost in those areas was high. But even as early as the 1880s there were important interstate differences in state aid which directly affected interstate comparisons of individual local school tax burdens.

The expansion of intergovernmental flows of funds and differential assignment of direct expenditure responsibilities has made it more difficult to determine the precise relationships between the various aspects of school finance. Nevertheless, there are a number of very important conclusions concerning school finances in the large cities relative to the nation as a whole and to the states and metropolitan areas in which they are located.

Rural and suburban school district expenditures are under-reported, relative to the large cities. This is primarily the case where rural and

18

suburban districts' retirement systems are financed by state government and those of large cities are self-financed.

From the development of free public education in the United States in the middle of the nineteenth century until well into the twentieth century, the relative position of the large city was preeminent from both an educational and fiscal point of view. Except for those cities located in the South, the large cities spent considerably more per pupil and more per resident than did the nation as a whole. There was one exception to this generalization; the Southern cities did not do well relative to the nation as a whole. However, they did well relative to their own section of the country. Further, because of their superior economic resources, the large cities could provide a greater amount of resources per pupil to a larger proportion of their population at an equal or lower tax burden to themselves than was the case in the rest of the nation. It should be noted that this was not the way the cities viewed their educational and fiscal problems at the time, but that this was the way their position was appraised by such knowledgeable contemporary observers as Cubberley, Strayer, and Adna Weber,[1] and it is certainly the way it appears from the vantage point of hindsight.

In the last two decades the position of the large central cities has shifted abruptly. At the beginning of the period it was possible for large cities to raise sufficient revenues from their own and state sources to maintain educational parity, with or without superiority, with their outside areas as measured in terms of current expenditures per pupil. During the period covered by the analysis, the levels of per-pupil expenditures are clearly lower in the large central city areas than in their suburban areas.

To understand the educational and fiscal position of the large city school system, it is essential to know its history, not only because it provides a perspective but also because many of these historical factors were incorporated into the political process and have been carried forward into the present.

THE EDUCATIONAL DIMENSION

From an educational point of view, it is not only important to know the total amount spent per pupil or other educationally appropriate unit, but it is also important to know the purposes for which it is spent. Once again it should be pointed out that detailed comparative information of expenditures on local public elementary and secondary schools is limited.

[1] This was especially true of that remarkable analyst of urban growth, Adna F. Weber, in his study *Growth of Cities in the Nineteenth Century* (New York: Columbia University Studies in History, Economics, 2nd Public Law, Vol. XI, 1899).

And ironically, as was implied earlier, it is more limited the closer we get to the operationally responsible unit of government. It is practically impossible to determine the expenditures in behalf of an individual school. As was already noted, educational expenditures are not only made by independent school districts, which are separate governmental units and report accordingly, but they also are made by governments which provide other services as well—that is, by dependent school systems. In the latter case, it is necessary to allocate the expenditures in behalf of local schools. This case involves a degree of arbitrariness as to what a local school expenditure is, and there is considerable variety among states, which can be reconciled in part. For the United States as a whole, this problem is relatively minor; for a state taken as a whole, this is more important; and from an individual school district or area point of view, it is even more important.

Not all expenditures made by local school districts are for educational purposes. There are expenditures for libraries, recreation, and other community purposes which would be considered noneducational expenditures if they were made by a noneducational unit of government. A knowledge of the individual state practices often provides clues to the problem. At times the opposite situation exists, when a noneducational government provides services for the public schools which do not appear in the school budget. Sometimes such expenditures made in behalf of either an independent or dependent school district could not be determined even if made by an overlying government. This is especially important in the case of state government contributions to teacher retirement systems.

These factors are not solely of academic interest; they have a direct bearing on the comparisons of large city and other school finances within and between states. An attempt will be made later in this chapter to indicate the specific nature and quantitative importance of this problem.

As reported by educational and fiscal agencies, local school expenditures are divisible into three broad categories—current expenditures, interest payments, and capital outlays. Expenditures in behalf of debt retirement and short-term interest are excluded; the former because it would involve some double counting, and the latter because it is involved in the borrowing process. However, from a current tax point of view, not only must the current expenditures and interest be financed but the payment of principal must be financed as well. There is thus no necessary equality between the expenditure and revenue sides of the picture; taxes may be relatively high as a result of past borrowing, or they may be low because of current borrowing.

The educational dimension of school finances is ordinarily measured by the current expenditures directly allocable to full-time day schools divided by the number of pupils or other appropriate educational units. The choice of measure depends on the purposes for which they are to be used. However, by starting with the most inclusive measure, that of enrollment, a number of important checks on the data emerge and these in turn show interesting differentials between the large cities and the rest of the nation, whether they be suburban or rural or smaller cities.

Even within the current expenditure category, some of the costs are not as readily identifiable with the current educational process as are others. This has led some observers to consider only instructional expenditures and to exclude other purposes of education. However, insofar as they are related to the fiscal problem, they must be considered in conjunction with each other. And since many of the expenditures for noninstructional purposes are in fact alternatives for instructional expenditures, a knowledge of their nature and effect is essential.

The standard breakdown of current expenditures developed by the Office of Education over time offers the following six major categories:

(1) Administration
(2) Instruction
(3) Plant Operation
(4) Plant Maintenance
(5) Fixed Charges
(6) Other School Services[2]

From a comparative point of view, two particular categories, (5) and (6), raise the most vexatious problems. The "Fixed Charges" category represents the most rapidly growing sector of education for which information is available, growing from 0.9 percent of the total in 1919–20 to 6.5 percent of all expenditures in 1965–66. Since this category shows a clear differentially greater burden on the large city schools as compared to other schools, it will be considered in detail later.

Recent developments have indicated that many of the traditional differences between expenditures in behalf of current full-time pupils in elementary and secondary schools and the expenditures which appear in the "Other School Services" category must now be more carefully evaluated than was done in prior years. Expenditures on prekindergarten enrichment programs such as Head Start provide difficult analytical problems. In the past, this category could be dismissed—in part because it was so small—but recent policy changes and the extension of public

[2] Prior to 1955–56 some of the items included under "Other School Services" were listed under "Auxiliary Services," a more comprehensive classification than the "Other School Services" classification in that it included community services.

monies to nonpublic schools have raised some serious analytical as well as policy problems. Thus, the amount of transportation and textbooks provided to private and parochial schools cannot be adequately evaluated except on an individual case-study basis, regardless of whether or not the school district is independent. On a quantitative basis, the problem was still relatively minor as late as 1964–65 but, once again, it might have been important for individual cities and their surrounding areas.

Variations in the range of instruction and variations in educational offerings within given ranges, which were implicit in the previous discussion, pose additional problems. Again, these range the large cities against other school districts within their states and in other states. Because some suburban districts are now so large, they are often able to provide offerings similar or superior to those of the large cities. There are, however, some significant differences to be noted later.

A public school system may provide educational offerings from a prekindergarten level through two or more years of college, or it may provide only a segment of that range of education. While most large central cities provide K-to-12-year range of education, this is not invariably the case even in those instances when such a range is permissible or urged by state law. In some parts of the country, including the large cities, public education may effectively begin at the first grade. While this is partly taken into account in some weighted averages used in computing the educational units, something is left out if the range of education is not taken into account as well.

Historically, the large city offered a greater range of education by providing high school, whereas its surrounding area usually had only elementary school facilities. The large city school system provided not only a greater range than schools elsewhere but also, within any given range of education, a wide variety of offerings and curricula. Because they were the leaders in education, the cities initiated a variety of costly programs which were more often than not excluded from the educational offerings of other school districts. These came to include some of the most costly of all programs—those for the special education of the mentally and physically handicapped, vocational education, and a broad variety of curricula on the high school level.

The problem of summing all the educational expenditures made in behalf of public school systems, whether they are independent or dependent, is integrally related to the measure of the school load. Total or aggregate expenditures provide no guide in making intercity or intrametropolitan comparisons. Further, even if a "correct" unit can be agreed upon, there is no guarantee that such information will be available.

While the only data uniformly and comprehensively available as between and within states are those for enrollment, other measures have been used to great advantage and some of these measures will be utilized in the historical analysis which follows. The choice of the unit of analysis is not an academic matter because the relationships between the various measures are not fixed, and they show important differences between the large cities, their suburbs, and the rest of the nation. Individual state policy shows great variety in the choice of unit with important consequences on the amount of state aid received by the large cities. As Charles Benson and others have shown so carefully,[3] Ellwood P. Cubberley, in his first work, devoted a considerable portion of his analysis to this precise problem as it affected the large cities and rural areas. Because of the relationship of this analysis to state aid, Cubberley's historically significant contribution will be considered in Chapter IV, but it should be noted that the problem can be considered with a fiscal emphasis, such as Cubberley conceived it, or in educational terms with fiscal consequences as it is being considered at this point.

Some of the more relevant educational questions which emerge are:

(1) Should the unit of analysis be in terms of the pupil or some other educational measure such as the classroom unit?

(2) If the pupil unit measure is chosen, should it be based on enrollment, membership, or attendance?

(3) Should all units be weighted equally regardless of the level of education?

Because of these and other questions, a number of alternative measures of current expenditures have been developed in theory, only a limited number of which are available in practice. Among the most commonly used and important of these measures are the current expenditure per:

(1) Enrolled pupil;

(2) Pupil in average daily membership;

(3) Pupil in average daily attendance;

(4) Pupil in weighted average daily membership;

(5) Pupil in weighted average daily attendance;

(6) Classroom unit;

(7) Teacher unit;

(8) School-age child;

(9) High school graduate.

Each of these measures has its proponents, purposes, and availability; singly, no one is completely adequate. However, each brings out certain aspects of large city behavior which were and are important.

---

[3] Charles S. Benson, *The Economics of Public Education* (Boston: Houghton Mifflin, 1961), 195–201.

The most comprehensive pupil data, and the only data available for a national or metropolitan analysis of large city behavior, are the enrollment data. While not as sophisticated as the average daily attendance or average daily membership data in either their weighted or unweighted forms, they are more readily available and have a more substantive connection to the problem today than they had at an earlier era. Also, the enrollment data are less subject to state and local vagaries than are other data.

As noted earlier, the educational dimension of school finances has been dealt with for a much longer period than has generally been appreciated. The Office of Education has not only produced the national data with which we are now so familiar but, almost from its very beginning in the early 1870s, it reported state and local educational data, including large city educational expenditures both by enrollment and average daily attendance as well as some of the fiscal data to be noted below. The Governments Division of the Census Bureau also produced remarkably detailed data on education in large cities at the turn of the twentieth century. But it is only for the years 1957, 1962, and 1964–65 that it has been possible to place the educational dimension of large city school systems in their metropolitan contexts on a common basis throughout the nation, and, in addition, to make the educational dimension consistent with the fiscal dimensions of school finances.

FISCAL DIMENSIONS

The fiscal dimension of education involves the sources and uses of public funds for education. In open systems involving intergovernmental flow of funds, there is no necessary relationship between the locally available resources and expenditures. From a fiscal standpoint, it is necessary to determine appropriate common measures in the same way as it was necessary to find standardized units for the educational dimension. The more or less traditional measure which preserves comparability as between different purposes for which public expenditures are made is, of course, the per-capita measure. Unfortunately, however, given the absence of school districts coterminous with other expenditure jurisdictions, it is difficult to determine the population of the school districts, and it is even more difficult to determine the expenditure within a given municipal area. While both of these approaches—the large city and the large city school district areas—are used in this study, it should be noted that they involved enormous effort and yet leave many fiscal problems unanswered.

If the problem of educational finances in large cities could be isolated from other local fiscal considerations, it would be much simpler to deal with. Analytically, though, this is far less meaningful than an approach which recognizes the interconnections between these two classes of local finances. Ultimately, the choice of the data was decided on this basis. While the Governments Division of the Census Bureau does not provide the expenditure data in the same detail as do the Office of Education and the National Education Association, it does provide the only fiscally comparable data which reflect the process by which funds are allocated to local schools in both independent and dependent school systems.

Expenditures are financed from a variety of revenue sources in addition to direct expenditures by governments of which they are part. Direct expenditures and indirect expenditure in the form of grants-in-aid or shared taxes are made by other governments. Indeed, a considerable part of the contemporary problem of school finance is a reflection of this last aspect of fiscal federalism, namely that, in addition to local sources, there is an intergovernmental flow of funds which directly and indirectly influences local fiscal behavior with respect to education. And there is considerable variation between and within states in the amount of aid received by the large cities relative to the rest of the state, particularly relative to their own outside areas.

The problem is additionally complicated for all areas by the fact that aid is received in behalf of other functions which have a direct or indirect bearing on the level of resources devoted to local public elementary and secondary education. It should also be noted that while a considerable part of school aid is designed for current purposes, state aid may be explicitly designed or used indirectly to influence the amount of capital outlay or debt charges. In fact, state aid is generally designed to reduce or equalize local tax burdens.

The existence of the intergovernmental flow of funds means that for any individual area, such as the large city or an individual suburb, there is no necessary relationship between the level of total expenditure and taxation. There is direct evidence as to the level of taxation for individual localities, but such information is not directly available in any truly comprehensive and comparable fashion except for the indirect evidence for the years 1957 and 1962. Detailed educational aid data are not available for 1964–65, hence the primary emphasis of this study is on the year 1962.

In contradistinction to national totals, and to a lesser extent to state totals, there are clear differences in the level of accessible sources to local governments, including school districts. In a closed national system, and to a lesser extent in the state system, it is possible to assume that such a measure as the gross national product, or national income, or personal income in the case of the states, represents a measure of the availability of resources for the financing of education as well as for other services.[4] This is not true for the individual local area such as the large city, for not only are there legal limitations on the accessible tax bases but there are major interstate differences between the property tax bases used by the schools and other governments. As a result, the principal local tax base—the property tax—shows great variation in its relation to income and other comparable measures, both between and within states, with important consequences for local school finance.

One of the great developments of the twentieth century has been the emergence of the interdependent system which we call metropolitanism. While the interdependence already existed on an economic and social level, in the earlier period it did not exist to the same extent in the case of public finance. In essence, this now means that local areas, particularly the large cities, respond not only to the educational demands made on them by their own residents in the light of their own resources, but that the demands reflect the fiscal behavior of other governments. The accessibility to, and availability of, resources in the large cities increasingly reflect forces outside their control.

The usual fiscal measures describing this interdependence are phrased in terms of resident population (per capitas), rates of taxation (per units of "equalized valuation"), or as a proportion of income. Given the absence of coterminous school districts, it is not directly possible to determine population, let alone such characteristics as income. The available tax-base information is not directly comparable as between states or, more often than not, within states. Further, unlike school enrollment data, which are available for every year, it is difficult to determine the population between censuses where the school district is not coterminous with the large city. Even where it is coterminous, it is difficult to determine populations on a uniform basis in noncensus years. Problems of coterminality and population estimates do not exist in the case of state-wide totals, which are accordingly easier to interpret but not directly relevant to the large city problems.

A consistent treatment of school districts, whether they are analyzed on the basis of the large city school districts or the school districts providing local school services in large cities, should lead to only modest differences in the results on the educational side, but they have a major effect on the noneducational side. If all aspects of educational finance in large cities—especially in its fiscal dimensions—could be isolated from other local fiscal requirements, the analytical problem would indeed be much easier. But one of the most important aspects of large city educational finances involves its relationship to local noneducational expendi-

---

4 See Advisory Commission on Intergovernmental Relations, *Measures of State and Local Fiscal Capacity and Tax Effort* (Washington, 1962) for a discussion of the difficulties in establishing measures of fiscal capacity on a state-wide basis.

tures and taxes. It is quite clear that if large cities devoted the same proportion of their total resources to education as do their surrounding areas, major inroads could be made in the current educational inadequacies of large city educational systems. If they spent the same amount per capita as the suburban areas they would also make a major improvement, but the cost would be far greater than that which could be financed out of local, or even out of state and local, resources.

Turning to the particular large cities which are the object of this study, a varying pattern emerges. In a few cases such as New York City, Boston, and Baltimore, not only does the municipality provide all the local government services in a given area, but its school district is an integral part of the municipal government. The school district boundaries in Philadelphia, St. Louis, and San Francisco, while coterminous with all other governments providing local government services in the area, are fiscally independent of the municipalities. Even in these coterminous areas, there are differences in the allocation of functional responsibilities between the states and their localities which affect the proportions devoted to education, which in turn have varying effects on the fiscal dimensions of education.

Where there are overlying levels of local government which are not coterminous with the large city boundaries, the problem becomes much more difficult. Following a general practice of many years' standing, the expenditures and taxes of the noncoterminous county and other governments are allocated on the basis of population, and checked against the direct information available in the case of taxes. Further, detailed intracensal population estimates have been made, with limitations to be noted later. When the county expenditures are allocated to the large city and its outlying areas on a per-capita basis, it is assumed that this does not represent the benefits (or burdens) on the constituent areas, but rather represents the fiscal totals allocable to them. In the case of taxes, they also appear to represent the burden on the areas. Even in the case of school districts coterminous with their overlying governments, the educational proportion of total local fiscal activity is fundamentally influenced by the expenditures and revenue responsibilities assigned to the local governments by the state. Thus, if local governments are assigned responsibility for public welfare, the educational proportion of total expenditures is accordingly reduced as compared to a city located in a state where public welfare is a state function. And since public welfare is not 100-percent aided by the state and federal governments, this leads to a higher local tax level. The major question becomes one of whether the local level of education is altered by the presence of these noneducational responsibilities.

This situation was not the case at the turn of the century, when the state and local sectors could be viewed as independent. The functions fell into more or less neat and exclusive categories, with the role of most of the state governments extremely limited. State aid certainly did exist, but its role was relatively restricted as compared to the period after World War II.

The three aspects just discussed—school coterminality, dependence, and city-county coterminality—are summarized in Table 1 for the large city school systems considered in this study. The school systems servicing all cities over 300,000 are included in the major sample with the exception of the special cases of Honolulu and Washington, D.C., where there are no overlying governments, and Fort Worth, Phoenix, and San Antonio, where data problems were insurmountable. In a minor sample, the large cities of the 37 major metropolitan areas of the nation are considered on a city rather than school system area basis.

The Educational Dimension in Historical Perspective

As part of the general study of policies and policy-making in large city educational systems, special attention was paid to the five large cities singled out for detailed analysis: New York, Chicago, Boston, San Francisco, and Atlanta. Their long-term behavior clearly demonstrates the evolution of the large central city from a position of ability to deal with unparalleled large numbers of students and more expensive education per pupil than the rest of the nation, to a position of relative inferiority except in special cases. And, as will be demonstrated later, even in the case where a city such as New York was able to maintain or improve its relative standing nationally, it found its standing reduced within New York State and, more particularly, within its own metropolitan area.

The long-term trend indicates that in terms of expenditures per pupil the latter part of the nineteenth and early part of the twentieth centuries represented the high points of educational expenditures of large cities relative to the rest of the nation. The national totals were influenced by the small rural school districts with their very numerous one-room schools and their extensive use of payments in kind.

Those cities (Table 2) which ranked first, second, fifth, and ninth among all 168 cities with populations over 30,000, ranked appropriately high in expenditures relative to all cities as well as to the United States average. This is indicated by their ranking in the year 1900.

Only Atlanta was relatively low, but it was a moderately sized Southern city of less than 90,000 at the turn of the century. It should be noted that the only cities to rank higher than the other large cities in

TABLE 1

Large City School Systems, 1967

Large City School System	Coter-minous	Fiscally Dependent	City-County
East			
Baltimore, Md.	Y	Y	Y
Boston, Mass.	Y	Y	Y*
Newark, N.J.	Y	Y	N
Buffalo, N.Y.	Y	Y	N
New York, N.Y.	Y	Y	Y
Rochester, N.Y.	Y*	Y	N
Philadelphia, Pa.	Y	N	Y
Pittsburgh, Pa.	Y	N	N
Midwest			
Chicago, Ill.	Y	N	N
Indianapolis, Ind.	Y*	N	N
Detroit, Mich.	Y	N	N
Minneapolis, Minn.	Y	N	N
St. Paul, Minn.	Y	Y	N
Kansas City, Mo.	N—	N	N
St. Louis, Mo.	Y	N	Y
Omaha, Neb.	N+	N	N
Cincinnati, Ohio	N+	N	N
Cleveland, Ohio	Y*	N	N
Columbus, Ohio	N	N	N
Toledo, Ohio	N	N	N
Milwaukee, Wis.	Y	N	N
South			
Birmingham, Ala.	Y	N	N
Atlanta, Ga.	Y*	N	N
Louisville, Ky.	N—	N	N
New Orleans, La.	Y	N	Y
Oklahoma City, Okla.	N—	N	N
Memphis, Tenn.	Y	Y	N
Dallas, Tex.	N+	N	N
Houston, Tex.	N—	N	N
Norfolk, Va.	Y	Y	Y
West			
Long Beach, Calif.	N+	N	N
Los Angeles, Calif.	N+	N	N
San Diego, Calif.	N—	N	N
San Francisco, Calif.	Y	N	Y
Denver, Colo.	Y	N	Y
Portland, Ore.	N	N	N
Seattle, Wash.	Y*	N	N

* Nominal difference.
+ School system larger than central city.
— School system smaller than central city.

TABLE 2

POPULATION, PER-PUPIL, AND PER-CAPITA EDUCATIONAL
EXPENDITURES, CITY RANK, 1901

City	Population Rank	Rank in Per-Pupil Current Expenditure	Rank in Per-Capita Expenditure
New York, N.Y.	1	4	6
Chicago, Ill.	2	20	25
Boston, Mass.	5	7	4
San Francisco, Calif.	9	6	27
Atlanta, Ga.	43	128	122

SOURCE: Edward C. Elliot, *Some Fiscal Aspects of Public Education.*

per-pupil expenditures were a select group located in New England and mining communities such as Denver and Butte, Montana. The data for this period are consistent with the image of the large city as being able not only to maintain high expenditures per pupil but high expenditures per capita as well, and these were financed primarily out of local revenues.

From 1912 to the beginning of World War II, large cities showed remarkable stability and in some cases a slight relative improvement. This is rather striking in view of the emergence of the high-income suburb with its attendant high expenditures on education, and the improvement of the small rural school district in response to the changes in state aid formulas. In spite of both of these developments, the large city school systems were able to maintain their position (Table 3).

The picture for 1910 is confirmed by more general statistics of current expenditure per pupil in regular ADA for all cities and for the United States as a whole (Table 4).

The much higher level of expenditures per pupil is brought out not only for the large cities relative to the nation as a whole, but also relative to the smaller cities as well. It should be noted that the contrast would be larger if the U.S. average were computed without the large cities.

The picture for 1910 also contains detail on the major source of expenditure change for the next three decades, *i.e.,* the much higher cost of secondary education relative to elementary education. As shown in Table 5, during the period 1910 to 1940 enrollment in public high schools increased from 5.1 percent of total enrollment to 26.0 percent in 1940, a level which was not attained again until 1964. These changes

TABLE 3

CURRENT EXPENDITURES PER PUPIL IN ADA AS A PERCENTAGE
OF UNITED STATES AVERAGE, SELECTED YEARS, 1880–1971*

Fiscal Year	Boston %	Chicago %	San Francisco %	Atlanta %	New York %	U.S. Average $
1880–81	226.2	153.3	212.3	NA	209.4	12.00
1909–10	160.6	159.0	144.5	NA	163.4	27.85
1921–22	155.1	133.5	141.2	77.3	154.0	66.98
1929–30	154.4	138.7	149.1	NA	163.8	86.70
1938–39	158.4	141.5	168.9	NA	183.2	88.09
1941–42	153.5	145.2	179.9	93.2	184.9	98.31
1949–50	134.6	129.6	143.6	66.6	144.5	208.83
1959–60	108.5	110.8	121.4	71.2	137.9	375.14
1965–66	103.2	94.0	120.4	77.7	150.9	532.00
1970–71	120.7	131.0	131.4	NA	170.2	858.00

* NA: Not available (used throughout).
SOURCE: U.S. Department of Health, Education, and Welfare, Office of Education.

TABLE 4

CITY SIZE AND CURRENT EXPENDITURE PER PUPIL IN ADA, 1910

| City Size, 1910 | Schools | | |
	All, $	Elementary, $	Secondary, $
Over 300,000	41.41	36.89	87.34
100,000–300,000	35.31	29.43	70.44
50,000–100,000	35.04	30.60	68.99
30,000–50,000	32.82	28.24	57.64
U.S. average	27.85	NA	NA

SOURCE: U.S. Bureau of the Census, *Financial Statistics of Cities, 1910.*

are also reflected in the use in per-pupil expenditures between 1928 and 1938 (Table 6).

In the early 1900s, the emergence of the very wealthy suburb with higher expenditures than the large central city was clearly indicative of what would happen later. During this period Oak Park and Winnetka (outside Chicago), Newton (outside Boston), Scarsdale, Great Neck, Westport, and Montclair (outside New York), and Shaker Heights (outside Cleveland) already spent more money per capita on education than their large city counterparts, and certainly evidenced considerable in-

TABLE 5

GENERAL CHARACTERISTICS OF PUBLIC SCHOOL ENROLLMENTS, 1870–1968

School Year End	Total Population Enrolled in Public Schools, %	Population 5–17 Enrolled in Public Schools, %	Total Enrollment in High School and Postgraduate (Public), %	Enrollment in Public High School and P.G. of Total H.S. and Postgraduate Enrollment, %	Average No. Days Attended Per Enrolled Pupil
1870	17.3	57.0	1.2	NA	78.4
1880	19.7	65.5	1.1	NA	81.4
1890	20.2	68.6	1.6	56.4	86.3
1900	20.4	71.9	3.3	74.2	99.0
1910	19.7	74.2	5.1	82.0	113.0
1920	20.6	78.3	10.2	88.0	121.2
1930	21.1	81.7	17.1	91.6	143.0
1940	19.4	84.4	26.0	93.2	151.7
1950	16.9	83.2	22.7	89.2	157.9
1960	20.1	82.2	23.5	88.9	160.2
1964	21.8	85.5	27.1	88.9	163.2
1968	22.6	86.7	27.9	89.7	163.2

SOURCE: *Statistics of State School Systems; 1967–68* (Washington, D.C.: U.S. Department of Health, Education and Welfare, Office of Education)

TABLE 6

CITY SIZE AND CURRENT EXPENDITURES PER PUPIL IN ADA, SELECTED YEARS, 1928–38

City Size	Number	1928 $	1930 $	1932 $	1934 $	1936 $	1938 $
Over 100,000	40	114.20	119.17	114.86	91.56	106.82	119.50
30,000– 99,999	212	94.97	98.03	97.02	83.25	89.67	98.72
10,000– 29,999	643	82.82	85.75	82.04	69.10	75.82	84.69
2,500– 9,999	1,944	75.69	79.02	73.09	63.55	68.10	75.23
U.S. Average		(87.00)	(90.00)	(83.00)	(65.00)	(75.00)	(86.00)

SOURCE: U.S. Department of Health, Education, and Welfare, Office of Education.

novative capacity. During this period, however, the central cities were more than able to hold their own compared to their metropolitan areas.

While the position of many central cities improved slightly during the World War II period, the general drift was downward. By 1950 the relative position of each city had clearly declined from its prewar position; and with the exception of Atlanta, which was low to start with, the decline continued during the next decade. To the wealthy suburbs were now added many newer suburbs which, even though not as affluent as some of their older neighbors, became educationally more attractive than the central city because they made education their principal public activity. Cities which had spent considerably more than the national average now spent at or near the average. Since the middle 1950s the large central cities have moved in a variety of directions relative to the national norms, but they all have moved approximately in the same downward direction relative to their own state and metropolitan contexts.

The movement in the direction of the national norm reflected the fact that the pace of change was no longer determined by the large cities—not by the five for which there is the long-term information, nor by the much larger sample which moved in the same direction and which indicated the basic behavior of the large city in general. The improvement of suburban and much of rural education was the result of a massive school-consolidation movement fostered by increased state aid and improved means of transportation—the school bus for pupils and the auto for teachers—as well as by improved economic status. Occasionally, where a large city was able to maintain its national position, it was often as a result of state aid policy and the effect of local action. But in general, the large city was not able to maintain its relative position in the metropolitan area.

The decline in the relative position of large central cities has been most evident in the past decade and a half. As late as 1957, central cities' spending was on a par with that of their surrounding areas. Based on a comprehensive cross-sectional sample and using central city and surrounding areas, the figures for 1957 were $309 and $303 per enrolled pupil, as compared to an estimated national norm of $277 per enrolled pupil in 1957.

Five years later, using the large city school districts of this study as the basis, the central cities spent $360 and their outlying areas $432, with a national norm of $376. By 1965 the gap had widened even more significantly. The central city average was $449 and that for surrounding areas was $577, with a computed national norm of $455 for the year.

The decided shift in favor of the outlying areas of the large cities occurred in a context in which, as will be shown in Chapter IV, there is a statistical bias in favor of larger current expenditures reported by the central cities. That is, the gap is actually larger than that observed.

The very rapid decline relative to the outlying communities after 1957 is perhaps the outstanding contemporary feature of large city school finances. It reflects not only the long-term increase in resources being allocated to education per pupil outside the central cities, but also the powerful interaction of the large cities and their suburbs. These have increased the costs of large city schools without improving their relative educational positions.

Our understanding of the position of the large city is enhanced by looking at the historical evolution of public education in the United States. The long-term trends for total enrollment show great stability over time. As shown in Table 5, from 1880 to 1968 the proportion of the total population enrolled in public schools remained virtually constant at around 20 percent. Part of the constancy of the figures is due to the increase in nonpublic school enrollment, particularly in the large cities, but it is also due to an upward change in the age distribution of the population of the United States (Table 7). And it should also be noted

TABLE 7

Enrollment in Elementary and Secondary Schools,
Selected Years, 1870–1970 (in millions)

School Year End	Total Enroll- ment	Public School Enrollment			Nonpublic School Enrollment
		Total	K–8	9–12	
1870	NA	7.6	7.5	0.1	NA
1880	NA	9.9	9.8	0.1	NA
1890	14.5	12.7	12.5	0.2	1.7
1900	16.9	15.5	14.0	0.5	1.4
1910	19.4	17.8	16.9	0.9	1.6
1920	23.3	21.6	19.4	2.2	1.7
1930	28.3	25.7	21.3	4.4	2.7
1940	28.0	25.4	18.8	6.6	2.6
1950	28.5	25.1	19.4	5.7	3.4
1960	42.0	36.1	27.6	8.5	5.7
1962	45.0	38.3	28.7	9.6	6.6
1964	47.8	41.0	29.9	11.1	6.8
1968	51.1	45.1	32.5	12.6	6.0*
1970	51.6	46.0	33.3	13.3	5.6

* Estimate.
Source: *Digest of Educational Statistics,* 1970 edition, National Center for Educational Statisics.

that enrollment did not mean attendance, for in the same period the average number of days attended per enrolled pupil almost doubled.

However, up to 1940 the proportion of the population between the ages of 5 and 17 enrolled in public schools increased dramatically, with the large cities leading the advance. The proportion of the 5–17 age group enrolled in public schools increased from 57.0 percent in 1870 to 71.9 percent in 1900; it then increased to 84.4 percent by 1940. Since 1940 the aggregate figure has remained quite constant, varying only between 82 and 87 percent. This proportion showed, however, and continues to show—depending on the age mix and the availability of nonpublic education—great variation between areas. From the point of view of expenditure, there is a major difference between nominal enrollment and actual attendance, particularly between unexpected or undesirable nonattendance and that which is expected as a result of climatic and health reasons.

While large cities clearly had a greater number and proportion of children attending nonpublic schools in the early period as well as at present, they had a much greater proportion of the population attending public schools than did the nation as a whole. However, if distinction between expected and unexpected nonattendance is accepted, then the central cities must have "budgeted" for longer terms than did the nation as a whole. In recent years the problem has been altered due to higher incomes, larger school districts, improved means of transportation, and the decline in the demand for school-age labor in agriculture. These changes have shifted the advantage to the outlying areas, particularly to the middle- and high-income suburbs. The effective length of the school term no longer shows an advantage in favor of the large cities as it did in earlier periods.

The position of the large cities has also been influenced by the changing quantity or range of education. In 1890 only a miniscule proportion of total enrollment was in high school and postgraduate education. High school education was less extensive and far more concentrated in the private sphere than was elementary education. In the initial surge of high school education there was a shift from private to public schools, which were located primarily in the large cities. The small size of the noncity school district and the unavailability of adequate transportation facilities guaranteed such a concentration of high school education in the large cities except in the most unusual circumstances.

It was the changing mix of large central city education, with a very considerable high school component, that probably maintained the relative position of the large city. The year 1940 probably represented the situation most dramatically as 26.0 percent of all pupils in the nation, and probably a large proportion in large city areas, were enrolled in public high schools and postgraduate courses. Thereafter, as the census data have indicated, the proportion attending high school moved definitely in favor of the areas outside the central city.

Especially striking was the fact that the relative position of the large city school systems remained as high as it was in the 1910–40 period in view of what Raymond Callahan has called "the cult of efficiency."[5] This involved the application of methods derived from industry to reduce central city education costs, methods that were not as applicable in local schools as in manufacturing. The stability of expenditures per pupil during the period 1930–40 is surprising considering the vast expansion of more costly high school education. This stability was a result of the use of a variety of cost-saving temporary expedients.

The period immediately after World War II was extraordinary. On a decennial basis, the proportion of the total population enrolled in public schools in 1950 was at an all-time recorded low—16.9 percent of the population. This was due to the low birth rate in the depression period, not to any basic reduction in the proportion of the school-age population (ages 5–17) attending public schools. At this time cities had a favorable age mix, as well as their school plant and teaching staffs, compared to the outside central city areas. The problems were focused on the suburban areas, especially the new growth areas, which were confronted with huge demands for building and expanding educational facilities as well as in the recruitment of staff. The central city, with its very low proportion of population attending school and its already built-up educational plant, could provide as good an education as the outlying areas at a lower per-capita total cost. The central cities appeared to be in a healthy fiscal position. They still were able to provide a range of educational opportunities which could not be matched elsewhere. The period from 1957 to 1965 represented the shift from the still-dominant city to the city as an unwilling laggard.

The suburban problem in 1957 was to provide facilities for an ever larger group of children attending their public schools. The schools were still characterized by a much younger age group than elsewhere. By 1962 the picture had changed in both the central city and suburb.

By 1964 the new facilities, except for the peripheral growing areas, were basically completed. Inadequate temporary facilities of the early and middle 1950s were replaced by much more modern facilities designed to keep class size down. As a result of the enormous growth in

[5] Raymond Callahan, *Education and the Cult of Efficiency* (Chicago: University of Chicago Press, 1962).

high school enrollment in the suburbs, by 1964 a greater proportion of those enrolled in public schools attended high schools than in any previous year. With few exceptions, the new suburb could and did provide the full range of education by 1964–65. In the meantime, the position of the central city was altered for, in spite of a decline in population, the number of pupils enrolled in large city public school systems began to increase (Table 14). The facilities which had been in use for a long time were found to be either inadequate or improperly located (Table 13). Cities found themselves confronted with new and unparalleled educational demands in a period of relative, if not absolute, decline within their borders and economic growth outside their borders.

What was clearly evident was the emergence of the state and metropolitan context now so essential in the evaluation of both the educational and fiscal dimensions of large city school finances. Whereas the state context could place a large city school district high or low relative to the national norm, the metropolitan context established its particular level within a state. Detailed intrastate analysis for Ohio and New York for the period from 1940 to the present, and more recent data for other states, indicates this to be the case. This is due to what may be called the demonstration and labor-market effects of the suburban districts on large city school finances. The current situation represents a reversal of the former relationship between cities and suburbs. In previous periods the central cities established the educational norms for themselves and for their surrounding areas, and if there was any labor market–demonstration effect in the earlier period, it moved outward from the city. This is an important concept which attempts to put in a single phrase the salary interactions that exist within a metropolitan area, as well as the extent to which pupil-teacher ratios of one district influence the surrounding districts. (In effect, school systems are also playing the "Keep up with the Joneses" game.) This is one of the basic arguments for metropolitanization.

The relative financial position of the large city school system is thus, from an educational perspective, far worse than it was prior to World War II and the early postwar years. From a historical perspective, the long-term economic and educational advantages enjoyed by large cities relative to the rest of the nation no longer exists.

FISCAL DIMENSIONS IN HISTORICAL PERSPECTIVE

The recent decline in the relative position of the central city as to the amount of resources provided per pupil understates the much more fundamental changes which have occurred in the fiscal position of education in the large city. At the turn of the century the large cities spent approximately the same proportion on education as they do today; whereas then they spent as much as or more than the nation as a whole, today they spend a smaller amount. At the turn of the century the large cities sent a greater proportion of their population to public schools and, in the period immediately afterwards to approximately the year 1940, a greater proportion to high schools. The limited proportion of the budget which they devoted to education did not restrict the city to lower levels of fiscal activity than was the case for the rest of the nation.

The relative decline in the position of the large cities reflected both a relative decline in the demand for education and an even greater relative decline in the resource base which could be devoted to education. The particular forces responsible for these developments will be considered in the succeeding chapters; in this chapter the over-all historical picture will be shown.

As shown in Table 8, there is stability in the proportion of local expenditures devoted to public education in large cities. In 1913 the average was 29.7 percent of all local expenditures for the large cities of this study, and a national figure of 29.5 percent. In 1962 the comparable figure for the same large city school districts was 32.4 percent, as against a national norm of 44.8 percent and 54.8 percent in their suburbs. Not only was there stability in the aggregate, but there was stability on an individual-city-areas basis as well. Changes in functional responsibilities of local governments over time have had a modest effect on the proportion of total local expenditures devoted to education by these large cities. The stability of these relationships raises the question of other demands on educational expenditures, a question which will be answered in Chapters V and VII.

Even in the period since 1957, the changes in the national patterns are not so much a reflection of the proportions devoted to education as they are of the much greater weight of the outlying areas in the national totals. The great problem involves a shift away from the central city to the surrounding areas.

While the precise data reflect the methodologies used, the general picture is very clear-cut for both central cities and their outlying areas. It is the emergence and widening of a gap which had emerged earlier between the two areas in amounts per resident of resources devoted to education in a period of enormous change.

The general picture for per-capita total educational expenditures is summarized in Table 9, using Census Bureau definitions for the period 1957–67.

The use of 1960 population figures tends to reduce the level of expenditures in the central cities and increase the level for the areas out-

TABLE 8
Local School Current Expenditures as a Percentage of Total Current Expenditures (School District Basis)

	1913 CC*, %	1962 CC†, %	1962 OCC†, %
East			
Baltimore, Md.	19.1	31.5	58.7
Boston, Mass.	24.6	18.8	49.1
Newark, N.J.	37.4	34.4	43.1
Buffalo, N.Y.	27.9	26.1	50.3
New York, N.Y.	27.1	24.7	53.8
Rochester, N.Y.	26.1	31.3	51.6
Philadelphia, Pa.	22.4	29.5	57.8
Pittsburgh, Pa.	33.4	28.1	57.5
Midwest			
Chicago, Ill.	28.0	28.6	51.9
Indianapolis, Ind.	33.8	40.8	63.7
Detroit, Mich.	24.1	38.1	53.9
Minneapolis, Minn.	36.7	30.2	55.7
St. Paul, Minn.	26.6	26.9	55.7
Kansas City, Mo.	32.1	38.0	57.5
St. Louis, Mo.	25.3	32.7	57.0
Omaha, Nebr.	31.0	33.0	20.1
Cincinnati, Ohio	30.3	29.4	51.8
Cleveland, Ohio	34.5	30.2	48.4
Columbus, Ohio	34.2	37.7	50.4
Toledo, Ohio	38.3	32.1	67.4
Milwaukee, Wis.	29.4	23.5	47.0
South			
Birmingham, Ala.	32.0	37.5	54.4
Atlanta, Ga.	23.8	33.9	52.2
Louisville, Ky.	24.4	26.4	75.7
New Orleans, La.	24.9	29.6	33.8
Oklahoma City, Okla.	41.3	46.1	64.4
Memphis, Tenn.	26.8	34.6	48.7
Dallas, Tex.	29.9	38.5	50.9
Houston, Tex.	27.0	39.8	73.2
Norfolk, Va.	29.7	23.1	65.0
West			
Long Beach, Calif.	48.7	34.2	45.6
Los Angeles, Calif.	46.9	37.5	45.6
San Diego, Calif.	31.4	34.5	52.2
San Francisco, Calif.	12.7	22.4	49.1
Denver, Colo.	29.4	35.1	57.6
Portland, Ore.	43.5	45.4	60.8
Seattle, Wash.	31.5	38.4	50.3
Average (unweighted)	29.7	32.4	54.8
National weighted average	29.5	44.8	

* City area basis. † School district basis.
Source: U.S. Bureau of the Census.

TABLE 9

PER-CAPITA TOTAL EDUCATIONAL EXPENDITURES

	Unweighted Averages		U.S. Weighted Average
Year	Central City, $	Outside Central City, $	Local Schools, $
1957	(A) 58.05* (B) 61.36*	(A) 85.83* (B) 80.19*	68.62
1962	(C) 68.69	(C) 126.17	95.46
1964–65	(D) 98.75*	(D) 140.78*	113.04
1966–67	(E) 137.00	(E) 178.00	139.44

* Includes a nominal amount of higher educational expenditures.

(A) = Sample of all metropolitan areas using 1957 population, municipal basis.

(B) = Sample of large metropolitan areas using 1957 estimates of population, municipal basis.

(C) = Sample of all large city school districts using 1960 population. School district basis (major sample of this study).

(D) = Same sample as (B), using 1964 estimates of population.

(E) = Same sample as (B), using 1966 estimates of population.

side the central cities for the year 1962 because of the decline in large city population and increase in population outside the central cities between these two years. Using the same sample, (B) and (D), the absolute gap for the outside central city areas increased between 1957 and 1967, but the proportionate increase was the same for both areas. Since the bias in the reporting of the expenditures is clearly in favor of the large cities, the actual size of the gap for local school expenditures was probably larger than that indicated.

The weighted average figures for 1967 are probably the most indicative of the current picture, for even with the inclusion of higher education and the built-in bias in favor of large central city expenditures, the large central cities in the United States spent $100.23 per capita on the average; their peripheral areas spent $146.62. The remainder of the nation—including the rural South—spent in excess of the central city figure, with local educational expenditures of $106.92.[6]

The level of expenditures on education is not only influenced by local and metropolitan conditions but is clearly influenced by state requirements and by state aid as well. Data for educational aid are difficult to

---

[6] *Fiscal Balance in the American Federal System*, Vol. 2, *Metropolitan Fiscal Disparities*, ACIR, p. 86.

ferret out, especially when the recipient government performs other functions in addition to education. Such an analysis was undertaken for both 1957 and 1962, the only years for which both comprehensive and comparable data were available. The picture which emerges is clear-cut; in both years educational aid was decidedly higher in the outside areas than in the central cities. In 1962 the central cities received $20.72 per capita and the outlying areas received $37.61 (Table 38), slightly less than twice as much. These figures not only reflect the higher enrollment ratios of the outlying areas, but they also reflect higher per-pupil aid. There are definite differences in aid levels by state, and these differences get absolutely and, generally, proportionately higher the greater the amount of state aid.

The specific problems associated with state aid will be dealt with at length in Chapters IV and VII, but their nature may be noted in lesser detail at this point. The principal question is whether aid stimulates, merely shifts responsibility from locality to state, or reduces the total amount of resources devoted to education. The problem can be re-phrased in terms of the local contribution to education. This can be done if educational aid is subtracted from total educational expenditures. Then one can approximate the local contribution to education by using the nonaided educational expenditures as a proxy for taxes or, in its own right, as an important variable. An alternative approach would be to analyze the taxes which reflect not only expenditures but also debt service charges for education. Such information is not available in detail, however, for the schools which are dependent and, when they are re-ported, there is no guarantee as to the uniformity with which they are reported. It is also very difficult to determine the levels outside the large central cities, not only because dependent school districts report school taxes in a haphazard manner, but because comprehensive data are often not available because of the enormous costs involved in compilation.

Insofar as these expenditures are being financed out of borrowed funds, as in the case of capital outlay, the expenditures are not reflected in local tax burdens at the time they are made but are reflected in the taxes levied at the time of repayment of principal and interest. As a result, contrary to usual assumptions, the current expenditures of an individual local school system may not be closely related to its tax burden. In the case of many suburban areas this was, and still is in some instances, un-doubtedly the case, but they clearly had a much more modern educa-tional plant to show for their high levels of taxation. In the case of the large cities, there is often a large debt-service component in their total local tax levy, but it is quite often associated with the noneducational portion of the local tax picture. Data for both 1957 and 1962 indicate

TABLE 10

CURRENT EDUCATIONAL EXPENDITURES PER STUDENT, TOTAL EDUCATIONAL AND NONEDUCATIONAL
EXPENDITURES PER CAPITA, AND TOTAL NONAIDED EDUCATIONAL EXPENDITURES
PER CAPITA (TAX PROXY) FOR CENTRAL CITY AND OUTSIDE CENTRAL CITY AREAS, 1962
(School District Basis)

	Current Education Expenditures Per Pupil, $		Total Education Expenditures Per Capita, $		Total Non-aided Education Expenditures Per Capita, $		Total Noneducation Expenditures Per Capita, $	
	CC	OCC	CC	OCC	CC	OCC	CC	OCC
East								
Baltimore, Md.	366	421	81	113	61	81	206	93
Boston, Mass.	385	465	50	101	44	93	227	142
Newark, N.J.	496	522	94	112	78	100	201	151
Buffalo, N.Y.	447	561	59	137	34	78	161	184
New York, N.Y.	537	684	77	194	47	128	276	161
Rochester, N.Y.	580	573	79	159	55	92	185	185
Philadelphia, Pa.–N.J.	398	493	55	106	37	81	154	84
Pittsburgh, Pa.	368	451	51	96	40	62	117	91
Midwest								
Chicago, Ill.	408	474	66	113	51	92	177	137
Indianapolis, Ind.	353	468	70	144	51	116	116	116
Detroit, Mich.	462	434	94	128	70	89	163	131
Minneapolis, Minn.	414	442	61	157	42	110	155	146
St. Paul, Minn.	416	442	58	157	40	110	143	146

City							
Kansas City, Mo.–Kans.	409	351	75	157	54	126	95	108
St. Louis, Mo.–Ill.	387	434	55	101	37	76	145	76
Omaha, Neb.–Iowa	283	395	49	137	44	126	128	101
Cincinnati, Ohio–Ky.–Ind.	373	398	63	118	55	95	171	151
Cleveland, Ohio	371	459	65	114	58	101	156	141
Columbus, Ohio	327	332	61	98	52	70	130	130
Toledo, Ohio	379	512	80	161	72	113	129	120
Milwaukee, Wis.	378	469	65	125	52	113	220	190
South								
Birmingham, Ala.	194	224	50	61	18	24	75	75
Atlanta, Ga.	273	288	57	90	36	51	147	121
Louisville, Ky.–Ind.	301	478	43	134	25	106	97	77
New Orleans, La.	272	233	42	67	13	28	131	98
Oklahoma City, Okla.	269	292	67	84	44	70	76	66
Memphis, Tenn.–Ark.	228	246	49	97	27	64	131	132
Dallas, Tex.	302	325	74	100	47	62	114	99
Houston, Tex.	290	450	64	144	32	92	116	116
Norfolk, Va.	265	289	47	88	30	59	347	72
West								
Long Beach, Calif.	426	555	86	132	50	72	180	199
Los Angeles, Calif.	437	555	101	132	50	72	204	199
San Diego, Calif.	414	539	105	156	68	82	168	168
San Francisco, Calif.	468	546	69	132	45	74	240	182
Denver, Colo.	418	381	81	151	67	116	164	94
Portland, Ore.–Wash.	422	480	79	149	58	96	111	105
Seattle, Wash.	410	416	89	138	47	59	153	121

SOURCE: U.S. Bureau of the Census, *Census of Governments, 1962.*

that the nonaided school expenditures are, on the average, closely related to total local school taxes in both central cities and peripheral areas.

The last dimension of school finance to be analyzed in historical perspective has been called the "municipal overburden," *i.e.,* the level of noneducational fiscal activity. While the problem has been dealt with implicitly, when the educational proportion of local finances was considered (as in Table 8), it emerges more importantly when viewed as an independent phenomenon.

Central city areas have specialized in noneducational expenditures in proportion as well as in amount, as shown in Table 10, the basic analysis table, which summarizes all the aspects of educational finance considered in this study. The former was clearly evidenced when it was noted that the educational expenditure averaged 32.4 percent in the central cities and 54.8 percent in the outlying areas (Table 8). From 1957 to 1964–65, using the only consistent available sample of large cities and their surrounding areas, the total increase in expenditures in both areas was almost identical on a per-capita basis, but the distribution of increases was quite different. Of the $118-increase in central city expenditures, $80 was devoted to noneducational purposes and only $38 to an increase in educational expenditure (including local higher education expenditure). The outlying area had an increase of $107 per capita, some $60 of which was for educational purposes and only $47 for noneducational purposes.[7] This situation has existed for a very considerable period of time.

SUMMARY

School finance has two primary dimensions—educational and fiscal. The former has a long tradition drawn from the various studies of educational finance; the latter principally has been considered as an aspect of finance. The relationship between these two aspects of school finance is extremely complex, especially when they involve the large cities in their metropolitan contexts. The relationship has been made increasingly even more complex as the flow of intergovernmental aid has increased in volume.

The position of the large cities has been preeminent historically from both an educational and fiscal point of view. Thus, large cities were able to spend more money for education than the rest of the country and perhaps, more relevantly, than their state and metropolitan areas. They were able to do this until almost the middle of the 1950s. Detailed analyses of large city educational finances indicate that the costs covered by these cities are higher than those in their surrounding areas, due to

[7] *Ibid.,* pp. 103–105.

greater assignment of responsibilities and to historically determined factors. Recent developments in educational finance have made their analysis much more complex as the range of services provided by school systems has broadened.

The fiscal dimension has been a kind of stepchild of school finances. Where the fiscal dimension has been introduced, it has not been systematically analyzed within the domain of school finance. In part, this is a result of the complexity of educational structure in the broader local fiscal context.

III. The Historical and Metropolitan Context

The financial problems of large city school systems are a reflection not only of their own characteristics and position in the metropolitan areas to which they give their name but also of their own past histories, extending from a time when most of the cities completely dominated their surrounding areas economically. While the contemporary emphasis is on the metropolitan nature of the central city, particularly the relationship between the city and its outside area, other factors—historically derived—continue to influence the fiscal behavior of the city, both for educational and noneducational purposes.

From an educational point of view, the historical development of the large city is clearly divisible into four periods. These were not the same for all areas but became more uniform over time as they merged into the metropolitan context. Indeed, some large cities were very late in developing, and they may have skipped one or two of the earlier periods, with important consequences for their current fiscal problems.

The first period, roughly to 1900, involves the growth and concentration of the American population in large cities. The period covers the evolution of urban America from a set of isolated cities in the wilderness to the city as the major characteristic of American society.

The second period, from about 1900 to 1930, involves the consolidation of the modern city in an era of growth. (See Table 11.) This is especially true of the central cities which were to become the large metropolitan areas of the bench-mark year 1960, i.e., those SMSA's with over a million persons in 1960. During this period the large cities grew at about the same very rapid rate of the over-all growth in population, but the period was also characterized by a buoyant growth of the peripheral areas as the development of interurban rail transportation continued apace. In the decade of the 1920s, the rate of growth outside the central city reached a level it was not to reach again until the late 1940s, but the cities continued to dominate the total growth. While the rural areas still persisted and the city continued to play its role as a marketplace, the era

46

TABLE 11

POPULATION GROWTH IN CENTRAL CITIES AND OUTSIDE CENTRAL CITY AREAS
OF STANDARD METROPOLITAN STATISTICAL AREAS, BY DECADES, 1900–70

Decade	SMSA's	Central Cities	Outside Central City Areas	Central City Growth per 100 Increase, Outside Central City Areas
		In Thousands		
1900–10	10,176	7,337	2,839	258.4
1910–20	10,496	7,519	2,977	252.6
1920–30	14,204	8,428	5,776	145.9
1930–40	5,864	2,403	3,461	69.4
1940–50	16,387	6,664	9,723	68.5
1950–60	23,421	5,573	17,848	31.2
1960–70	19,152	850	18,301	4.6

SOURCE: U.S. Bureau of the Census, *U.S. Census of Population. Selected Area Reports: Standard Metropolitan Statistical Areas,* Final Report PC(3)–1D. U.S. Bureau of the Census, *Current Population Reports,* Series P–23, No. 37, "Social and Economic Characteristics of the Population in Metropolitan and Nonmetropolitan Areas: 1970 and 1960."

was characterized by the emergence of a social and economic interdependence and a change from a nominal metropolitan area to a functional metropolian area.[1] The year 1930 represented a peak in the proportion of the total population residing in cities of over 100,000. During this period, cities established or introduced levels of local public services which were to be irreversible over time, as they were to discover during the next decade.

The third period, from 1930 to 1950, contains both the Great Depression and World War II. The rates of population growth were considerably below the prior period, but not very different from the national norms. Even the suburban growth was below that of earlier periods. During this period, in spite of the enormous changes taking place in the economy, with unemployment during the Depression and then full

---

[1] The change was recognized by a series of studies published in the early 1930s. The most important of these from an analytical point of view is that of Paul Studenski, *The Government of Metropolitan Areas in the United States* (New York: National Municipal League, 1930).

employment during World War II, the large city was characterized by an apparent stability or equilibrium which differentiated it from its preceding and succeeding history. The forces which had made for such great growth in the preceding periods—immigration from abroad and from rural America, the natural increase in population, and the expansion of the city borders by annexation and consolidation—came to a virtual standstill. Despite the fiscal traumas in the early 1930s and the fiscal euphoria in the early 1940s, hindsight suggests that the period was one of unique stability of the large city relative to its outlying areas and the nation as a whole.

The last period, from 1950 to the present, is characterized by a major change in the large central city relative to its suburbs and to smaller central cities. The change actually started a few years before 1950, when the enormous movement away from the central city began in earnest. The magnitude of change for several individual areas is hidden by the reemergence of annexation, which had not been a strong factor during the prior two decades. Between 1960 and 1970, central cities' population declined by 2.0 percent in the largest areas, and in all the other areas the central city populations grew by 8 percent or more. Further, unlike all other areas (Table 15), the large cities in the aggregate showed a decline in their white populations (13 percent) and an increase in their black populations (37 percent). The period from 1970 to the present has shown an acceleration of the pattern.

During this last period the large central cities, although they have remained important, no longer represent the main thrust of economic development. As shown in Table 15, the principal population growth during the 1960s occurred in the suburbs of the large metropolitan areas (*i.e.,* those with over 1 million population), which grew by 11 million, while their cities grew by only 610,000. And, of the latter growth, a good part was accounted for by cities in the West and Southwest—including Houston, San Jose and Los Angeles—and by a series of large annexations outside the Northeast. The enormous growth of an automobile-oriented suburbia provided the opportunity for a massive change in suburban public elementary and secondary education. The provision of public education had been one of the attractions of the central city in an earlier era; this attractiveness declined abruptly during this period. Earlier examples of the educational appeal of individual suburbs existed, but this period witnessed a massive shift in attitude as to the educational attractiveness of the suburban areas.

The changing racial and ethnic character of the central city was associated with an enormous amount of intracity movement. In terms of movement, as opposed to net addition to the population, there was no fundamental difference between the large cities and their suburbs.

Each of these periods under discussion has given its own unique stamp to large city education. During the first three periods, large city education was the principal instrument of educational innovation and change. Cities alone had the resources to provide the complete range of education. Even the few exceptions that existed outside the central cities reflected the behavior of their central cities and school systems with a full range of educational opportunities, and were available to only a very small portion of the peripheral population. The growth of the suburbs since the end of World War II changed the pattern by the 1960s.

ECONOMIC AND SOCIAL CHANGES

The large central city, more than its smaller counterparts, has undergone a major set of changes in its economic and social structure. These were associated first with the growth and then with the decline of their population, and were to have severe educational consequences.

The first period witnessed the establishment of the city in North America. Its development roughly coincides with the formation of the United States. In 1790 there were only 12 places in the United States with populations in excess of 5,000 persons, and they contained but 4.0 percent of the population enumerated in the First Census. For the first 50 years, *i.e.,* to 1840, the pace of urban change was modest as the number of places with populations over 5,000 increased to 48, but, due to the enormous rural growth, they still comprised less than 10 percent of the population.

However, during this period there was a concentration of the urban population in a limited number of communities. In 1840 there were 5 communities with populations in excess of 50,000—cities large enough to meet our contemporary standards for central cities of metropolitan areas. These contained 41.0 percent of the total urban population. While the number of places with populations over 5,000 increased to 905 in 1900, the concentration of the urban population in the large cities increased. Using 100,000 population to define a large city, these contained 47.1 percent of the total urban population of the United States. By 1900 the large city had shifted from being a special case to a major social and economic force.

As shown in Table 12, the cities in metropolitan areas with population over 3 million in 1960 contained 81.1 percent of their total metropolitan population in 1900 and 60.0 percent in the 1–3 million class. As late as 1930 these proportions had not changed very much. The metropolitan

TABLE 12

CENTRAL CITY AS A PERCENTAGE OF STANDARD METROPOLITAN
STATISTICAL AREA POPULATION, 1900–70

	1900 %	1930 %	1950 %	1960 %	1970 %	City Rank 1900	City Rank 1970
East							
Baltimore, Md.	73.8	77.6	67.6	54.4	43.7	6	7
Boston, Mass.	42.5	36.0	33.2	26.9	23.3	5	16
Newark, N.J.	47.0	35.4	29.9	24.0	20.2	16	36
Buffalo, N.Y.	69.3	62.9	53.3	40.8	34.3	8	28
New York, N.Y.	90.1	86.9	82.6	72.8	68.2	1	1
Rochester, N.Y.	74.6	77.4	68.2	54.3	33.5	24	49
Philadelphia, Pa.–N.J.	68.4	62.2	56.4	46.1	40.5	3	4
Pittsburgh, Pa.	41.7	33.1	30.6	25.1	21.7	11	24
Midwest							
Chicago, Ill.	81.5	74.9	69.9	57.1	48.2	2	2
Indianapolis, Ind.	85.8	86.2	77.4	70.6	67.1*	21	11
Detroit, Mich.	66.9	72.0	61.3	44.4	36.0	13	5
Minneapolis–St. Paul, Minn.	79.6	83.4	72.4	53.7	41.0	19 / 23	32 / 46
Kansas City, Mo.–Kans.	63.6	60.1	56.1	45.9	40.4	22	26
St. Louis, Mo.–Ill.	69.6	59.3	49.8	36.4	26.3	4	18
Omaha, Neb.–Iowa	50.3	68.3	68.5	65.9	64.3	35	41
Cincinnati, Ohio–Ky.–Ind.	61.8	63.8	55.7	46.9	32.7	10	29
Cleveland, Ohio	82.8	72.4	62.4	48.8	36.4	7	10
Columbus, Ohio	76.3	80.5	74.7	69.0	58.9	28	21
Toledo, Ohio	85.8	83.6	76.8	69.6	55.4	26	34
Milwaukee, Wis.	78.1	74.4	66.6	62.1	51.1	14	12
South							
Birmingham, Ala.	27.4	60.2	58.3	53.7	40.7	94	48
Atlanta, Ga.	45.3	58.5	45.6	47.9	35.8	43	27
Louisville, Ky.–Ind.	68.5	72.1	64.0	53.9	43.7	18	39
New Orleans, La.	93.4	90.8	83.2	72.3	56.8	12	19
Oklahoma City, Okla.	17.2	67.5	62.0	63.4	57.2	19	37
Memphis, Tenn.–Ark.	66.6	82.6	82.1	79.3	81.0	37	17
Dallas, Tex.	20.2	56.8	58.4	62.7	54.2	58	8
Houston, Tex.	70.0	81.4	73.9	75.5	62.1	85	6
Norfolk, Va.	50.8	76.4	65.8	72.7	49.5	80	47
West							
Los Angeles–Long Beach, Calif.	55.1	59.3	50.9	41.9	45.1	—	3 / 40
San Diego, Calif.	50.4	70.6	60.1	55.5	51.3	—	14
San Francisco–Oakland, Calif.	75.5	68.1	51.8	41.8	34.6	9	13 / 38
Denver, Colo.	72.8	74.8	67.9	53.1	41.9	25	25
Portland, Ore.–Wash.	60.0	66.3	53.0	45.3	37.9	42	35
Seattle, Wash.	60.2	67.4	55.4	50.3	37.4	48	22

	1900	1930	1950	1960	1970†
U.S. Total, SMSA	62.1	64.6	58.6	51.4	45.8
Over 3,000,000 in 1960	81.1	75.8	68.5	56.1	44.4 (over 2,000,000)
1,000,000–3,000,000 in 1960	60.0	57.0	50.5	42.6	44.1
500,000–1,000,000 in 1960	57.6	65.5	59.0	52.7	49.2
250,000– 500,000 in 1960	48.6	58.0	52.9	49.0	44.3
100,000– 250,000 in 1960	50.3	59.9	57.5	56.8	—
Less than 100,000 in 1960	63.4	69.1	74.1	77.0	55.5 (less than 250,000)

* Consolidation   † 1970 categories are not identical with those of earlier years due to definitional changes.

SOURCE: U.S. Bureau of the Census, *Selected Area Reports: Standard Metropolitan Statistical Areas,* Final Report PC(3)–10.

areas with 500,000 to 1 million fell somewhere between the higher and lower group. Starting with 1930, the proportion of the total population residing in the central cities began to decline precipitously relative to the position they held at the beginning of the century.

The decline in their position was reflected not only in a loss of population but in a loss in their share of economic activity. While initially the loss in population was more severe, the loss in economic activity is now more serious. However, the situation as it existed from 1900 to 1930 was to have an enormous impact on educational financial policy. During the period of overwhelming large city dominance, Cubberley, who was to become the leading figure in educational administration and finance, commented that this resulted in relative superiority of the large city school systems on a comparatively small tax effort.[2] This too was the result of a great deal of educational adaptation in the large central cities which was still not characteristic of the rest of the nation.[3]

During this period the central city grew in area from its original comparatively small size, and this expansion involved the annexation of surrounding lands and population. During the nineteenth century the unified large city school system evolved, a process which is still not complete. Apart from a few instances in New England, the unified large city school system did not emerge full-blown. The large city had to undergo a basic set of changes during the middle of the nineteenth century, evolving from the "ward system" to a unified city school system.

Again quoting Cubberley concerning the large city:

> As the people in each ward felt willing to provide school facilities for their children they were permitted by law to call a meeting, organize a school district in the ward, vote to erect a school building, employ teachers, and vote to tax themselves to maintain the school. Some wards thus had public schools and others did not.
>
> The different cities thus came to contain a number of what were virtually country school districts, each maintaining an ungraded and independent district school. As the city grew, these ungraded and independent schools increased in number and size. Later the situation became impossible, the city was unified by law for education as it previously had been for city government.[4]

The unification of the city area for "city government," combined with the unification of the school systems, was to have serious consequences

[2] Ellwood P. Cubberley, *School Funds and their Apportionment* (New York: Teachers College, Columbia University, 1905), 2.

[3] See Edward A. Krug, *The Shaping of the American High School, 1880–1920* (Madison: The University of Wisconsin Press, 1969).

[4] Ellwood P. Cubberley, *Public Education in the United States* (Boston: Houghton Mifflin, 1934), 316.

at a later time, especially in the large central cities. This unification called for a much greater range of municipal services than existed in their outside areas or in smaller cities. Some of the programs were virtually irreversible once they were introduced.

But while the school system was unified, it hardly solved all the problems of a growing, socially heterogeneous large city. Among these, growth and the problem of Americanization of the immigrant bulked large and were especially marked in the second period, from 1900 to 1930. During this period, the aggregate growth of the central cities—and of these, primarily the large cities—was considerably in excess of their outside areas. A considerable portion of the growth reflected immigration from Eastern and Southern Europe to the large cities. To this was added a large migration from rural America.

The huge growth in enrollment for individual cities is shown in Table 14. During this period the increased enrollment of the cities paralleled and indeed was a major contributor to the growth in aggregate enrollment shown in Chapter II.

EXPANSION OF CAPITAL FACILITIES

The growth in this period was also responsible for a large building boom in public schools, which in part explains the currently aged school plants in many large cities. Thus, in Boston, Cleveland, Pittsburgh, and St. Louis, over 50 percent of the school plant in 1965 was built prior to 1920. And considering that this date represented the end of World War I, most of it must have been built prior to 1917. Logically enough, the figure is even higher for elementary schools (as shown in Table 13) than it is for high schools.

Starting in 1900, the growth of school enrollment reflected not only the increase in city population but also the extension of secondary education from a minority institution to a mass phenomenon. Estimates of school enrollment as late as 1912 indicated that the proportion of total enrollment in high schools was still limited to 6 percent of the total. Large cities generally exceeded that level, and a few, such as Boston and Cleveland, by a considerable amount; but the provision of secondary education was to engender a major set of fiscal problems due to the growth that was beginning to accelerate—a phenomenon which was to lead to a preoccupation with educational finances.

Of comparable importance was the effect of the great wave of immigration from Southern and Eastern Europe. The language problem—which today is agitating contemporary Britain, with only a few thousand children involved—had to be dealt with on an unparalleled scale by the large American cities in the first two decades of the twentieth century.

TABLE 13

PERCENTAGE OF PUBLIC SCHOOL BUILDINGS OVER 45 YEARS OLD,
15 SELECTED LARGE CITIES, AS OF JUNE 1965*

City	Schools		
	Elementary	Junior and Senior†	All‡
Baltimore, Md.	47.3	41.5	46.1
Boston, Mass.	64.0	38.9	53.7
Buffalo, N.Y.	35.2	47.1	36.6
Chicago, Ill.	46.9	46.4	46.9
Cleveland, Ohio	61.6	44.4	58.0
Detroit, Mich.	38.0	27.1	35.8
Houston, Tex.	23.3	13.2	20.8
Los Angeles, Calif.	9.0	6.3	8.4
Milwaukee, Wis.	49.6	22.2	44.6
New York, N.Y.	36.8	26.9	34.0
Philadelphia, Pa.	46.9	11.1	39.6
Pittsburgh, Pa.	54.3	46.2	52.3
St. Louis, Mo.	55.7	41.7	54.7
San Francisco, Calif.	38.0	12.5	33.1
Washington, D.C.	46.6	20.9	40.3
15-city total	39.6	25.5	36.7

*Excludes additions.   †Includes vocational schools.   ‡Excludes 13 junior colleges.

SOURCE: *School Construction,* Hearings Before the General Subcommittee on Education of the Committee on Education and Labor, House of Representatives, 89th Cong., 1st Sess., July and August 1965 (Washington, D.C.: Government Printing Office, 1966), 357.

In the most widely read educational textbook of its time, *Public Education in the United States,* Elwood P. Cubberley stated in 1934:

> As a result we had, in 1930, almost 13 and a half million of foreign-born people in our population, of whom practically forty-five per cent had come from the South and East of Europe. Of the immigration since 1900 almost eighty per cent has come from there. In addition to these thirteen and a half millions of foreign-born, an additional nine and a half million were native-born but the children of foreign parents, and of another six million one parent was foreign-born.
>
> These Southern and Eastern Europeans were of a very different type from the North and West Europeans who preceded them. Largely illiterate, docile, often lacking in initiative, and almost wholly without the Anglo-Saxon conceptions of righteousness, liberty, law, order, public decency, and government, their coming has served to dilute

TABLE 14

LARGE CITY SCHOOL DISTRICTS, MEASURES OF PUPIL ENROLLMENT,
1900–70 (in Thousands)

	1900 ADA	1930 ADA	1940 ADA	1950 ADA	1959 ADM	1967 ENR	1970 ENR
East							
Baltimore, Md.	53.7	98.4	102.4	107.9	160.9	191.0	192.2
Boston, Mass.	78.7	121.3	111.8	97.5	86.8	91.4	94.8
Newark, N.J.	25.8	69.3	61.1	59.4	63.7	75.8	76.0
Buffalo, N.Y.	41.2	75.5	78.9	59.8	66.1	73.3	71.8
New York, N.Y.	378.2	971.7	967.3	766.8	946.6	1,074.0	1,116.7
Rochester, N.Y.	18.7	46.4	42.2	30.5	41.1	45.0	45.7
Philadelphia, Pa.	126.1	241.0	234.2	191.4	235.2	276.2	288.8
Pittsburgh, Pa.	35.3	89.5	93.3	62.2	71.1	75.6	74.6
Midwest							
Chicago, Ill.	199.8	431.8	411.6	342.1	440.2	548.2	554.5
Indianapolis, Ind.	21.6	51.8	53.4	54.4	78.6	105.0	97.6
Detroit, Mich.	29.4	233.9	239.0	216.8	285.9	294.8	294.1
Minneapolis, Minn.	29.2	76.2	70.6	58.9	70.7	77.8	73.0
St. Paul, Minn.	20.3	36.4	35.3	34.3	41.9	48.5	51.2
Kansas City, Mo.	19.9	59.0	53.2	49.1	63.9	71.2	79.0
St. Louis, Mo.	57.1	92.7	93.9	81.0	100.9	116.2	124.7
Omaha, Neb.	NA	34.9	34.6	29.7	44.2	59.0	61.5
Cincinnati, Ohio	35.9	51.9	54.1	54.5	76.5	89.1	86.6
Cleveland, Ohio	45.1	139.6	122.3	93.4	126.8	152.7	153.3
Columbus, Ohio	15.0	41.4	40.6	43.4	74.9	104.9	109.1
Toledo, Ohio	16.5	41.7	39.7	35.8	48.6	61.5	61.5
Milwaukee, Wis.	30.7	74.1	77.3	67.1	89.8	122.4	130.6
South							
Birmingham, Ala.	3.2	43.4	44.8	43.8	66.2	71.1	65.7
Atlanta, Ga.	9.8	46.1	44.7	61.9	93.3	110.4	114.1
Louisville, Ky.	22.1	37.1	37.6	38.2	45.7	50.2	54.7
New Orleans, La.	22.2	51.4	55.9	55.7	86.3	107.4	112.3
Oklahoma City, Okla.	0.9	28.5	34.8	39.9	58.7	74.0	78.5
Memphis, Tenn.	6.8	29.6	37.4	53.0	92.8	124.3	116.8
Dallas, Tex.	5.0	38.0	43.6	57.9	112.0	150.3	158.8
Houston, Tex.	4.2	44.7	60.0	87.2	156.7	228.2	223.8
Norfolk, Va.	2.7	22.6	21.1	23.6	NA	56.7	51.1
West							
Long Beach, Calif.	NA	24.0	24.2	43.9	68.5	72.9	71.4
Los Angeles, Calif.	15.2	214.8	249.5	331.7	488.1	620.3	656.1
San Diego, Calif.	2.6	22.3	27.8	48.0	91.0	118.5	128.8
San Francisco, Calif.	32.4	64.6	63.3	71.2	87.5	93.6	93.7
Denver, Colo.	19.1	41.1	44.3	49.8	83.5	95.8	97.3
Portland, Ore.	9.6	45.7	39.5	49.9	61.5	79.0	75.4
Seattle, Wash.	8.0	55.5	49.4	59.0	99.9	83.4	94.0

SOURCE: Office of Education.

tremendously our national stock and to weaken and corrupt our political life. Settling largely in the cities of the North, the agricultural
regions of the Middle and the Far West, and the mining districts of
the mountain regions, they have created serious problems in housing

and living, moral and sanitary conditions, and honest and decent government, while popular education has everywhere been made more difficult by their presence. The result has been that in many sections of our country foreign manners, customs, observances, and language have tended to supplant native ways and the English speech, while the so-called "melting-pot" has had more than it could handle. The new peoples, and especially those from the South and East of Europe, have come so fast that we have been unable to absorb and assimilate them, and our national life, for the past quarter of a century, has been afflicted with a serious case of racial indigestion.[5]

American Negroes have not been the first ethnic group to bear the burden of blame for cities' educational and social troubles.

ECONOMIC STABILITY OF LARGE CITIES

A combination of factors led to the already noted unprecedented interest in educational finances. Along with an unparalleled expansion of their educational systems, the large cities showed a vast expansion of their resource base. Of exceptional importance was the increase in land values in the central city areas. At the end of this period, Cubberley could still assert the educational primacy of the central cities.

At the same time it should be noted that while the central cities maintained their domination, Paul Studenski, writing in behalf of the National Municipal League in 1930, could note the emergence of the high-income metropolitan suburb. But the over-all economic preeminence of the large city was not really challenged.

The period from 1930 to 1950, when viewed independently of the events surrounding it, appears as a period of great educational stability. The great wave of economic growth that had characterized the first three decades came to a grinding halt; there was a similar end to the growth in the central city areas; and for the first time the amount of suburban growth exceeded that of the central city. From the standpoint of public education, the major development during the period was an absolute decline in the elementary school enrollment with an offsetting growth in secondary education. Both these changes were due largely to shifts in the age composition of the population.

The period from 1930 to 1950, which appears so stable in terms of its population growth, presented unprecedented problems for local governments. The solutions—a set of limitations on local government—were carried over into later years and into the present. The decline in national income and the increase in unemployment during the early part of the 1930s, and the slow improvement for the rest of the decade, had a

[5] *Ibid.*, 485–86.

deleterious effect on local government finances as demands on local government increased and the resource base contracted.

The decline in national income and the increase of unemployment placed new burdens on local governments, especially in the large cities. This was accompanied by a belated but very severe decline in the real property tax base. Because of the lag in the response, this did not lead to anything like a proportional decline in local government expenditures, especially those in public welfare and education. High tax rates and extensive local borrowing characterized the early and middle 1930s. The result was anomalous, unless one recognizes that the slow response of the political process to economic changes was a reflection of the nature of the political decision-making structure. Where there was a breakdown, of course, educational expenditures—like other governmental expenditures—were very low. But the over-all effects were very high local property tax rates and historically high local government expenditures as a percentage of income. In both cases the large cities were a major contributory factor.

The tensions engendered by the severe decline in personal income and the real property tax base, combined with the increase in local government requirements other than education, led to more stringent controls over local tax and debt policies, which were made especially applicable to the large cities. These limits have directly and indirectly served as limits on local government's fiscal activity since that period, including the expenditures on education and especially in large cities.

The over-all stability in this decade was associated with a change in the distribution of public school enrollment between elementary and secondary education. In the most dramatic part of the period, 1933–34 to 1937–38, elementary school enrollment in city public schools dropped 8.2 percent; special schools were virtually eliminated, dropping some 56.6 percent; but ninth grade was up 7.8 percent and tenth grade up 13.8 percent. Eleventh grade was up 19.1 percent and twelfth grade up 18.9 percent. In the light of the declining group of elementary school pupils and the school systems' own financial position, this shift was dealt with by resort to a number of temporary expedients, including the creation of enormous schools. This was accomplished by a set of multiple sessions and annexes with multiple sessions, but the temporary nature of the phenomenon is indicated by the fact that, as late as 1967, many large cities had not again reached the attendance levels of 1940.

Assessed property values, the resource base for education as well as for other local government functions, disintegrated during this period. The low point for any individual city depended upon the local circumstances surrounding the assessment of its property tax base. The situation of the central cities was no different, and was better for some, than that of suburban and rural areas. As was indicated earlier, school costs were reduced during the period from 1930 to 1934, for perhaps the only time in the twentieth century, although not nearly as rapidly as the decline in the resource base. The reduction in costs was not as rapid as the changes in the tax base because it was impossible immediately to change plans made earlier; and when policies *were* changed, the economy began to improve from its low point. Where information is available, there is clear indication that the period represented a unique interval in modern American history, one which we remember because of the financial changes that followed in its wake. The decade from 1930 to 1940 was basically a time of great difficulty, and that difficulty was translated into a set of severe limitations on the ability of local governments to handle local fiscal problems by the end of the decade. At the same time state aid grew from 19.6 percent of local educational expenditures in 1932 to 36.0 percent of the total in 1942.

The decade from 1940 to 1950 introduced an air of euphoria into large city finances which was also to have deleterious consequences. The early 1940s were characterized by great improvement in the economy. The exceptional welfare and welfare-oriented expenditures of the 1930s were reduced in the wake of the improvement in economic activity. While some cities did not show any immediate improvement in their real property tax base, the decline characteristic of the 1930s came to an end. Further, during World War II the large cities were urged not to spend any additional sums on either capital improvements or on salaries and wages. From a fiscal point of view, this provided the needed breathing space for many large cities and their surrounding areas. By the time World War II was over, the underlying fiscal resource position had improved immensely in the large cities. The period 1946–48 probably marked the actual watershed in the position of the large city.

There is reason to believe that, in terms of their relative position, the large cities were then at their historical zenith and that the period from 1948 to 1950 began to show the characteristics of the succeeding decade. As to resources, most large cities were able to adjust to the great demands placed on them in the immediate postwar period. In particular, the demands on schools were reduced in the older large cities. Even the increase in population in the 1940s was not associated with any generalized increase in large city school enrollment at that time. The reduction in debt charges and in local financed welfare also brightened the large city's financial position.

This favorable financial position was in contrast to the then unfavorable position of the new suburbs. At the outset, the outward movement of families with school-age children was not accompanied by anything like an adequate resource base to both build and run a quality educational system such as then existed in the large cities. In addition to the costs of education, the costs of building an infrastructure suited to an automobile-oriented society were clearly beyond the means of those who were moving into these areas. The costs of highways, water, and sewage taxed the budgets of these new communities to the breaking point. The result was a set of decisions by the state legislatures to provide them with the kind of direct and indirect state assistance which earlier had been provided to rural areas. Based on the criteria established, the position of the large cities was clearly superior to that of their surrounding areas. However, like the legal constraints of the 1930s, the aid policies of the late 1940s were to operate to the disadvantage of the large cities even after the cities had lost their favorable position.

REDISTRIBUTION OF POPULATION

The period from 1950 to the present represents a basic change insofar as the central city is concerned. As shown in Table 11, central city population has been estimated to have grown by 6.4 million from 1950 to 1970, while the population outside the central city grew by 36.1 million during the same period. The increase in city population represents an overstatement in terms of their 1950 boundaries, and it also shows important differences by size.

Based on the comprehensive data for the decade 1960–70, central city population growth occurred primarily in smaller cities and in suburban areas which were annexed by the central city areas during the period. Population in all cities over 100,000 grew by only 0.1 percent (or by only 69,804) within their 1960 boundaries, although, as shown by the unadjusted statistics, the increase over-all was 5.3 percent. Even some of the most rapidly growing cities in the United States, such as Memphis, Toledo, Omaha, Indianapolis, Jacksonville, and Nashville, showed declines within their 1960 borders: the first three increased because of annexation, the last three because of consolidation. Population growth throughout the United States has been extensive (area) rather than intensive (density), i.e., cities are now less densely populated but larger in size. This is particularly true of the central cities of the older metropolitan areas as measured by the Census, using the decade in which Standard Metropolitan Statistical Area population first reached 100,000 as a criterion of age. These areas had practically no increase in central city population even if account is taken of annexation. For those SMSA's with over two million, large city population decreased 2.0 percent during the sixties, and for those between one and two million the increase was 10.0 percent (Table 14), reflecting the annexations of the 50s and 60s.

From an educational standpoint, the change of racial distribution of the population is extremely important. The white population in the central cities in all metropolitan areas declined 1.2 percent between 1960 and 1970; however, in the case of the largest metropolitan areas (those over one million persons in 1970) the white population declined by 13.0 percent. It was only in those with populations of less than two million that the white population increased (Table 15). There was a further regional bias, reflecting the use of annexation and/or special circumstances.

While the white population declined or remained static, the black population in the large central city areas grew considerably, except in parts of the South (Table 16). In fact, the larger the metropolitan area, the greater the rate of increase in the black population in the central city (Table 15). Estimates for the 1970s indicate that there has been a continuation of the trend. In 1970 the black population was 25 percent of the total population of central cities in metropolitan areas of over one million.

The effects of the changing ethnic composition of the central city population have been an increase in the proportion of blacks in total public school enrollment and an increase in the total size of public school enrollment. This is because the Negro, unlike many ethnic groups before him, has made relatively little use of the parochial or private school systems. The basic shift occurred between the middle 1950s and 1967. As is shown in Table 14, from 1958–59 to 1966–67 there is a clear indication of major increases in large city public school enrollment. These increases occurred even in the cities which had major decreases in total population, such as Cleveland, St. Louis, and Buffalo. In fact, there was not a single large city surveyed which did not show a major increase in public school enrollment during this period. From a long-term point of view, however, in some cases the 1967 levels did not exceed those of 1930 or 1940, and the 1970 figures show a decline for a dozen cities from the 1967 levels and a smaller rate of increase for the others. It should be noted that the earlier period is measured in terms of average daily attendance, and the later period in terms of membership and enrollment.

The importance of the increase in total enrollment is that it has taken place in the context of an absolute decline in over-all population and, at best, a relative decline in the availability of total local tax resources. Further, it has a qualitative dimension in the level of income and asso-

TABLE 15

Population Change, Central City (CC) and Outside Central City (OCC) of Cities of Standard Metropolitan Statistical Areas, by Race and by Size, 1960–70

Size of Area	All Classes			White			Negro		
	Total	CC	OCC	Total	CC	OCC	Total	CC	OCC
				Numbers in Thousands					
2,000,000 or more	5,590	−424	6,013	2,773	−2,489	5,262	2,302	1,755	547
1,000,000–2,000,000	5,966	1,034	4,931	4,940	295	4,645	820	637	182
500,000–1,000,000	3,346	763	2,583	2,767	299	2,468	437	407	30
250,000–500,000	2,769	768	2,002	2,238	462	1,875	321	248	72
Less than 250,000	2,122	1,053	1,070	1,877	826	1,051	174	186	−11
U.S. Total	19,793	3,194	16,598	14,695	−607	15,300	4,054	3,234	820
				Percent Change					
2,000,000 or more	12	−2	29	7	−13	24	40	37	59
1,000,000–2,000,000	27	10	42	24	3	41	39	39	38
500,000–1,000,000	18	8	30	17	4	31	22	26	8
250,000–500,000	17	10	22	15	7	22	20	24	13
Less than 250,000	14	13	16	14	11	17	13	21	−2
U.S. Total	17	5	28	14	−1	27	32	33	29

SOURCE: U.S. Bureau of the Census: *1970 Census of Population.*

ciated socioeconomic characteristics of a growing inner city Negro, Puerto Rican, and Mexican-American population (Table 17). This is a school population which is more difficult to teach because of the destructive effects of much large-scale and long-term poverty.

METROPOLITAN CONTEXT OF EDUCATION

The position of the large city is most clearly demonstrated by analyzing income in the large city and comparing it to its outlying area; that is, by utilizing its metropolitan context. Income is important because of its effect on the demand for education as measured by the expenditure for, and presumably also the quality of, education as well as the proportion attending public schools, especially high school. The common metropolitan environment, which in former years had a salutary effect on suburban education, now has a debilitating effect on central city education as the metropolitan area determines the level of costs without providing the resources for meeting those costs.

In national aggregates, the stereotype of the high-income suburb and the low-income central city emerge. For the year 1967 it is estimated that central city areas had a median family income of $7,813, while for the outlying areas the figure was $9,367. It is quite clear that if the rural components of the outlying areas were taken into account, the difference would be much larger, as evidence for 1959 and 1964 indicated, since the rural component shows a lower income than either central city or suburb. Adjustments of this sort were made for the 37 largest metropolitan areas for the year 1964, and they indicate the extent of the discrepancies.

The socioeconomic position of the large cities is best interpreted as having high income relative to other central cities in the nation, although that gap is narrowing; but low income relative to their own suburbs, a gap which is expanding. The detailed data for 1959 indicate that, as shown in Table 18, in the case of both white and black, the proportion of families with incomes under $3,000 decreases and the proportion of families with incomes over $10,000 increases as metropolitan area and central city size increases. However, the relative position of the central city in the large metropolitan area declines and is reversed compared to that of the central city in the smaller area. Thus, while the central cities of the larger metropolitan areas are relatively better off than their smaller counterparts, they are distinctly worse off compared to their surrounding areas. This combination of attractiveness and income inferiority has had profound effects on the provision of education in large central cities. The peripheral areas, which formerly were characterized by small units, now can compete with much larger central city educational units

TABLE 16

RATE OF CHANGE OF POPULATION, CENTRAL CITY (CC) AND OUTSIDE CENTRAL CITY (OCC), 37 LARGEST STANDARD METROPOLITAN STATISTICAL AREAS, 1960 THROUGH 1970

Area	Total Population		White		Negro		Growth in CC Without Annexations, %
	CC %	OCC %	CC %	OCC %	CC %	OCC %	
East							
Washington, D.C.	−1.0	61.9	−39.4	57.9	30.6	102.2	−1.0
Baltimore, Md.	−3.5	34.7	−21.4	35.7	29.1	15.9	−3.5
Boston, Mass.	−8.1	13.4	−16.5	13.3	69.9	81.1	−8.1
Newark, N.J.	−5.6	14.8	−36.7	10.8	50.3	63.7	−5.6
Paterson–Clifton–Passaic, N.J.	0.9	18.7	−9.1	17.6	89.2	89.2	0.9
Buffalo, N.Y.	−13.1	14.5	−20.7	22.1	34.1	40.8	−13.1
New York, N.Y.	1.1	25.7	−9.3	21.7	61.6	59.0	1.1
Rochester, N.Y.	−7.0	41.7	−17.1	54.2	115.1	374.5	−7.0
Philadelphia, Pa.–N.J.	−2.7	20.7	−12.9	17.0	23.5	34.1	−2.7
Pittsburgh, Pa.	−13.9	4.4	−18.0	4.5	4.2	6.9	−13.9
Providence, R.I.	−13.6	15.4	−17.5	14.9	49.3	60.2	−13.6
Midwest							
Chicago, Ill.	−5.2	35.3	−18.6	32.0	35.7	65.5	−5.3
Indianapolis, Ind.	11.7	31.4	7.3	30.1	34.5	112.9	−8.0
Detroit, Mich.	−9.5	28.5	−29.1	21.8	37.0	26.1	−9.5
Minneapolis–St. Paul, Minn.	−6.5	55.9	−9.0	55.4	49.5	222.5	−6.5
Kansas City, Mo.–Kans.	6.6	21.0	0.0	−1.5	34.7	14.9	−8.1

St. Louis, Mo.–Ill.	−17.0	28.5	−31.6	22.5	18.6	126.2	−17.0
Cincinnati, Ohio–Ky.–Ind.	−10.0	21.7	−17.2	21.4	15.0	25.9	−10.2
Cleveland, Ohio	−14.3	27.1	−26.5	23.4	14.8	452.8	−14.2
Columbus, Ohio	14.5	32.8	11.3	32.4	29.2	41.8	8.9
Dayton, Ohio	−7.1	30.5	−17.7	29.7	29.7	53.8	−8.3
Milwaukee, Wis.	−3.3	27.7	−10.4	13.9	68.3	101.5	−4.0
South							
Miami, Fla.	14.8	45.0	13.5	43.0	16.8	57.6	14.8
Tampa–St. Petersburg, Fla.	8.3	64.0	5.2	66.0	23.2	24.8	4.9
Atlanta, Ga.	2.0	68.6	−20.0	72.5	38.2	23.6	1.2
Louisville, Ky.–Ind.	−7.5	39.0	−14.3	39.8	22.8	16.1	10.7
New Orleans, La.	−5.4	61.8	−17.6	68.8	14.4	27.4	−5.4
Dallas, Tex.	24.2	61.8	14.2	67.3	62.8	4.8	22.6
Houston, Tex.	31.4	56.7	25.3	63.3	47.4	7.7	27.6
San Antonio, Tex.	11.3	63.4	9.8	62.9	20.2	40.6	8.8
West							
Los Angeles–Long Beach, Calif.	12.5	20.0	4.6	14.4	51.7	105.2	11.8
San Bernardino–Riverside–Ontario, Calif.	38.4	42.2	33.7	44.4	83.7	59.8	17.2
San Diego, Calif.	21.6	43.8	17.2	41.4	53.8	82.7	19.8
San Francisco–Oakland, Calif.	−2.7	31.9	−17.2	26.9	39.7	60.7	−2.7
Denver, Colo.	4.2	63.7	−0.1	55.4	55.4	141.7	−7.3
Portland, Ore.–Wash.	2.7	39.5	0.2	39.3	38.0	64.9	−1.4
Seattle–Everett, Wash.	−2.2	64.3	−6.2	62.9	41.0	194.6	−8.6

SOURCE: U.S. Bureau of the Census, *1970 Census of Population and Housing: General Demographic Trends for Metropolitan Areas, 1960 to 1970.*

TABLE 17

Large Central City Population, Percentage Negro, 1900–70

	Percent of Population				Percent of Public Schools, 1968–69†
	1900 %	1950 %	1960 %	1970 %	%
East					
Baltimore, Md.	16	24	35	46.4	65.1
Boston, Mass.	2	5	9	16.3	27.1
Newark, N.J.	3	17	34	54.2	72.5
Buffalo, N.Y.	1	6	13	20.4	36.0
New York, N.Y.	3	10	14	21.2	31.5
Rochester, N.Y.	0*	2	7	16.8	28.9
Philadelphia, Pa.	5	18	26	33.6	58.8
Pittsburgh, Pa.	5	12	17	20.2	39.2
Midwest					
Chicago, Ill.	2	14	23	32.7	52.9
Indianapolis, Ind.	9	15	21	18.0	33.7
Detroit, Mich.	1	16	29	43.7	59.2
Minneapolis, Minn.	0*	1	2	4.4	7.5
St. Paul, Minn.	0*	1	3	3.5	35.8
Kansas City, Mo.	11	12	18	22.1	46.8
St. Louis, Mo.	6	18	29	40.9	63.5
Omaha, Neb.	3	7	8	9.9	18.1
Cincinnati, Ohio	4	16	22	27.6	42.9
Cleveland, Ohio	2	16	29	38.3	55.9
Columbus, Ohio	7	12	16	18.5	26.0
Toledo, Ohio	1	8	13	13.8	26.7
Milwaukee, Wis.	0*	3	8	14.7	23.9
South					
Birmingham, Ala.	43	40	40	42.0	51.4
Atlanta, Ga.	40	37	38	51.3	61.7
Louisville, Ky.	19	16	18	23.8	46.1
New Orleans, La.	27	32	37	45.0	67.1
Oklahoma City, Okla.	12	9	12	13.7	21.8
Memphis, Tenn.	19	37	37	38.9	53.6
Dallas, Tex.	21	13	19	24.9	30.6
Houston, Tex.	33	21	23	25.7	33.0
Norfolk, Va.	40	32	28	28.3	41.9
West					
Los Angeles, Calif.	2	9	13	17.9	22.6
Long Beach, Calif.	2	2	3	5.0	7.6
San Diego, Calif.	0*	5	6	7.6	11.6
San Francisco, Calif.	1	6	10	13.0	27.5
Denver, Colo.	3	4	6	9.1	14.1
Portland, Ore.	1	3	4	5.6	8.1
Seattle, Wash.	1	3	5	7.1	11.0

* Less than one-half of 1 percent.   † School District basis.

Source: U.S. Bureau of the Census: *1970 Census of Population; Directory of Elementary and Secondary Public Schools in Selected Districts, With Enrollment and Staff by Racial/Ethnic, Fall 1968.*

TABLE 18

Percentage of Families with Incomes Under $3,000 and Over $10,000, by Race of Head of Family and Size of SMSA for Central Cities (CC) and Outside Central Cities (OCC), 1959

Size of Area	All Classes			White			Negro		
	Total	CC	OCC	Total	CC	OCC	Total	CC	OCC
Percentage Under $3,000									
3,000,000 and over	12.6	15.4	8.9	10.6	12.7	8.3	27.9	28.6	24.0
1,000,000–3,000,000	13.0	17.1	10.0	10.8	13.4	9.2	32.6	32.6	32.5
500,000–1,000,000	17.2	19.8	14.2	14.7	16.4	13.1	37.9	37.8	38.3
250,000–500,000	17.6	18.7	16.6	15.3	15.3	15.2	46.1	44.4	51.0
100,000–250,000	19.5	19.6	19.3	16.1	15.6	16.6	52.3	49.5	59.3
Less than 100,000	20.7	18.8	27.2	18.2	16.6	24.1	57.2	54.5	64.5
U.S. Total	15.2	17.6	12.5	12.8	14.4	11.4	36.7	35.8	40.4
Percentage Over $10,000									
3,000,000 and over	23.0	19.5	27.6	24.9	21.9	28.3	7.4	7.2	9.1
1,000,000–3,000,000	20.8	16.6	23.9	22.5	19.2	24.5	6.2	6.0	6.9
500,000–1,000,000	16.4	14.6	18.4	17.6	16.3	19.0	6.0	5.9	6.5
250,000–500,000	14.6	14.7	14.5	15.6	16.2	15.0	2.8	2.8	2.8
100,000–250,000	13.7	14.3	12.9	14.9	15.9	13.6	2.3	2.4	1.9
Less than 100,000	13.8	14.4	12.0	14.7	15.2	12.8	1.6	1.6	1.7
U.S. Total	18.8	16.5	21.2	20.3	18.5	21.9	5.3	5.2	5.3
Ratio: Number Over $10,000 Per 100 Under $3,000									
3,000,000 and over	183.0	126.7	311.5	234.1	172.8	340.4	26.6	25.1	37.7
1,000,000–3,000,000	160.5	97.3	238.9	208.5	143.3	265.9	19.0	18.4	21.3
500,000–1,000,000	95.6	73.8	129.3	120.0	99.6	144.9	15.9	15.7	16.9
250,000–500,000	82.8	78.6	87.4	101.8	105.7	98.3	6.1	6.3	5.6
100,000–250,000	70.3	73.1	66.6	92.5	101.5	82.0	4.3	4.9	3.2
Less than 100,000	67.0	76.3	44.0	80.5	91.4	53.2	2.8	2.9	2.7
U.S. Total	123.9	93.5	169.4	157.9	128.9	191.9	14.3	14.6	13.1

Source: U.S. Bureau of the Census, *U.S. Census of Population: 1960. Selected Area Reports. Standard Metropolitan Statistical Areas.* Final Report PC(3)–1D.

TABLE 19

Percentage Increase in Retail Sales, Deflated by General Price Increase,
Central City (CC) and Outside Central City (OCC) Areas, 1958–67,
and Percentage Retail Sales in Central City (CC) 1958 and 1967,
37 Largest Standard Metropolitan Statistical Areas

Area	% Retail Sales in CC (CC/SMSA)			% Increase (Real) Retail Sales, 1958–67	
	1958	1963	1967	CC	OCC
Washington, D.C.	52.1	42.1	32.9	10.5	134.8
Baltimore, Md.	71.4	58.1	53.4	4.9	128.2
Boston, Mass.	38.9	31.2	26.0	−1.4	79.2
Newark, N.J.	30.0	25.8	21.2	−14.1	37.1
Paterson–Clifton–Passaic, N.J.	36.0	23.9	24.6	0.9	74.5
Buffalo, N.Y.	52.2	40.1	38.9	−9.9	54.7
New York, N.Y.	72.9	67.1	64.8	9.7	60.2
Rochester, N.Y.	60.4	52.9	48.5	18.1	91.3
Philadelphia, Pa.–N.J.	51.1	43.4	40.2	6.2	65.4
Pittsburgh, Pa.	37.5	34.1	33.5	7.8	28.7
Providence, R.I.	55.7	50.4	31.2	−36.3	73.1
Northeast	(50.7)	(42.6)	(37.7)	(−0.3)	(75.2)
Chicago, Ill.	65.3	56.9	51.5	5.3	86.6
Indianapolis, Ind.	76.8	65.5	60.4	20.0	160.8
Detroit, Mich.	51.1	42.7	36.1	0.7	86.4
Minneapolis–St. Paul, Minn.	73.4	61.5	54.4	7.9	149.7
Kansas City, Mo.–Kans.	59.9	63.3	50.1	55.2	64.3
St. Louis, Mo.–Ill.	48.1	37.5	32.7	−7.6	76.2

Cincinnati, Ohio–Ky.–Ind.	64.2	57.0	45.0	4.6	129.4
Cleveland, Ohio	74.0	54.8	39.6	−15.2	269.1
Columbus, Ohio	80.2	69.0	67.2	22.8	141.9
Dayton, Ohio	60.5	47.4	41.3	3.6	125.5
Milwaukee, Wis.	73.1	63.1	58.4	7.5	108.3
Midwest	(66.0)	(56.2)	(48.8)	(9.5)	(127.1)
Miami, Fla.	54.9	40.4	37.5	−2.5	98.2
Tampa–St. Petersburg, Fla.	75.4	66.6	65.8	30.9	108.9
Atlanta, Ga.	71.4	62.8	57.6	37.7	153.9
Louisville, Ky.–Ind.	70.5	64.0	57.5	14.0	101.8
New Orleans, La.	79.0	71.3	65.3	21.0	141.9
Dallas, Tex.	77.7	71.2	68.4	36.6	119.2
Houston, Tex.	75.7	82.4	74.8	55.9	63.3
San Antonio, Tex.	91.2	90.0	89.6	36.4	79.9
South	(74.4)	(68.6)	(64.5)	(28.7)	(108.3)
Los Angeles–Long Beach, Calif.	48.8	41.3	39.9	22.2	75.4
San Bernardino–Riverside, Calif.	44.9	42.1	NA	NA	NA
San Diego, Calif.	64.0	56.4	53.9	25.6	91.8
San Francisco–Oakland, Calif.	54.5	48.0	43.4	16.3	81.6
Denver, Colo.	70.5	55.9	53.3	11.1	132.4
Portland, Ore.–Wash.	76.3	58.8	59.6	28.1	180.3
Seattle, Wash.	71.7	63.5	54.3	18.0	152.5
West	(61.5)	(52.3)	(49.0)	(20.2)	(119.0)
Unweighted average, 37 SMSA's	63.0	54.1	49.3	12.6	105.8

SOURCE: U.S. Bureau of the Census. *Census of Business—1958*, Vol. II, *Census of Business—1963*, Vol. II, and *Census of Business—1967*, Vol. II.

TABLE 20

MANUFACTURING EMPLOYMENT, CENTRAL CITY (CC) AND OUTSIDE CENTRAL CITY (OCC),* 1958, 1963, AND 1967 (in Thousands), 37 LARGEST STANDARD METROPOLITAN STATISTICAL AREAS

	1958		1963		1967		% Increase, 1958–67	
	CC	OCC	CC	OCC	CC	OCC	CC	OCC
East								
Washington, D.C.	21.3	13.4	22.1	28.0	23.1	32.4	+8.5	+141.8
Baltimore, Md.	113.4	84.4	103.9	86.6	106.7	103.0	−5.9	+22.0
Boston, Mass.	90.2	210.8	82.5	210.9	79.6	236.6	−11.8	+17.0
Newark, N.J.	78.8	166.8	73.7	176.5	68.5	195.2	−10.3	+12.2
Paterson–Clifton–Passaic, N.J.	62.9	95.6	62.8	113.7	62.1	127.9	−1.3	+33.8
Buffalo, N.Y.	68.0	105.9	57.0	105.9	66.7	109.5	−1.9	+3.4
New York, N.Y.	998.6	185.4	927.4	219.8	895.3	252.1	−10.3	+36.0
Rochester, N.Y.	96.5	20.2	97.3	24.0	114.2	31.5	+18.3	+55.9
Philadelphia, Pa.–N.J.	298.5	238.4	264.9	270.9	263.9	309.9	−11.6	+30.0
Pittsburgh, Pa.	99.3	206.4	81.7	190.5	85.6	214.0	−13.8	+3.7
Providence, R.I.	62.6	64.6	65.0	60.9	65.4	72.6	+4.5	+12.4
Midwest								
Chicago, Ill.	569.4	287.8	508.4	352.2	546.9	436.2	−4.0	+51.6
Indianapolis, Ind.	70.1	35.5	70.2	45.6	86.3	48.4	+23.1	+36.3
Detroit, Mich.	213.5	253.9	200.6	293.3	209.7	374.8	−1.8	+47.6
Minneapolis–St. Paul, Minn.	113.5	32.5	110.3	53.5	123.6	80.0	+8.9	+146.2
Kansas City, Mo.–Kans.	64.9	38.2	62.1	49.0	65.1	64.3	0	+68.3
St. Louis, Mo.–Ill.	146.8	115.7	129.1	130.6	131.9	163.6	−14.9	+41.4
Cincinnati, Ohio–Ky.–Ind.	76.4	80.1	76.6	77.5	84.5	82.3	+10.6	+2.7

Cleveland, Ohio	180.8	92.9	168.9	111.4	171.3	135.5	−5.3	+42.6
Columbus, Ohio	55.4	17.6	65.9	14.3	65.4	17.6	+18.1	0
Dayton, Ohio	78.2	19.0	81.2	23.0	88.3	37.9	+12.9	+99.5
Milwaukee, Wis.	126.6	63.9	119.3	74.5	118.6	97.9	−6.3	+55.6
South								
Miami, Fla.	19.4	17.4	19.2	24.0	20.5	37.8	+5.7	+116.0
Tampa–St. Petersburg, Fla.	23.7	8.5	23.8	12.9	24.6	24.1	+3.8	+280.0
Atlanta, Ga.	49.6	33.9	52.4	43.3	54.0	63.2	+8.9	+86.4
Louisville, Ky.–Ind.	55.7	31.0	58.0	29.6	64.0	46.0	+16.7	+48.4
New Orleans, La.	30.1	16.8	31.1	18.0	33.8	21.7	+12.3	+29.2
Dallas, Tex.	79.7	15.5	86.3	23.2	113.1	35.8	+41.9	+131.0
Houston, Tex.	68.8	35.7	77.3	31.3	97.9	40.2	+41.6	+12.6
San Antonio, Tex.	19.3	1.6	21.4	2.2	24.8	2.6	+28.5	+62.5
West								
Los Angeles–Long Beach, Calif.	327.2	401.8	304.0	538.9	361.0	494.4	+10.3	+23.0
San Diego, Calif.	56.8	14.6	48.7	11.6	42.9	20.6	−24.5	+27.5
San Francisco–Oakland, Calif.	99.5	90.8	91.6	104.6	80.5	117.4	−23.5	+29.3
San Bernardino–Riverside–Ontario, Calif.	11.7	17.5	14.0	23.5	18.4	28.0	+57.3	+60.0
Denver, Colo.	37.9	15.8	36.1	33.4	40.5	33.6	+6.9	+112.7
Portland, Ore.–Wash.	35.2	23.1	35.6	29.7	41.0	38.8	+16.5	+68.0
Seattle–Everett, Wash.	86.5	28.4	84.1	37.5	64.3	97.9	−25.7	+244.7
Weighted Average	—	—	—	—	—	—	−1.8	+36.0

* Not adjusted for annexation.

Source: U.S. Census of Manufacturing.

and are capable of holding and attracting—by virtue of their higher income and other advantages—the more affluent parent and the better teacher.

In addition to increasing enrollment, the changing racial distribution in the central city has changed the geographic distribution of the population within the large cities. Counter to the general outward movement of population, the black population tends to be concentrated in dense ghettoes in the inner city areas where the available educational facilities are generally quite old and insufficient.

While there has been a major increase in the number of children attending large city public schools, the property tax base on which the large central city school districts depend for local revenues has not expanded proportionately. This has been true of each of three major components of the property tax base: commercial uses—including primarily retailing—manufacturing, and housing.

Given the tremendous increase in retail activity in recent years, it is not surprising that in most large central city areas there was an increase in the value of retail activity between 1958 and 1967 (Table 19). However, in 6 of the 37 largest SMSA areas, central city retail activity in real terms actually declined in dollar volume. The average increase adjusted for price changes for these central city areas was 12.6 percent, as compared to a 105.8-percent increase in activity for their outside areas. The large increase outside the large central cities represented a shift in the location of retail activity which had consequences both for the income generated to the residents of the central city and the size of the tax base, since commercial uses have traditionally played such an important role in the central city real property tax base. It should also be noted that these do not separate out the effects of annexation on the growth of many of the cities in the South and West. The magnitude of the changes is indicated by the fact that in 1958, 63.0 percent of all retail transactions were in these large central cities but had fallen to 49.3 percent in 1967.

The greatest decrease in the dollar volume of retailing occurred in the central business districts. The crucial role of this area with regard to the city tax base is a matter of historical record. The large city central business district which recorded anything more than a nominal increase in retail sales activity during the period 1958–67 was the exception. In most of them the decrease was greater than that of the city as a whole and, in all cases, even if it did record an increase this was far less than that for the Standard Metropolitan Statistical Area taken as a whole. The downward pressure on the local property tax base, especially one adjusted to current conditions, is thus obvious.

The reduction in manufacturing employment in the large central cities and the increase in such employment in their outlying areas imposed increased pressures on the large city tax bases and led to improvement in those of the outside areas. The picture of the changes would be even more pronounced if adjustments could be made for the annexations. However, insofar as the school district contained any part of the growth areas, as in the case of the noncoterminous large city school districts such as Los Angeles, its base would be improved accordingly. Finally, it is probably true that part of the price which large cities have paid to retain manufacturing businesses is lower assessed values than would otherwise be the case. As in the case of retailing, this has meant a downward pressure—not only in older central cities but also in those where the school districts were unable to capture any of the suburban growth.

The pattern of change in manufacturing is similar to the one in retailing, although the magnitude is considerably less due to the much greater difficulty of relocating manufacturing activity (Table 20). In the aggregate, manufacturing employment in the large central cities declined by 1.8 percent while their outside areas increased by 36.0 percent. Special circumstances including annexation brought about increases in several cities. The largest increases occurred in extended cities which, because of peculiarities of definition are considered central cities, such as the San Bernardino–Riverside–Ontario complex, and cities such as Columbus and Houston where annexation played a major role. Once again the changes in employment were to be reflected in downward pressures on the large city tax bases.

To the relative and oftentimes absolute declines in the retailing and manufacturing components of the tax base was added a number of absolute declines in the values of the central city housing stock. This was in part associated with the decline in total population and the abandonment of a number of housing units, but it was also a result of the nominal increase in the value of housing in the large central cities. The only exceptions occurred in California.

This is shown in Table 21, using the change in the median value of housing of central cities for the period 1960–70 as compared to their outside areas. In large city communities there was an increase in housing values, but in general, they were a fraction of the amount of increase outside their boundaries. In Baltimore, Buffalo, Pittsburgh, Indianapolis, St. Louis, and Cincinnati, housing values registered only a very nominal increase relative to the general price level.

The various forces thus far noted are brought together in their effect on the local property tax base. School districts depend on the real property tax base almost exclusively for their local resources and state aid

TABLE 21
CHANGE IN MEDIAN VALUE HOUSING, CENTRAL CITIES
(CC) AND OUTSIDE CENTRAL CITY AREAS (OCC), 1960–70,
37 LARGEST STANDARD METROPOLITAN STATISTICAL AREAS

	Change in Median Value Housing 1960–70		Residential as % of Total Value, 1966
	CC	OCC	
East			
Washington, D.C.	5,900	11,700	51.0
Baltimore, Md.	1,000	6,400	53.5
Boston, Mass.	6,000	7,900	37.2
Newark, N.J.	3,700	10,200	41.4
Paterson–Clifton–Passaic, N.J.	6,300	10,800	59.0*
Buffalo, N.Y.	1,200	3,200	51.0
New York, N.Y.	8,700	11,300	53.9
Rochester, N.Y.	3,000	7,500	49.4
Philadelphia, Pa.–N.J.	2,000	5,700	63.3
Pittsburgh, Pa.	1,800	2,300	50.4
Providence, R.I.	4,700	6,200	41.3
Midwest			
Chicago, Ill.	3,200	7,100	42.4
Indianapolis, Ind.	2,800	3,800	42.2
Detroit, Mich.	3,600	7,000	41.9
Minneapolis–St. Paul, Minn.	4,400	8,000	38.6
Kansas City, Mo.–Kans.	3,000	4,300	37.1
St. Louis, Mo.–Ill.	1,300	4,100	36.9
Omaha, Neb.–Iowa	2,800	3,800	54.5
Cincinnati, Ohio–Ky.–Ind.	1,500	3,000	45.8
Cleveland, Ohio	2,900	5,500	29.7
Columbus, Ohio	3,900	5,000	48.1
Dayton, Ohio	3,100	5,800	33.6
Milwaukee, Wis.	3,100	6,600	47.8
South			
Miami, Fla.	3,600	5,000	53.5
Tampa–St. Petersburg, Fla.	1,500	3,200	56.2
Atlanta, Ga.	5,200	8,300	22.5
Louisville, Ky.–Ind.	2,900	4,100	50.4
New Orleans, La.	5,000	4,700	37.9
Dallas, Tex.	5,400	7,000	51.7†
Houston, Tex.	3,600	5,300	38.7†
San Antonio, Tex.	2,900	5,600	63.3†
West			
Los Angeles–Long Beach, Calif.	9,100	8,200	55.3
San Diego, Calif.	4,800	6,100	54.6
San Francisco–Oakland, Calif.	9,100	10,800	37.0
San Bernardino–Riverside–Ontario, Calif.	4,900	5,900	46.4†
Denver, Colo.	4,800	6,000	48.3
Portland, Ore.–Wash.	3,600	7,000	47.8
Seattle–Everett, Wash.	6,100	7,800	43.6*

* Principal city only   † County average.
SOURCE: U.S. Bureau of the Census, *1967 Census of Governments: Taxable Property Values; 1970 Census of Population and Housing: General Demographic Trends for Metropolitan Areas, 1960 to 1970.*

is dependent to an extraordinary degree on a measure of the "equalized" per-pupil values. Also, while the amount of valuation per pupil has been declining, the decline has not led to any relative increase in the amount of aid. This particular problem will be considered in more detail in Chapter IV.

THE TAX BASE

These factors all combine to affect the position of the large city tax base and its related school district tax base. However, it should be noted that insofar as the school district goes beyond the city border to include the growing retailing, manufacturing, and suburban housing developments, the large city school tax base would appropriately be enhanced. The general over-all effect of all these factors on large city tax bases is shown in Table 22. For the more current 1961–66 period, the only period for which comparable data on central cities and suburbs is available, the growth in the levels of the city base are certainly nominal in terms of the educational and noneducational tax burdens placed upon them. Reassessments account for the more spectacular changes, as in the case of Newark and Louisville, but the relative decline of the large cities is shown by their falling share of the total metropolitan tax base. Annexations also account for a redistribution of the tax base from what were formerly suburbs of the central cities. This explains most of the cases in which the central city areas grew relative to their suburbs. Unless these two factors are taken into account, the position of the large city is overstated.

The last aspect of large city tax base to be considered shows the great dependence on their presently declining nonresidential portion of the property tax base. This is best seen by analyzing the residential and non-residential portions of the total tax base, rather than the locally assessed real property portion alone. In some states, such as Pennsylvania, this does not make any difference at all; in others, such as New York, it is of nominal importance; but in still other states, such as Georgia and Ohio, it may make a major difference.

What is clear is the large city dependence on property other than that used for residential purposes. This dependence is exaggerated in individual communities where, by custom and practice, nonresidential properties have been assessed at higher levels than residential. In recent years, however, changes in laws and practices have reduced the importance of the nonresidential sector, as is evidenced by the practices in Minnesota, Michigan, and Ohio, by removing certain personal property from the tax roles.

TABLE 22

Taxable Real Property Values, 1961–66, School District Basis, Central City (CC) and Outside Central City Areas (OCC)

	% Values in CC		% Growth in Real Values	
	1961	1966	CC	OCC
East				
Baltimore, Md.	47.9	40.6	4.3	40.3
Boston, Mass.	23.1	16.7	2.3	52.8
Newark, N.J.	20.8	17.6	109.0†	157.9†
Buffalo, N.Y.	44.6	42.1	0.3	11.0
New York, N.Y.	79.8	78.3	22.1	48.5
Rochester, N.Y.	49.4	41.6	2.5	40.8
Philadelphia, Pa.–N.J.	58.4	48.4	8.8	62.6†
Pittsburgh, Pa.	30.2	27.9	2.2	14.5
Midwest				
Chicago, Ill.	49.4	44.5	4.5	26.8
Indianapolis, Ind.	50.1	43.4	14.0	49.5
Detroit, Mich.	48.9	37.2	−4.6	54.3
Minneapolis, Minn.	37.9	31.3	2.0	56.0
St. Paul, Minn.	21.7	17.8	1.5	56.0
Kansas City, Mo.–Kans.	55.0	52.8	13.8*	24.1
St. Louis, Mo.–Ill.	32.8	29.8	5.7	21.2
Omaha, Neb.–Iowa	66.2	67.2	53.3*,†	46.6†
Cincinnati, Ohio–Ky.–Ind.	42.3	30.6	7.4	67.5†
Cleveland, Ohio	40.4	34.3	−5.1	23.6
Columbus, Ohio	57.9	56.0	21.9*	31.6*
Toledo, Ohio	51.8	67.7	24.2*	−11.6*
Milwaukee, Wis.	51.6	46.5	9.7	34.9
South				
Birmingham, Ala.	55.1	44.3	4.9	64.5
Atlanta, Ga.	43.5	33.7	24.7	88.4
Louisville, Ky.–Ind.	50.9	49.1	227.3†	251.8†
New Orleans, La.	83.0	78.2	10.2	49.6
Oklahoma City, Okla.	NA	61.1	NA	NA
Memphis, Tenn.–Ark.	76.0	76.3	33.2	31.8*
Dallas, Tex.	NA	NA	31.8	NA
Houston, Tex.	NA	NA	41.7	NA
Norfolk, Va.	NA	45.7	20.5	NA
West				
Long Beach, Calif.	4.3	4.8	57.0	39.4
Los Angeles, Calif.	36.4	36.8	43.0*	39.4
San Diego, Calif.	54.5	54.3	26.2	27.3
San Francisco, Calif.	27.9	23.0	17.7	57.4
Oakland, Calif.	11.7	10.2	24.2	57.4
Denver, Colo.	55.7	49.0	11.2*	40.8
Portland, Ore.–Wash.	53.0	40.2	−23.4*,†	28.8†
Seattle, Wash.	55.5	46.7	21.2	72.4
Average	47.0	40.8		

* Annexation.   † Reassessment.

Source: U.S. Bureau of the Census, *Census of Governments: Taxable Property Values.*

SUMMARY

There has been a notable increase in the demands for public education as enrollments have increased and relative incomes in the central cities have declined. The reduction in the property tax base has exacerbated the problem without any compensatory state policy. The reduction in income inevitably has been associated with a decline in the value of private housing and an expansion of the amount of public housing. The latter is concentrated in a few cities, where it is often of extraordinary importance both in its effects on public school enrollment and its reduction of the property tax base.

However, the reduction in the underlying nonresidential portion of the property tax base has been far greater than the reduction due to public housing and other exemptions. This has resulted from the declines in retailing and manufacturing activity, key factors in preserving the fiscal viability of the large cities.

IV. The Role of the State

The differential role of the state with regard to school finances is quite clear as between states, although the many ways in which states enter into the picture have not been elaborated.[1] More appropriate for this study is the state government's differential role between the large cities, their suburbs, and the rural portions of the state. The purpose of this chapter is to indicate the many ways in which the state affects large city school finances, with particular emphasis on the differential role of the states with regard to the large cities and other areas.

THE STATE AND THE STRUCTURE OF EDUCATION

The system of governing and organizing local education in the United States is ultimately a state-determined function. The tradition of local government of education, while virtually universal, has assumed a variety of forms with important consequences for local school finances; in no state is it possible to decide on the size, organization, and other aspects of local school government outside of the framework established by the state. While there is a considerable literature on the problem of fiscal independence of school systems, which will be considered in Chapter VI, there are many more basic ways in which the state government has directly and indirectly influenced large city school finances.

States determine the size and organization of local school systems by constitutional provision, statutes, and court decisions; in one case, Hawaii, a state has reserved the provision of all public education to itself. In this latter case, the financial problems of providing education in the large city of Honolulu are thus different in kind from all other large cities in the country. The situation in Washington, D.C., also deserves special consideration because the arrangements with the federal government and the absence of overlying state governments are unique. In Florida and West Virginia, the school districts are coterminous with county borders;

---

[1] For a general analysis of these relationships, see Fred F. Beach and Robert F. Will, *The State and Education* (Washington, D.C.: U.S. Department of Health, Education, and Welfare, Office of Education, 1955); Council of State Governments, *The Forty-Eight School Systems* (Chicago: The Council, 1949).

in Georgia, Maryland, and Tennessee, education is provided by a combination of county-wide and city-wide school districts; and in New England they are city- and town-defined. At the other extreme there are the small school systems, most of which are not coterminous with any municipal boundary, as in Minnesota, Wisconsin, and Michigan. These latter states are important because they, with the Great Plains states, contain a very large proportion of all the school districts in the United States.

State policies governing the nature and size of school systems have an important bearing on the distribution of local and state fiscal resources. In the extreme case of Hawaii, all schools have basically the same level of educational resources per pupil throughout the state. This situation exists to a lesser extent when school systems are county-wide. Considerably greater variation is possible where school systems are fragmented. School systems may be coterminous with other jurisdictions as a result of state law, may be noncoterminous, or may follow a variety of other arrangements. In the case of the large city school districts which are not coterminous with municipal boundaries, a number of important possibilities emerge which, in turn, have fiscal implications. The school district may go beyond the city boundaries to include tax-base wealthy industrial enclaves, as is the case with the City of Vernon which is part of the Los Angeles School District. Or it may include some very poor areas outside the city, as, for example, Linndale in the Cleveland School District. Finally, the state may permit the central city area to be serviced by a number of school districts, as in San Antonio and Kansas City; some with relatively large bases compared to their needs, and others with small bases and large needs. The extent to which these developments are permitted to take place is a function of the local response to state laws and practices.

In addition to its direct effect on the size and nature of the school organization in the large cities, state policy also has important indirect effects. Many of the special problem areas of school finance, in addition to those in large city areas, arise from state permissiveness on inclusion or exclusion of areas from school districts. In recent years, the extent to which suburban areas have school districts made up of low-income bedroom communities with restricted tax bases and a large proportion of their total population attending public schools is partly a result of state policy. Similarly, the extent to which there are high-income suburbs and industrial and commercial enclaves which do not share their tax base is a function of state policy. These are important because so much of state policy has been focused on redressing the fiscal disparities among suburban school systems, especially in formulation of recent state educational aid policy.

The extent to which each of the above-named situations can and does occur, clearly reflects state policy modified by local response. The measurement of the direct and indirect effects of state policy raises both substantive and analytical issues. If the large city school system provides educational services to smaller, lower income, lower valuation areas than the city itself, then it can be responsible for a lowering of its own position. In an earlier era, when the large cities were wealthier than their surrounding areas, the expansion of the city school district was clearly to the benefit of the outlying area. However, in terms of current needs and resources, the situation is often fundamentally different. Nevertheless, state policy generally persists in overstating large city fiscal resources for educational purposes, usually by using a simple per-pupil valuation measure. The precise effects on state aid will be considered later, but it should be sufficient to note at this time that because the ratio of school enrollment to total population is generally lower in the school systems serving cities than in their outside areas, the valuation per pupil is accordingly higher. If all other things were equal, then the presumption of greater fiscal capacity would be warranted; however, other factors cannot be presumed to be equal and this is in part due to other aspects of state policy.

The question of independence or dependence of a school system raises another problem. The latter implies some initial degree of coterminality with another unit of government—city or county. But regardless of its effects, the independence or dependence of the school systems and their relationships with other local governments is a function of state policy.

As was already noted, there are fundamental differences in the non-educational fiscal responsibilities among the large central cities of different states, and among the large central cities and their outlying areas within states. These differences arise because the field of educational finance has basically given only limited recognition, except in a few very important cases, to the problem of noneducational expenditures supported by local governments. This problem, which will be dealt with in detail in Chapter V, arises because of differential state policy and local responses to that policy. While very difficult to deal with, it is nevertheless central to an understanding of large city finances.

The state may designate that all or nearly all local services must be provided by a single local governmental unit. This is basically the case in New England, where the city or town provides the whole range of local government services. This is especially true when the county has either atrophied or has been abolished, as in the case of Connecticut. There are, of course, important differences in the assignment of local government functions and the state-local fiscal arrangements between states. In all these cases, the school district is coterminous with the local government and is also generally a dependent school system. In New England there are no basic differences in the functions assigned to large cities as compared to other areas of the state, but there are different local responses to the assignment patterns. Apart from New England, there are a number of other jurisdictions in the country where state policy has integrated educational and noneducational finances, such as the independent cities and counties of Virginia.

In most of the large cities of the country, as well as in most of the country outside of New England, noneducational services are provided by a set of noncoterminous governments—county, city, and special districts—whose assignment function and revenue responsibility reflect the local responses to differentials in state policy. This, in turn, reflects the size of the area directly benefiting from the expenditure and the size of the areas providing the local tax resources. In fact, it is possible to be an enclave for noneducational purposes, as is the case for the City of Vernon even though it is a component part of the Los Angeles School District.

From the standpoint of educational finance, it is thus necessary to know not only the levels of government providing local government services but also the services which are provided by local government. The most important single competitor of education for local tax funds in large cities since the latter half of the 1930s has been public welfare, but there were and are differences among and within states in the assignment of the public welfare function to local governments. The state may also differentially assign parts of public welfare, such as general assistance, and other functions between the large central city and other governments.

This differential assignment of functional responsibilities both between and within states clearly helps explain both the level of noneducational expenditures and the proportion which education makes up of total local expenditures. Unfortunately, the knowledge that there is a differential assignment of functional responsibilities is not easily quantifiable when the expenditures must be allocated among different levels of local governments. Thus, county-wide expenditures on public welfare, health and hospitals, and highways, as well as county-wide expenditures on schools, pose some analytical problems. For the purpose of this study, county-wide expenditures—taxes and aid-received—are assumed to be equally distributed between the central city and the remainder of the area.

The picture which emerges indicates a long-term interaction between the state assignment of both local educational and noneducational responsibilities and the local response to these assignments. In the case of the large cities, there is an indication that in many instances responsibilities were legally assigned after they had in fact been assumed. But once they were assumed they were often irreversible. And in many cases the differential responsibilities were a reflection of municipal versus non-municipal, rather than specifically large city versus other areas. However, in practice this resulted in differentials in the actual distribution of responsibilities by state governments to the large cities, differentials which are in part a result of a failure to recognize, let alone coordinate, policy at the state level.

LOCAL SCHOOL COSTS

As has already been noted, state policy not only has differential effects as among states, but it also has a differential effect between the central cities and their outlying areas within states. In some cases the principal differences are among states, whereas in others the more important policy differentials are between the central cities and their outlying areas.

States establish and enforce ages of compulsory and permissive school attendance, both for those who attend public schools and those who do not. The problems raised by these differences are not as great today as they were earlier. Although the 12-year sequence is generally accepted, the required period of attendance may be considerably shorter. The problem becomes much more confusing at the extremes. At the entrance age there are questions which involve the extent of kindergarten and pre-kindergarten education as well as the precise age at which children must be accepted. In terms of actual behavior, *The Census of Population* indicates that there are important regional differences, although in some instances the state laws sometimes show very little variation. In addition to the mandatory age of acceptance, there is the permissive age of kindergarten and prekindergarten education and its recognition for school aid. At the other end of the spectrum, states also establish minima and maxima for leaving schools. States also provide the possibility of higher education, which in turn has consequences for those continuing through high school. State policy is also in evidence in large cities, where the problem of retaining students is much greater than it is in the suburban areas whose high schools and student bodies are much more college-oriented. The differential effects on the cost of education resulting from such mandates as vocational education must be much more carefully studied than has been historically the case.

The existence of nonpublic elementary and secondary education is also a product of state policy and local response. There are clear differences among states, and just as clear differences within states, as between the central city and outside central city areas. The recent expansion in the use of federal, state, and local funds for nonpublic schools or for nonpublic school pupils has created analytical as well as substantive problems in evaluating school finances. In states such as Pennsylvania the problem may be massive, but similar problems have existed and will continue to exist elsewhere.

The state also plays a very important role in the specific operational level of education. In establishing, encouraging, and enforcing standards, not only for school system size but in school size, class size, length of the school year, and the nature and kinds of offerings, the states influence the costs of operation per pupil and, through their relationship to the total population, influence the fiscal dimensions of education as well.

The issue of school district size historically has been one of inadequate size to provide an appropriate range and variety of courses. In recent years new issues involving the size of large city school systems have become the object of state policy. While the question of the small school district is almost academic in the case of large city areas, the problem is not academic in the suburban areas. In general, there is a feeling—especially in the case of systems with small high schools—that these are not only inordinately costly but that they do not provide satisfactory educational programs. On the other hand, the question of city systems which are "too large" has become a question of major state concern in recent years, as exemplified by decentralization in New York and Michigan.[2]

As part of their response to the "Cult of Efficiency" which dominated state and large city educational policy during the period between 1900 and 1930, large cities developed larger schools and larger class sizes than their counterparts in the rest of the states.[3] State-established maxima, as well as policy as to desirable size, had broad effects on the costs of education. In fact, one of the major trade-offs of educational costs involves those of salaries of instructional personnel and class size. Salaries can be kept high, other things being equal, by increasing class size. And the reduction of class size, concomitantly, would be at the expense of salaries. State mandating of maximum class size has had an effect on the amount expended per pupil and the amount expended per capita to be raised from local and state sources.

The effects of state policy on the pupil-teacher ratio is shown in Table 23. Estimates of the pupil-teacher ratio are shown for the large central cities and for the entire state in which they are located. The averages are for 1967–68. The state averages are overstated relative to the city

[2] For an analysis of the fiscal aspects of school decentralization see John J. Callahan and Donna E. Shalala, "Some Fiscal Dimensions of Three Hypothetical Decentralization Plans," Education and Urban Society, II (November 1969), 40–53.

[3] See Raymond Callahan, *op. cit.*, for an educational interpretation of the phenomenon.

TABLE 23

PUPILS PER CLASSROOM TEACHER, LARGE CITY SCHOOL SYSTEM
AND STATE AVERAGE, FALL 1967–68

	City System	State Average
East		
Baltimore, Md.	27	24
Boston, Mass.	25	25
Newark, N.J.	21	22
Buffalo, N.Y.	22	20
New York, N.Y.	20	20
Rochester, N.Y.	21	20
Philadelphia, Pa.	27	25
Pittsburgh, Pa.	28	25
Midwest		
Chicago, Ill.	28	22
Indianapolis, Ind.	28	25
Detroit, Mich.	31	24
Minneapolis, Minn.	25	23
St. Paul, Minn.	25	23
Kansas City, Mo.	27	25
St. Louis, Mo.	30	25
Omaha, Neb.	29	22
Cincinnati, Ohio	28	25
Cleveland, Ohio	28	25
Columbus, Ohio	25	25
Toledo, Ohio	27	25
Milwaukee, Wis.	28	21
South		
Birmingham, Ala.	28	26
Atlanta, Ga.	27	27
Louisville, Ky.	29	25
New Orleans, La.	25	25
Oklahoma City, Okla.	28	24
Memphis, Tenn.	27	27
Dallas, Tex.	28	23
Houston, Tex.	29	23
Norfolk, Va.	24	24
West		
Long Beach, Calif.	27	26
Los Angeles, Calif.	27	26
San Diego, Calif.	27	26
San Francisco, Calif.	26	26
Denver, Colo.	25	24
Portland, Ore.	24	22
Seattle, Wash.	28	25

SOURCE: National Education Association.

in that they include the large city behavior with which they are being compared. However, with a few notable exceptions, it appears that the over-all effect of state policy has been to reduce the pupil-teacher ratio to a greater extent outside the large cities than in them. In 1968, 29 of the 37 largest central city areas had systems with pupil-teacher ratios higher than their state averages; in only 1 case (Newark), did a large city have a pupil-teacher ratio lower than its state average.

Not only do states influence class size and the range of offerings, which in some cases are very expensive, but they also influence the nature and the quality of teachers through state control over teacher certification provisions and, more directly, by mandating the level of teacher salaries. This occurs not only on the minimum levels but also in the extent to which increases are automatic or merit, and these work out through state aid policy. It was a striking change when in the 1950s, the large cities, which had a waiting list of teachers during the 1930s, became relatively unattractive places to teach. As a result, in recent years states have allowed large cities to make more extensive use of part-time and substitute teachers than has been the case in other systems.

Furthermore, during the period of this analysis, the length of service of many central city school teachers has gone up considerably and with it their average compensation. This, in part, is due to the fact that the teachers in large city schools have been "locked in" by retirement systems.

The factors thus far enumerated in the context of direct state control over local expenditures do not have as much of a differential effect with the cities and their outlying areas as they do among large cities in different states. There are clearly different responses of the large cities compared to their suburban areas in the number of pupils per teacher than appear when cities are compared to states as a whole.

The direct effect of the states can be most clearly seen in the case of the financing of employee retirement systems, for not only are there major differences among states, but there are also significant differences between the treatment of the central cities and of their outlying areas. In some states, neither the large cities nor their other districts are responsible for raising revenues for the employee retirement systems. In some of these states there are social security contributions, in others there is no social security contribution at all. In some, the governmental share of employee retirement may be made only by local governments. Consequently, comparative data on per-pupil expenditures is not always an accurate indicator of the total expenditures made on behalf of school children.[4] If an expenditure is financed on a state-wide basis, there is no

---

[4] The University of the State of New York, State Education Department, *Educational Expenditures: Interstate Comparisons* (Albany, 1969).

way of determining directly the amounts which should be allocated to any individual local school district, whether it be a large city district or any other district in the state. Further, there are major differences in financing arrangements which do call for differential burdens of the local governments involved and, it should also be noted, on the teachers themselves.

Another element enters into the aspect of large city finances, however, for in a number of instances the only school systems in a state which must bear the responsibilities for financing employee retirement systems are the large city school districts. In some cases, even where all local school districts are given this responsibility, a differential responsibility may be assigned to the large city school district or its overlying government. As has been noted, the expenditure on fixed charges (mainly those arising from employee retirement systems) grew more rapidly than any other class of expenditure in recent years.

The differential effect on large cities of state mandating of educational costs is most clearly evident in the case of a number of employee retirement costs. The reason for this situation lies in the histories of the large cities. One of the major deficiencies was the absence of adequate local retirement systems apart from a few of the larger cities. Since local units could not finance them, the states undertook this task. Initially, it was not as costly as the financing of the much more highly developed large city retirement systems. However, as time wore on and this financing became more costly, the rural and suburban districts did not wish to share their advantage with the larger cities. It should also be noted that the large cities often carry similar differential burdens for their non-educational personnel as well. These costs also have to be financed almost universally out of local taxes. Some recent changes in this responsibility have been a major step forward insofar as the large city governments are concerned.

Local School Revenues

The states not only influence the level of educational costs, both directly and indirectly, but also the revenue side of the picture directly and indirectly. The direct influence is most evident in the complex case of state aid, which is considered in the last part of this chapter. The indirect influence is most powerfully exerted in the context of the local accessibility and use of the property tax and other tax sources, which are a product of state policy.[5]

As shown in Chapter III, the accessibility of the property tax base varies among the states and, as a consequence, among the large cities

[5] Advisory Commission on Intergovernmental Relations, *The Role of the States in Strengthening the Property Tax*, 2 vols. (1963); *Local Non Property Taxes and the Coordinating Role of the State* (1961).

as well. This tax, which clearly provides the bulk of all local taxes devoted directly to education, varies from a general property tax (one inclusive of both real property—land and buildings), and a personal property (business and individual—tangible and intangible), to an almost exclusively real property tax in the states of New York and Pennsylvania. Not only do the states influence the inclusiveness of the tax, but they also influence in a most complex way the level of assessing that property. In addition to determining the level of assessments, the state also determines the over-all exemption policy to be followed. While certain classes of property are exempt from property taxation as a result of federal constitutional provisions, others are a function of individual state practices. In a state with "Homestead" exemptions there may be very serious inroads into the local revenue sources and profound distortion of the use of the property base for state aid purposes.

A combination of all these factors has influenced the level and behavior of the real property tax base in recent years. Even interstate comparisons are very difficult to interpret exactly, though a number of important generalizations may be drawn from recent data. They show great differences in the amount of assessed valuation per pupil among the states, and since James and his colleagues found assessed valuation to be as good a measure as equalized full valuation in explaining variations among large city school districts, the finding is rather noteworthly.[6] The differences in assessed and equalized valuations clearly reflect state differences modified by local practices in assessment ratios. The presumptive "full" valuations per pupil are indicated for information only, since special care must be taken in their interpretation because of basic underlying differences in the assessed valuations.

The extent to which different classes of property are included in the tax rolls has profound consequences for the elasticity of the tax base with respect to economic growth; but regardless of the situation, there seems to be a clear indication of the differential growth of the large cities and their surrounding areas. As shown in Table 22, with a few exceptions the growth rates in locally assessed real property outside the central cities were considerably more rapid than in the city areas. If years other than 1961 and 1966 were taken, this would lead to a modification of some individual results but not in the general pattern. New York City stands in marked contrast with most other large cities which had neither annexations, reassessments, nor underlying population growth. The growth of its tax base is due to the exceptional building program in one part of New York City (Manhattan), and a continuous process of reassess-

[6] J. Thomas James, James A. Kelly, and Walter I. Garms, *Determinants of Educational Expenditures in Large Cities of the United States* (Stanford: Stanford University, 1966), 100–104.

ing real property which differentiates New York City from virtually all other central city areas of the country. However, even in the case of the New York Standard Metropolitan Statistical Area, the growth outside the central city areas was considerably in excess of that of New York City, even when not adjusting for the effects of the reassessment.

The reasons for the sluggish growth in central city property values partially involve the size of the state-determined exempt portion of the tax rolls. On the exemption side, state policy decisions as well as the traditional kinds of exempt property have had a major effect. In particular, new highways, urban renewal projects, schools, and a massive number of higher educational facilities have replaced properties which were previously on the rolls. In the case of urban renewal there is, of course, the hope that this fall will be arrested and reversed. There is evidence that this stage has already been reached in a number of cities, but it is of limited importance compared to the over-all downward trend in city property values.

Exemptions and withdrawal of property from the rolls show an asymmetry in their effects on the central city and the outside areas. This is particularly evident in the case of highways. The construction of highways in the large cities generally involves a reduction in existing total property values while sometimes maintaining some central business district commercial values. In the case of suburban areas, the effect of new highways is to enhance the value of existing land uses and to make new land uses more valuable. While this is not directly a state problem, the extent to which they are made manifest is influenced by over-all state property tax policy.

Finally, in some states such as New York, certain classes of property have been withdrawn from the tax rolls by state law. This was the case for certain classes of railroad property, withdrawal of which had an important effect on the tax bases of large cities. State policies have also had an enormous effect on large city assessments in recent years as certain classes of personal property have been withdrawn from the rolls, as in Minnesota. This is particularly true of Minneapolis and St. Paul, and is true of some of the more rapidly growing cities located in other states as well.

States not only control the size of the tax base, but state policy also determines the extent and the manner in which local taxes may be levied. Complex tax limits are a common feature of state-local tax laws throughout the nation.[7] As already noted in Chapter III, many of these came

[7] Thomas L. Johns, *Public School Finance Programs, 1968–1969* (Washington, D.C.: Department of Health, Education, and Welfare, Office of Education, 1969), for the most recent analysis of state aid programs and the tax limits associated with those programs.

into being in the 1930s, although some had their origin as far back as the nineteenth century. These limits have resulted in a set of rules and regulations which are, in some cases, operative only insofar as they affect the large cities and other communities with similar characteristics. At times they are imposed on school taxes, although more generally they are imposed on the total of school and municipal taxes. These tax limitations, operative for both legal and political reasons, can be avoided in a great variety of ways, but clearly they have the greatest effect on the large cities and on the school taxes of these large cities.

The effect of the tax limits on large cities has been inhibiting for large city school finances, which depend almost exclusively on the real property tax base. It should be noted that in some of the few cases where nonproperty taxes have been used for school purposes, they have been far more inhibiting than the property taxes themselves after their initial stimulative effects wear off.

STATE AID

Direct state expenditures in behalf of local school systems have been relatively minor apart from the acceptance of responsibility for employee retirement systems, the exception of the State of Hawaii having been noted earlier.[8] The indirect expenditures in the form of state aid have, however, been a major element, if not the most important element, in the state's influence on the total amount of resources devoted to education and the distribution of resources between the large central cities and the suburban and rural areas. Further, many of the controls over local education occur in the context of the provision of state aid. Thus, there is the mandating of a variety of costs, levels of service, minimum tax rates, etc., which takes place in the context of state aid.

State aid is the vehicle through which much of state policy toward education is carried out *de facto*. By the leverage of changing and withholding aid, state policy is in many instances made more powerful. The requirements for participation provide a set of controls over such variables as school system size, class size, teacher training, and minimum tax rates. The carrot of additional state aid is made available if certain types of programs are undertaken. The expansion of aid programs has also been a principal factor in the improvement of property tax equalization and assessment procedures.

The preoccupation of the analytical literature on state aid has been on the equalizing nature of the programs but, as Benson has indicated, there are other goals of aid policy, and there are a number of meanings,

---

[8] Direct state expenditures in behalf of individual school districts have not been adequately treated by the various reporting agencies. Even state totals have not been adequately reported by the Office of Education.

often conflicting, attached to the concept of equalization. Historically, much of this is premised on the multiple and not necessarily consistent objectives of stimulation, equity, efficiency, and tax relief or tax sharing.[9]

As shown in Table 24, there are not only differences between states but, much more important, there are clear differences between the central city and outlying areas in the amount of aid per pupil and per capita.

State aid, as it interacts with the tapping of the local resources, clearly provides one of the central themes of school finances in the United States. The problem this interaction presents has special relevance to the school systems in large city areas since the effectiveness of state aid for education is complicated by the existence of other aids which, while not directly related to education, may have a definite effect on it.

The analysis of state aid to education in large city areas assumes more meaning when it is viewed in its historical context. This problem, which was raised earlier in Chapter II, will now be analyzed in considerably more detail. Charles Benson has divided the history of state grants-in-aid for education by looking at the "major landmarks"—Cubberley, Strayer and Haig, and Paul Mort and his associates.[10] However, unlike Benson's, the prime emphasis of this analysis is on the relationship between aid to the large cities and the aid to the rest of the states.

The first of the three landmarks was Cubberley's analysis in *School Funds and Their Apportionment,* which was referred to earlier. In this volume Cubberley "sought a plan which would reduce the extremes of financial inequality." Insofar as inequality existed at the time of his writing (1905) it was in favor of the rich cities, plus a few isolated special examples, as against the towns and other rural districts. At this stage of the analysis the primary purposes of aid were dual in nature—equalization and encouragement of local expenditures. Insofar as school expenditures were encouraged, the large cities would be the beneficiaries. As a result, Cubberley developed an ingenious scheme combining teachers employed and aggregated days of attendance. While the Cubberley aid program did not achieve its goals, he did provide a basis of an argument for giving lesser aid to the large cities in his text, if not in the formula itself.

As Laszlo Ecker-Racz and Eugene McLoone have recently indicated, "in the 1920's, the goals of equalization and encouragement were thought to be in conflict. States moved almost exclusively toward equalizing a minimum foundation program." In that context Strayer and Haig[11] pro-

---

[9] Benson, *op. cit.,* 215–49.
[10] *Ibid.*
[11] *The Financing of Education in the State of New York.* Educational Finance Inquiry Commission, Vol. I (New York: The Macmillan Company, 1923).

TABLE 24

PER-PUPIL AND PER-CAPITA* EDUCATIONAL AID, 1962
(School District Basis)

	$ Per Pupil		$ Per Capita	
	CC	OCC	CC	OCC
East				
Baltimore, Md.	106	162	20	32
Boston, Mass.	50	42	6	8
Newark, N.J.	50	66	16	12
Buffalo, N.Y.	194	288	25	60
New York, N.Y.	234	297	30	66
Rochester, N.Y.	186	305	24	67
Philadelphia, Pa.–N.J.	140	132	18	25
Pittsburgh, Pa.	93	184	11	34
Midwest				
Chicago, Ill.	111	103	15	20
Indianapolis, Ind.	97	126	21	28
Detroit, Mich.	137	163	24	39
Minneapolis, Minn.	133	218	19	47
St. Paul, Minn.	129	218	18	47
Kansas City, Mo.–Kans.	130	89	21	31
St. Louis, Mo.–Ill.	129	141	18	25
Omaha, Neb.–Iowa	33	40	5	11
Cincinnati, Ohio–Ky.–Ind.	51	145	8	23
Cleveland, Ohio	50	66	7	13
Columbus, Ohio	50	114	9	28
Toledo, Ohio	52	202	8	48
Milwaukee, Wis.	93	55	13	12
South				
Birmingham, Ala.	154	152	32	37
Atlanta, Ga.	102	152	21	49
Louisville, Ky.–Ind.	95	137	18	28
New Orleans, La.	194	200	29	39
Oklahoma City, Okla.	96	61	23	14
Memphis, Tenn.–Ark.	107	119	22	33
Dallas, Tex.	140	172	27	38
Houston, Tex.	143	201	32	52
Norfolk, Va.	101	117	17	28
West				
Long Beach, Calif.	114	316	36	59
Los Angeles, Calif.	172	316	51	59
San Diego, Calif.	195	282	37	74
San Francisco, Calif.	189	254	24	59
Denver, Colo.	74	122	14	35
Portland, Ore.–Wash.	123	217	21	54
Seattle, Wash.	234	289	42	79

* Based on 1960 population.

posed that state aid be used to provide standardized educational programs based on uniform local tax rates. The state would mandate a set rate of local school taxation which all school districts would have to levy in order to qualify for state aid. Having qualified for aid, the state would guarantee the foundation level of school expenditures in a given school district. The large city with above-average resources, New York City in this case, would be the primary agent in a redistribution in favor of raising the minimum level of the smaller and poorer school systems. Insofar as the Strayer-Haig formula in New York concentrated on relieving high property tax rates, large cities with high tax rates were able to benefit to some extent. But the general data for the period, then and now, clearly indicate that it was the smaller, poorer, rural school district that was to benefit most, and that the large central city was to be placed eventually in the same resource position for state aid purposes as the wealthy emerging suburb. We find that Scarsdale, Bronxville, and Great Neck even in the 1920s were clearly able to support considerably higher levels of school expenditures per pupil and per capita than their large city counterparts.

The evolution of state aid for education not only reflected the work of the leading theorists but also began to follow political realities as state aid became more important in the aggregate for local school finances. It grew from 13.0 percent in 1922, immediately prior to the Strayer-Haig Report, to 19.6 percent of total local educational expenditures by 1932. An even more massive growth occurred between 1932 and 1938, when state aid grew from 19.6 percent of local educational expenditures to 30.6 percent of expenditures as Strayer-Haig types of formulas were more widely adopted. Between 1938 and 1948 it grew to 37.2 percent, a figure which it has more or less maintained. In 1964–65 it was 36.6 percent of all local educational expenditures. Since then the comingling of federal and state money has made this proportion difficult to interpret.

The amount of state aid has gone up tremendously since 1948. This is due to the growth in educational expenditures in the aggregate from 37.4 percent in 1948 to 44.8 percent of total local expenditures in 1962 and 48.0 percent in 1966–67. Yet both direct and indirect evidence suggest that, for the years 1957 to 1964–65, large city education expenditures as a percentage of total expenditures have remained virtually unchanged. The effect of state aid on this relationship is clearly significant, involving a large part of the urban population and, with the outlying areas, a large proportion of the national population.

The stability of state aid as a proportion of local educational expenditures obscures the most massive change in state aid which occurred during the era of the last major figure in school finance,[12] Paul Mort. At the outset, Mort was involved in the refinement and expansion of the Strayer-Haig minimum foundation program, then in its adaptation to the 1930s, and finally in its application to the suburban boom of the late 1940s. This last period appears to have been crucial in the establishment of the national pattern of state aid. The vast expansion and development of suburban school systems led to major upward revisions in the levels but not the concepts of the foundation aid program. This came about as the numbers of students and the cost of education began to move upward very rapidly. The special problems of the suburban districts during the period led to a revival of interest in general-purpose percentage equalization that involved state sharing of school system expenditures. At the same time, Mort and his colleagues also showed interest in the special problems of the large city school systems. Specifically, with the idea of a "valuation reduction ratio (VRR)"[13] to correct for the fact of municipality, primarily large city, tax differential, as a correction for the impact of municipal government, *i.e.,* for the "municipal overburden."[14]

State aid has been considered from a number of points—especially the extent to which it is or is not equalizing. Other approaches have analyzed the form of the grant. In addition, there are the controls implicit in the state aid system and their effects on the delivery of local educational services. Thus, an elegant formula like that of Wisconsin is quantitatively unimportant, whereas some of the more restricted formulas are of much greater importance. The principal emphasis in this analysis is on the differential treatment of large city and outside large city school systems within individual states.

In particular, the emphasis will be placed on the effect of state aid on the behavior of current expenditures per pupil. However, because of objections raised in the literature, the relationship between aid and locally raised revenues will also be considered. The impact of aid for capital outlays will not be considered in detail, although the distorting effects, both in the case of explicit capital aids and general purpose educational aids which might be used for capital purposes, have generally been recognized.

The specific relationship between aid, expenditures, and locally raised

[12] Two of his most important statements are contained in *The Foundation Program in State Educational Policy* (The State Education Department, 1957), and *A New Approach to School Finance* (Albany: New York State Education Conference Board, 1961), 9–20.

[13] *A New Approach to School Finance, op. cit.*

[14] Erick L. Lindman, *State Support and Municipal Government Costs* (Los Angeles: University of California, Los Angeles, 1964).

funds has been measured in a number of ways. Following recent practices, the comparisons will be made in terms of current expenditures on
education plus interest payments, which are generally much larger in the
suburban areas because of the extensive building program of the latter
half of the 1950s. The crucial question is to measure the effects of aid,
not to assume the problem away as has been characteristic of a number
of studies.

The pattern of state aid for the large cities analyzed in this study is
shown in Table 24. On a per-pupil basis, the aforementioned effect of
state boundaries is clearly evident in a number of ways. Certain states
stand out in the amount of aid they gave per pupil, notably New York,
Louisiana, California, and Washington; at the other extreme is Nebraska.
It is quite clear that when a large city receives a considerable amount of
aid, the outlying area usually receives a considerably larger amount of
aid. When the level of aid is low, as in Massachusetts, Wisconsin, Oklahoma, and Ohio, the large city may often receive a larger amount of aid
on a per-pupil basis.

Of the 37 large city areas, the central cities received larger aid per
pupil in 7 cases and the outside areas received greater aid in the remaining 30; in 2 of the 7 central city cases this is due to the bi-state nature of
the area. The extent of the aid to the outside areas is, however, under-
stated in fiscal terms, because not only do they receive larger amounts of
aid per pupil but the ratio of pupils to total population is greater in the
peripheral areas. The per-capita value of the aid is accordingly enhanced.
On a per-capita basis, only 3 of the 37 central city areas have greater aid
than their outlying areas. Of these, Oklahoma City represents a very
special case and, because of its enormous area, there is some question as
to whether it should be included with the other central cities. Milwaukee
represents a very insignificant amount as there is a difference of only one
dollar. On the average, per-capita aid in the large city areas was $20.72,
while in their outlying areas it was almost twice as great, $37.66.

The question of aid as a proportion of current expenditures has also
been raised. In this case it is quite evident that both the large central
cities and their outlying areas receive a much smaller proportion of their
current expenditures in the form of aid than does the nation as a whole,
for if the aid figure for the nation is computed on a current expenditure
basis, it amounts to some 44.5 percent of the total. Only six of the large
city areas in the entire sample received that proportion of aid. It should
be noted that if the large cities were excluded from the picture, as well
as the outlying areas, the figure for the rest of the nation would accordingly have to be raised.

The effect of state aid policy is brought out more clearly on a regional basis, where state boundaries intervene in school financing to a greater extent than they do in their underlying economic conditions. By looking at the broad concept of the New York Metropolitan Region, as developed by the Regional Planning Association, we can determine the working of three different systems of state aid and how they affect the central cities and the outlying areas in each of three states: New York, New Jersey, and Connecticut.

There are clearly striking differences between the amounts of aid received per pupil in the three states. Indeed, there is no overlap in the aids received when measured across state boundaries. Further, using the 1959 average of incomes, it is clear that New York City, with an average income of $2,306, received almost the same amount of aid as Westchester County (less Yonkers), which had an average income figure of $3,427 —almost 50 percent higher (Table 25). Further, the system was capable of generating aid of $359 per pupil when the national figure for current expenditure per enrolled pupil was $418.

TABLE 25

Sᴄʜᴏᴏʟ Sʏsᴛᴇᴍs ɪɴ ᴛʜᴇ Mᴇᴛʀᴏᴘᴏʟɪᴛᴀɴ Nᴇᴡ Yᴏʀᴋ Aʀᴇᴀ,* 1964

	Current Educational Expenditures Per Pupil, $	School Taxes Per Capita, $	Educational State Aid Per Pupil, $	Income Per Capita, $
New York State				
New York SMSA				
New York City	(759.31)	(67.87)	(250.23)	(2,306)
Nassau County	826.74	133.30	364.74	2,874
Rockland County	719.44	128.47	333.33	2,109
Suffolk County	696.07	119.04	406.86	1,964
Westchester County	805.36	116.81	261.74	3,252
Yonkers	(517.98)	(58.64)	(233.81)	(2,685)
Westchester less Yonkers	871.28	134.78	264.46	3,427
New York SMSA less New York City and Yonkers	790.35	129.90	358.59	2,738
New Jersey				
Newark SMSA				
Essex County	547.34	94.91	68.41	2,452
Newark	(516.03)	(85.43)	(71.52)	(1,792)
Essex less Newark	572.24	102.31	65.79	2,967
Morris County	557.20	141.98	84.88	2,527
Union County	521.44	107.54	69.13	2,631

TABLE 25 (Cont.)

SCHOOL SYSTEMS IN THE METROPOLITAN NEW YORK AREA,* 1964

	Current Educational Expenditures Per Pupil, $	School Taxes Per Capita, $	Educational State Aid Per Pupil, $	Income Per Capita, $
Newark SMSA less Newark	548.33	112.45	72.13	2,746
Paterson–Clifton– Passaic SMSA				
Bergen County	553.64	113.85	68.85	2,721
Passaic County	500.66	84.27	71.03	2,088
Clifton	(436.50)	(73.17)	(58.35)	(2,378)
Paterson	(451.88)	(63.89)	(83.24)	(1,840)
Passaic	(521.20)	(72.22)	(71.03)	(2,093)
Passaic less Clifton, Paterson, Passaic	562.09	119.68	78.82	2,181
Paterson–Clifton– Passaic SMSA less Paterson, Clifton, Passaic	555.02	114.66	70.48	2,646
Jersey City SMSA				
Hudson County	501.89	60.06	65.32	2,039
Jersey City	(473.68)	(53.27)	(56.47)	(1,964)
Hudson County less Jersey City	523.28	66.26	72.03	2,101
Other Metropolitan Counties				
Middlesex County	445.08	107.14	84.26	2,073
Somerset County	506.60	133.33	82.10	2,381
Connecticut				
Fairfield County	517.10	81.96	112.88	2,792
Stamford	(578.64)	(82.80)	(113.65)	(2,860)
Bridgeport	(388.54)	(42.04)	(112.08)	(1,955)
Norwalk	(520.60)	(88.23)	(111.33)	(2,523)
Fairfield less Stamford, Bridgeport, Norwalk	549.21	99.11	114.71	3,208

* Fourteen counties; parentheses indicate central cities.

SOURCE: Financial Data for School Districts, Year Ending June 30, 1964 (Albany, N.Y.: Department of Audit and Control, 1965); New Jersey Taxpayers Association, Financial Statistics of New Jersey Local Government, 1964 ed. (Trenton, N.J., September 1964); Connecticut Public Expenditure Council, Local Public School Expenses and State Aid in Connecticut, School Years 1960–61 through 1964–65 (Hartford, Conn., January 1966).

The New Jersey levels in 1964 were much lower than those in New York, but the aid per pupil in Newark, with a per-capita income of $1,792, was slightly lower than the aid received by the rest of the Newark SMSA, which showed an income average of $2,746. Similar results occurred in the other parts of the New Jersey areas analyzed.

An almost identical situation occurs in Connecticut for, in the case of Bridgeport, the aid was almost identical with that portion of Fairfield County not including any of the Census-designated central cities. However, in Bridgeport the average income was $1,955 and in the remaining part of the area it was $3,208.

High state aid per pupil does not necessarily mean low per-capita taxes. Looking at the "large cities" in the three states studied, the figures are:

	Aid Per Pupil, $	Taxes Per Capita, $
New York City, N.Y.	250	68
Yonkers, N.Y.	234	59
Newark, N.J.	72	85
Paterson, N.J.	83	64
Clifton, N.J.	58	73
Passaic, N.J.	71	72
Jersey City, N.J.	56	53
Bridgeport, Conn.	112	42

Per-capita school taxes are a function of enrollment ratios to a much greater extent than they are of aid, but the enrollment ratios in these cities are fairly similar except for Clifton, New Jersey. And there is little indication that the level of aid noticeably influences the level of taxation downward in the large cities. In the suburban areas there is an indication that the level of aid does not reduce taxes for school purposes.

This raises the question of the relationship between aid and taxes in large cities. While it is impossible to obtain directly comparable data on school taxes for all the large city areas considered in this study, indirect data based on revenues from own sources not financed from aid were computed in terms of "nonaided" educational expenditures in this detailed analysis of the three states, and it has been possible to determine the actual school taxes per capita. The picture which emerges in the three states is that the higher aid is not reflected in lower taxes of the areas studied.

In an important study of state school foundation programs in 1962–

63, Albert R. Munse[15] showed, for both elementary and secondary schools, that the allowances for small districts are in excess of those of the large school districts for every state for which the ratio was computed except Wisconsin. In Wisconsin the aid for education was quite small, being dwarfed by a "perverse" system of noneducational state aid which favors industrial and high-income suburbs. The state aid formula, in the last analysis, still places the city of Milwaukee in the least favored class. This problem will be considered in Chapter VII.

The question of state aid is central to a discussion of school finances in the United States. Considered in the restricted framework of educational aid alone, the problem overlooks the fact that there are other claims on the local areas which finance education. As stated, the analysis did not deal with the emergence of differential needs which are rendered only partially evident by a knowledge of income, racial balance, etc., and fails to take into account the deteriorated and often inappropriately located physical plants which provide education.

SUMMARY

State governments play a basic role in differentiating school systems. Within their boundaries, they also act to differentiate school systems located in large central cities from those located in suburban and rural areas. The full set of effects are most clearly apparent when the educational and fiscal aspects of school finances are considered, but other measures also indicate the effects of state policy on variations within and between states.

The analysis in this chapter indicated the importance of the state governments in determining the size and organization of school systems within their borders. Recent developments on the decentralization of large city school systems at the State House level in New York, Michigan, and elsewhere, are merely a continuation of that tradition, recognizing ultimate state power. On the other hand, the decision as to the minimum size of school systems has important consequences for the distribution of state aid and indirectly for the amount that can be distributed to the large central cities with their concentrations of poverty. The existence of school systems which extend beyond the central city also has important consequences for both the meaning and the amount of aid. However, where this situation exists at present, it is generally to the fiscal benefit of the surrounding areas.

Similarly, it is state policy which determines whether schools are

[15] "Weighting Factors in State Foundation Programs" *Proceedings of the Eighth National Conference on School Finance* (Washington, D.C.: National Education Association, 1965), 56–62.

fiscally independent and, if the alternatives are available, whether it is the large city or other government entities that may exert fiscal prerogatives.

States determine the "basic" average in addition to minimum ranges of educational service and hence the levels of school finances. This involves the minimum ages for compulsory attendance as well as the minimum ages for leaving school; it establishes a context for education. Thus, the extent to which nursery school and kindergarten education are used is clearly state-determined. Similarly, the effect of state policy is also evident in the determination of the pupil-teacher ratio and its consequences on per-pupil costs. Busing, high-priced courses, vocational and special education courses are state-determined in many instances. Often these have a differential effect on large cities as opposed to other areas.

Further, states establish differential accessibility to the property tax base as well as the rules governing rates. In many instances these operate differentially between large cities and other areas within a state. Similar situations exist in the case of debt.

State aid, perhaps the most important aspect of state policy, is considered because it is often the vehicle by which the state exerts its power, and because it provides a large but differential portion of the revenues received by large cities as compared to other school systems. The historical analysis of state aid brings out the basic set of factors which have led to a differential treatment of large cities compared to other school systems. This is brought out by the higher suburban levels of aid per pupil, and even more by the much higher per-capita levels received in suburban and rural school systems than in the large city school systems.

The multiple goals of state aid policy—tax sharing, equalizing tax burden, and providing incentives for policy—make the analysis of state aid quite difficult. In this chapter the pattern of aid, rather than the effects of state aid policy, has been considered. The problem of effects will be considered in detail in Chapter VII. The much higher level of aid in suburban areas and the built-in set of factors which favor them are of fundamental importance in understanding the contemporary fiscal position of large city school systems.

V. Noneducational Expenditures

One of the most consciously neglected areas in the study of contemporary large city educational finances—and one of the most important—is the complex set of relationships between educational and noneducational finances at the local government level. While these relationships have been partially considered by scholars, going back to the origins of the systematic study of educational finances, the analyses have been restricted by the complexity of the problems involved as well as by a desire to isolate and insulate educational finances from other local government demands.

The early work of Cubberley, already cited, as well as that of Edward C. Elliot at the turn of the twentieth century, either implicitly or explicitly, recognized and appreciated the problems raised by a dominant noneducational sector in large cities. This was especially true for the work of Elliot, whose study, *Some Fiscal Aspects of Public Education in American Cities,* specifically dealt with the interaction of educational and noneducational finances in large cities. The much simpler systems of local government finances in large cities at the turn of the century made the comparisons more meaningful than they would be today. In recent years the work of Paul Mort, Arvid Burke,[1] and Erick L. Lindman, individually and in association with others, has also dealt with the problems raised by the interaction of educational and noneducational finances at the local level—but this work is the exception rather than the rule. Unfortunately, there are severe limitations in attempting to generalize about noneducational behavior patterns unless the variation in the assignment of the responsibilities for the spending and the raising of local government funds for noneducational purposes, both among and within states, is explicitly recognized. In no areas are these differences as important as in the case of the large cities.

Students of government and public finance have dealt somewhat more extensively with the relationships between the educational and nonedu-

---

[1] See especially Arvid Burke's chapter on the application of Erick L. Lindman's formula to New York State in the latter's *State School Support and Municipal Costs.*

cational aspects of local governments and their finances than have scholars of educational finances. The work of Roscoe Martin and other political scientists has helped explain the isolation and insulation of educational finances from noneducational finances.[2] The major area where the question of the relationship of educational to noneducational finances has surfaced is in the considerable literature on "fiscal independence" and the autonomy of local educational government. (This literature is considered in Chapter VI.) However, most of these analyses are mainly concerned with qualitative differences in control and their effects on school finances; they tend to ignore the over-all differential quantitative effects occasioned by noneducational behavior. Perhaps the only area where the problem of the relationships has been touched on in depth is in the burgeoning literature in economics and political science on the determinants of governmental finances. But again, most of these analyses have been limited in their approach to the relationships between the educational sectors of local finance.

The purposes of this chapter are: (1) to explain the nature and the behavior of noneducational finances in the large cities and in their surrounding metropolitan areas in a manner compatible with the discussion of educational finances; (2) to provide some empirical evidence of the factors that determine noneducational fiscal behavior in large cities; and (3) to determine the relationship between educational and noneducational finances. A more systematic statistical analysis involving a whole matrix of variables will be considered in Chapter VII.

The noncoterminality of the governments providing local noneducational services, inherent definitional problems, and their isolation of educational finances have made the analysis of the relationship between educational and noneducational finances more difficult in recent years. The problem of the definition of noneducational finances is, of course, related to the questions as to what educational finances are, a subject which was discussed in the first two chapters. There it was analyzed in the context of educational behavior; here the focus will be on noneducational fiscal behavior.

There are two different classes of problems associated with local noneducational finances. The first is definitional and involves distinguishing among the governmental units responsible for expenditures and taxes; the second involves the nature of the specific operations involved. Even in the case of independent school districts which are full-fledged local governmental units, there is a variety of fiscal operations which, if they

[2] For an incisive statement of the reasons for this development from a political scientist's point of view see Roscoe C. Martin, *Government and the Suburban School* (Syracuse: Syracuse University Press, 1962), Ch. IV.

were undertaken by other local governmental units, would not be classified as educational or, more specifically, as "local school" expenditures. These include library, health, recreation, child care, and manpower development and training, as well as junior college and other higher educational operations. Expenditures on behalf of these functions have become quantitatively more important since 1965, but in fact and in principle, these expenditures existed in prior years. On a fiscal basis, it is difficult to differentiate and to analyze the noneducational operations of independent school systems by function unless such information is specifically forthcoming as a result of more detailed reporting than is usually the case; and once again there are major differences across state boundaries in such reporting. Thus, it is very difficult to determine the inherent noneducational expenditures being carried on by independent school systems, although the concept of "current expenditures for full-time elementary and secondary day schools" is specifically designed to achieve that goal by providing a standard definition.[3]

The problem of definition and differentiation of educational and non-educational expenditures becomes even greater in the case of fiscally dependent school systems. On the basis of past and present practices, it appears that there is an enormous variety in what cities, towns, and counties with dependent school systems classify and report as noneducational and educational expenditures. In some instances, certain classes of expenditures such as capital outlay, interest, principal payments, and local governments' payments to retirement systems never appear as educational expenditures, even when they are made in behalf of local schools in the purest sense of the concept. On the other hand, it is possible to credit local schools with expenditures, or with fiscal responsibility, as a result of certain definitional practices such as the allocation of certain costs to education because they are politically or fiscally more palatable or legally more possible. The problem of definition has been handled mainly by detailed analyses of individual school systems such as those carried on by the Office of Education and the National Education Association, but the major emphasis in both cases is to distinguish different classes of educational expenditures rather than to deal with noneducational expenditures.

The differences in the assignment of functional responsibilities are more important than the definitional differences in determining the level of noneducational expenditures in large cities. These differentials in state-assigned responsibilities for local expenditures and revenues vary both

---

[3] There are also great allocational difficulties when physical plant can be used for both educational and noneducational purposes. These difficulties occur on both current and capital accounts.

among and within states, and also in the differences in the local subsystems providing noneducational services at the large city level. Far more than in the case of educational expenditure and revenue responsibilities, there are differentially greater noneducational responsibilities assigned to the largest cities of the various states as compared to other local governments of the same states. But the differentials in the assignment of fiscal responsibilities among states clearly dominate the levels of local noneducational finances in cities and suburban areas. The most important quantitative variation among states occurs in the assignment of the responsibility for public welfare.[4] In some states it is almost entirely a state-administered program jointly financed by the federal and state governments, whereas in other states it is a locally administered program jointly financed by federal, state, and local governments. The effect on expenditure levels of local governments is substantial. This is reflected in the aid as well as in the expenditure patterns. There are other functions which fall into the same category as public welfare, although to a lesser extent.

In addition to the state differentials, there are variations in the local government subsystems providing services to the large cities. In a limited number of cases where there is coterminality between the city and the county—or in New England, where there is little or no county responsibility—there appears to be a different kind of relationship than when there are noncoterminous overlying local governments sharing in benefits and costs. The basic question which emerges is whether the concentration of the spending and revenue responsibility is proportional to the extent of responsibility in its effect on the noneducational and educational fiscal patterns of the large cities. The question of the absence or the presence of coterminality, which bulks so large in the analysis of educational finances, is even more important in the case of noneducational fiscal behvavior. And it is more than a measurement question. It is also a question of whether there are quantitative differences in local finances which emerge from different types of local governmental subsystems.

The last part of this chapter is an analysis of the extent to which the characteristics of the large cities—as measured by their size, density, income, surrounding areas, and history—determine their fiscal behavior. Only after all these definitional, structural, and empirical factors are considered is it possible to interpret the effects of noneducational fiscal behavior on educational behavior.

---

[4] Alan K. Campbell and Seymour Sacks, *Metropolitan America: Fiscal Patterns and Governmental Systems* (New York: The Free Press, 1967), 47.

THE MUNICIPAL CONTEXT

Local noneducational finances have been studied most carefully and extensively in their "municipal" framework. There is a vast body of information on municipal finances in both federal government documents and the counterpart state and local reports centering on municipal finances.[5] While the basic purpose of this analysis will be to deal with the total local system of governments providing local government services and collecting revenues in large city areas, the first step will be to look at the problem of municipal or city finance itself. This is the fundamental building block in the understanding of the noneducational and, in a few instances, the educational fiscal behavior of large city areas.

The first step of this particular analysis will be to clarify the observed pattern of municipal finances in large city areas, the conventional, if not always accurate, measurement unit in the analysis of large city school finances. In the case of municipal finances, the data must be carefully interpreted because they

> relate only to municipal corporations and their dependent agencies, and do not include amounts for other local governments overlying city areas. Therefore, expenditures here for "education" do not include spending by the separate school districts which administer public schools within municipal areas. Variations in the assignment of governmental responsibility for public assistance, health, hospitals, public housing and other functions to a lesser degree also have an important effect upon reported amounts of city expenditure, revenue, and debt.[6]

A very influential body of literature has emerged which presumes a relationship between population size and local governmental costs without recognition of the assignment differences involved. There are other influential generalizations involving the expenditure effects of density, as well as the proportional relationship between the size of the central city and of the SMSA of which it is a part. Because most of these generalizations concerning local noneducational expenditures have been made in the context of municipal finances, the problems initially will be so considered.

The pattern of municipal finances is reported on a municipal population size basis by the Census Bureau. As shown in Table 26, per-capita general expenditures range from $95.70 in the "less than 50,000" class

[5] U.S. Bureau of the Census, *1967 Census of Governments State Reports on State and Local Government Finances,* Vol. VI, No. 3 (Washington, D.C.: Government Printing Office, 1969)

[6] U.S. Bureau of the Census, *City Government Finances in 1966–67* (Washington, D.C.: Government Printing Office), 3.

to $320.00 in the "over one million" class. The former class represents 17,690 municipal-type governments of all sizes and kinds, many with only minimal fiscal responsibility. Furthermore, the figure for this class is estimated and subject to sampling variation. These considerations are important because, as will be shown, the major differences in expenditure and other aspects of fiscal behavior arise from comparisons of other population size groups with this group.

TABLE 26

PER-CAPITA CITY GOVERNMENT EXPENDITURES,
BY POPULATION SIZE CLASS, 1966–67

Municipalities Having a 1960 Population	Total $	Educational $	Noneducational $	Noneducational %	Number of Cities
Over 1,000,000	320.81	67.89	252.92	78.83	5
Over 1,000,000*	(149.12)	(1.65)	(147.47)	(98.89)	4
500,000– 999,999	232.71	35.74	196.97	84.64	17
500,000– 999,999†	(168.82)	(1.29)	(167.53)	(99.23)	(14)
300,000– 499,999	175.20	32.12	143.08	81.66	21
200,000– 299,999	160.18	24.13	136.05	84.93	19
100,000– 199,999	176.61	36.04	140.56	79.58	68
50,000– 99,999	161.13	29.73	131.40	81.54	180
Less than 50,000	95.70	8.37	88.33	92.29	17,690
Average	164.75	26.81	137.94	83.72	18,000

* Excluding New York. †Excluding Baltimore, Boston, and Washington, D.C.
SOURCE: *City Government Finances in 1966–67.*

In the case of other population size groups there is an apparent upward drift of total, educational and noneducational, expenditures with population size. If, however, New York City is removed from the over-one-million category, and Baltimore, Washington, D.C., and Boston are removed from the next size category because they perform county, school district, and—in the case of Washington—state functions, the picture is radically altered. There is little or no pattern relating size to per-capita total expenditures, or size to per-capita noneducational expenditures. The expenditure picture is blurred for cities over 50,000, and it is presumed that a similar blurring would occur if other aspects of finance were considered.

This obscurity is much more decidedly indicated in Table 27, where the individual large cities serving the 37 largest Standard Metropolitan Statistical Areas in 1966–67 are analyzed.[7] There areas contained almost 41 percent of the nation's population in 1967, and, hence, a considerable portion of what has been designated as the "metropolitan problem." In this table the large-city portions of these areas are grouped by region, and the noneducational functions are analyzed in more detail. There are two major subgroupings of functions. The first has been called "Common Functions," and represents what are generally considered the core functions of municipal governments, although even here there are some departures from a consistent pattern. The other major grouping includes the principal noncommon functions—public welfare and local schools—and implicitly the other functions cited by the Census Bureau as limitations in the analysis of municipal finances.

The range of direct general expenditures, including education when it is a municipal function, is from $67 per capita in San Antonio to $561 in the comprehensive governmental system of Washington, and $564 in the county-city school district of New York City. If education is excluded, the range is reduced from the $67-level in San Antonio to $414 in Washington, and $389 per captia in Boston. If state and local assignment systems for public welfare were taken into account, the range of expenditures would be further reduced because these expenditures are most important in Washington, Baltimore, Boston, New York City, San Francisco, and Denver, all of which appear at the upper range of municipalities with high noneducational expenditures. These are all municipalities which reflect the entire public welfare expenditure in their cities, as opposed to county or state assumption of the expenditure responsibility. In no instance does this reflect total revenue responsibility.

The range and the variation in expenditures are still further reduced if only the common functions are considered. These are the functions presumed to be carried on by almost all municipal governments, and include police, fire, sewage, sanitation, highway (other than capital),

[7] These findings were reported in part in the Advisory Commission on Intergovernmental Relations: "Metropolitan Disparities—A Second Reading" (Washington, D.C.: Bulletin 70–1, 1970).

TABLE 27

Per-Capita Expenditures, Principal Central Cities of the
37 Largest Standard Metropolitan Statistical Areas, 1967

	Total Direct General $	Non-education $	Common Functions $	Public Welfare $	Local Schools $	City-County
Northeast						
Washington, D.C.	561	411	140	49	144	Y
Baltimore, Md.	375	248	88	63	121	Y
Boston, Mass.	482	389	111	107	92	Y
Newark, N.J.	351	182	109	13	169	N
Paterson, N.J.	200	82	84	0	116	N
Buffalo, N.Y.	272	143	78	0	129	N
New York, N.Y.	515	351	107	89	128	Y
Rochester, N.Y.	343	185	83	0	157	N
Philadelphia, Pa.	171	166	81	7	5	Y
Pittsburgh, Pa.	135	135	71	0	0	N
Providence, R.I.	242	148	82	0	94	Y
Midwest						
Chicago, Ill.	127	127	71	3	0	N
Indianapolis, Ind.	101	101	52	0	0	N
Detroit, Mich.	170	167	78	10	3	N
Minneapolis, Minn.	116	116	64	0	0	N
Kansas City, Mo.	140	140	79	7	0	N
St. Louis, Mo.	158	158	73	2	0	Y
Cincinnati, Ohio	264	114	68	3	4	N
Cleveland, Ohio	128	128	75	1	0	N
Columbus, Ohio	135	135	88	0	0	N
Dayton, Ohio	141	141	64	0	0	N
Milwaukee, Wis.	157	151	84	0	0	N
South						
Miami, Fla.	109	109	65	0	0	N
Tampa, Fla.	115	115	59	0	0	N
Atlanta, Ga.	105	105	57	0	0	N
Louisville, Ky.	183	68	53	0	3	N
New Orleans, La.	141	138	73	1	0	Y
Dallas, Tex.	93	93	56	0	0	N
Houston, Tex.	98	98	58	0	0	N
San Antonio, Tex.	67	67	35	0	0	N
West						
Los Angeles, Calif.	124	124	74	0	0	N
San Bernardino, Calif.	130	130	72	0	0	N
San Diego, Calif.	122	122	52	0	0	N
San Francisco, Calif.	340	334	110	108	6	Y
Denver, Colo.	210	210	67	54	0	Y
Portland, Ore.	147	147	71	0	0	N
Seattle, Wash.	119	119	81	0	0	N
Also						
St. Paul, Minn.	121	116	74	0	5	N
Long Beach, Calif.	179	179	62	0	0	N
Oakland, Calif.	147	147	68	0	0	N

Detail does not add to totals because of exclusion of Higher Education category.

SOURCE: U.S. Bureau of the Census, 1967 *Census of Governments.*

financial administration, general control, and general public building. City-county types of areas appear to have higher levels of expenditures on common functions than other municipal areas. What is clearly evident, even without recourse to statistical analysis, is the importance of the assignment of responsibilities as compared to all other characteristics. The picture is confirmed by an analysis of the relative variation of the total expenditures as compared to the common functions, each as measured by their coefficients of variation. In the former case, the coefficient of variation is 58.6 percent, while for the common functions it is considerably less, standing at 29.4 percent.

The high coefficient of variation is in part caused by the dependent school systems in the Northeast but, almost equally, by the over-all mix of expenditures for other than local schools, such as public welfare, higher education, hospitals, housing and urban renewal, and a variety of other lesser functions which were noted by the Census Bureau. This is reflected in the coefficient of variation of 74.0 percent for the noncommon functions. Some of these reflect the city-county nature of the city and the assignment of functional responsibilities far more than they reflect local conditions.

These local conditions, however, figure importantly in the now extensive literature on the determinants of expenditures. While most of the literature has concentrated on the problem of state-local totals of expenditures, with the avowed purpose of getting around the assignment problem, there are studies on the determinants of municipal expenditures alone. Further, there are also analyses of the over-all behavior of all local governments in large city and outlying areas.

The most recent addition to the literature on the determinants of municipal expenditures, as well as the most comprehensive, is that of Roy Bahl.[8] This volume represents a replication and extension of the earlier work of Harvey Brazer and Amos Hawley. With the exception of the treatment of common functions, where a common assignment system is implied, Bahl's study, like the work of most of his precedessors, omits the effects of structural differentiation in the assignment of expenditure and revenue responsibility among and within states. His analysis of municipal expenditures in 190 metropolitan centers in 1960 shows a reduction of the coefficient of variation for total expenditures from 41.7 percent in the case of per-captia total municipal expenditures to 30.1 percent in the case of per-capita common-function expenditures. This latter figure is very close to the 1967 observed coefficient of variation of

---

[8] Roy Bahl, *Metropolitan City Expenditures* (Lexington: University of Kentucky Press, 1969).

29.4 percent of this study for common-function expenditures of large city governments.

It is a widely held assumption, not shared by this author, that expenditures are a function of population size. The assumption is not supported by correlations between city population and the level of per-capita expenditures. For the various expenditure categories analyzed by Bahl, the simple correlations between population, density, and per-capita intergovernmental revenues and the several expenditure categories are as shown in Table 28.

TABLE 28

Correlations Between Population, Density, and Intergovernmental Aid, and Selected Per-Capita Expenditure Categories, 1960

Expenditure Category	Population	Density	Per-Capita Intergovernmental Revenue
Total	0.3300	0.4441	0.6046
Operating	0.3224	0.5242	0.6490
Common Functions	0.2325	0.3994	0.3668
Police	0.4118	0.6148	0.3251
Fire	0.0552	0.3796	0.4261
Sanitation	0.2222	0.3264	0.2381
Highways	0.0379	0.0321	0.3290
Parks and Recreation	0.0246	0.0291	0.0511
General Control	0.2823	0.4151	0.4153

Source: Roy Bahl, *Metropolitan City Expenditures*, 31.

The relationships between size and per-capita expenditures are quite insignificant in the case of fire, highways, and parks and recreation, and not very striking except in the case of expenditures on police.

In part, the significant results with respect to size may be due to the relationship between density and population rather than to the direct relationship between population and the observed expenditure category. This is because the correlation between population and density is 0.51 for the Bahl sample of 190 central cities. In fact, the density aspect—which is only partially related to size—appears consistently more significant than does the size of the city.

In the absence of any direct measure of the assignment of expenditure responsibility, the per-capita governmental revenues, which reflect the extent to which municipalities undertake educational and/or public welfare functions, appear clearly as a proxy for the assignment variable; they are also the most important determinant of the aided functions, which are not analyzed, and of the total level of municipal expenditures. This is brought out by the simple coefficients between the aid variables and the observed behavior of per-capita total and per-capita operating expenditures. The magnitude of the importance of the aid variable is indicated by the fact that Bahl's complete system of 17 variables explains 40.8 percent of the variation in total expenditures, $R = 0.6387$, and that intergovernmental aid alone explains 37.0 percent of the variation, $r = 0.6046$. Similarly, in the case of the total operating expenditures the figures are $R = 0.6752$ for a 17-variable model and $r = 0.6490$ for the intergovernmental aid variable taken alone. And the single most significant variable in both comprehensive models, as measured by its T or significance value, is the ratio of intergovernmental revenue to total general revenue. The question as to whether aid should be included as an independent variable is answered in the negative by Bahl in his model, but, as indicated, he does include an aspect of aid in his analysis. However, the argument is more complex if the role of aid is a specific object of discussion. Under such circumstances, its inclusion is virtually mandatory. At this point, though, the aid variable appears to be of importance because it most closely approximates the differentials in assignment of expenditure responsibilities among municipalities. Unless this type of variable is included, the effect of other less important variables cannot be determined.

The importance of placing local fiscal behavior in a context which recognizes and incorporates differences in local government responsibilities for providing noneducational public services seems to be essential if analyses of school finances, especially those of large city systems, are expected to be meaningful. Further, it is also necessary to recognize and incorporate, if possible, differences in the state assignment of expenditure and revenue responsibilities for analyses which cross state boundaries. While this has been done in a number of studies, the relationship of the large cities to their surrounding metropolitan contexts has been dealt with primarily in terms of their proportion of the total metropolitan population, and the degree of central city or suburban "exploitation."[9]

The most detailed analyses of large city and outlying areas were

[9] James M. Banovetz, *Governmental Cost Burdens and Service Benefits in the Twin Cities Metropolitan Area* (Minneapolis: Public Administration Center, University of Minnesota, 1965).

undertaken for the year 1957 as well as for 1962, and for the year 1964–65 at Syracuse University.[10] Starting with the 1967 Census of Government, the promise of the 1957 Census is fulfilled, and the detailed state and federal information necessary for future integrated studies of local finance is now available.[11]

As in the case of educational expenditures, the crucial data problem involves the apportioning of not only the fiscal operations of the large city municipality but also of those expenditures and taxes collected by other local governments overlying the central city, county, special districts, and school districts. The principal result of such an operation is to clarify the patterns which reflect the assignment of responsibilities to the local government, and only indirectly does it reflect differences in state-local expenditure and revenue responsibilities. Insofar as such information is available, it shows a generally consistent pattern, with the large cities showing a higher per-capita noneducational expenditure than their surrounding areas. Based on two different samples for the year 1957, the observed relationship shows that the level of per-capita noneducational expenditures in large city areas is between 172 and 180 percent of that of their outside areas. The figure for 1965 is of the same order of magnitude at 165 percent. This notes the fiscal differences and does not represent the areas necessarily receiving the expenditure benefits or those which bear the fiscal burdens. However, a direct comparison based on taxes which are actually allocated, indicates that the tax side at least is accurately stated.

The 1957 data represent one of the few published attempts to determine both the over-all level of noneducational expenditures and the behavior of some of the principal components of large city and suburban noneducational fiscal behavior.[12] As shown in Table 29, the major differences are contained in the nonaided functions, although the figures for Health and Hospitals appears to show a higher level of expenditures in the central city areas than outside. And because of the allocation of responsibilities to the counties, there were no major differences between the cities and their outside areas in either Highway or Public Welfare expenditures. However, where the cities are also counties and are assigned public welfare responsibilities, the differences between central cities and their suburbs are evident. The major difference between the cities and their

[10] Campbell and Sacks, *op. cit.*, and A.C.I.R,, "Metropolitan Disparities—A Second Reading," *op cit*.

[11] The 1967 Census collected, but has not published, detailed expenditure data for local schools for all governments providing such services, *i.e.*, states, counties, cities, towns, and school districts. Of special importance are the detailed breakdowns of federal and state educational aid.

[12] Campbell and Sacks, *op. cit.*

TABLE 29

EDUCATIONAL AND NONEDUCATIONAL FISCAL CHARACTERISTICS, CENTRAL CITY AND OUTSIDE CENTRAL CITY AREAS, 1957, 1965, AND 1967

| | Per-Capita Amount, $ | | Central City as % Outside Central City | Percent — Large SMSA — Central City as % Outside Central City | | |
| | Central City | Outside Central City | | | | |
	1957 (A)	1957 (A)	1957 (A)	1957 (B)	1965 (B)	1967 (C)
Total Expenditures	185.49	159.83	116.05	127.02	114.77	110.31
Education	58.02	85.84	67.59	76.51	70.14	80.59
Noneducational	127.48	73.95	172.38	180.36	165.39	166.73
Highways	16.55	14.41	114.85	NA	NA	NA
Health and Hospitals	14.84	7.09	209.38	NA	NA	NA
Public Welfare	10.22	8.34	122.54	NA	NA	NA
All Other	85.70	43.80	195.66	NA	NA	NA
Taxes	109.07	88.78	127.15	146.13	126.42	128.81
Property Taxes	92.06	78.58	117.15	NA	NA	NA
Nonproperty Taxes	17.01	7.20	236.25	NA	NA	NA
Nonaided Education	42.24	56.43	74.85	NA	NA	82.13
Nonaided Noneducation	108.33	60.39	179.38	NA	NA	190.91
Total Nonaided Expenditures	150.57	116.82	128.89	NA	NA	NA
Total Aid (State and Federal)	34.65	39.72	87.23	99.25	99.84	NA
Education Aid	16.12	28.43	55.70	NA	NA	NA
Noneducation Aid	18.60	11.83	157.27	NA	NA	NA

SOURCE: (A) Campbell and Sacks, *Metropolitan America*. (B) Advisory Commission on Intergovernmental Relations, *Fiscal Balance in the American Federal System, Vol. II*. (C) Advisory Commission on Intergovernmental Relations, *Metropolitan Disparities: A Second Reading*.

outside areas is contained in the "All Other" category. This category is made up of the "Common Functions" and other functions which are principally locally financed. This category is also the principal source of difference between city areas and their suburbs in the locally raised noneducational revenues and taxes.

The most recent data (1966–67) indicate that there is no basic change in the position of the large cities in their noneducational load.[13] Noneducational expenditures exceeded educational expenditures in 36 of 37 SMSA's. Only in the case of the New Orleans area, where a major capital program financed out of borrowed funds was being undertaken outside the central city, were per-capita noneducational expenditures higher outside the central city. The noneducational taxes, however, were higher in New Orleans than in its suburbs. And based on the 1967 data, per-capita taxes (inclusive of those for schools) in all the cities of the largest metropolitan areas, for which data were available, exceeded those of their outside areas. The summarizing data indicate that per-capita noneducational expenditures in the central cities were 166.7 percent of noneducational expenditures in their outside areas, and that noneducational taxes in the central city areas were 190.9 percent of their outside areas.[14]

For the year 1964–65, the coefficients of partial determination of educational and noneducational expenditures on total taxes were quite different in the large cities as compared to their outlying areas.[15] In the large city areas, the coefficients of partial determination (the partial correlations squared) were 0.0350 for educational expenditures and 0.6265 for noneducational expenditures. That is, the variations in large city taxes are primarily accounted for by variations in noneducational expenditures. This is reversed in the suburban areas, where educational expenditures account for 0.3583 of the variation and noneducational expenditures account for only 0.0906 of the variation in taxes. It is presumed that a variety of nonsystematic factors account for the variation. The same type of relationship exists in the case of total expenditures, where it is presumed that aid plays a more important role.

EDUCATIONAL AND NONEDUCATIONAL FINANCES

The last and perhaps most important question in this chapter involves the relationship in the large central cities and elsewhere between educational and noneducational finances, especially the extent to which they

[13] Advisory Commission on Intergovernmental Relations, "Metropolitan Disparities—A Second Reading," *op. cit.,*

[14] *Ibid.*

[15] Seymour Sacks, "Metropolitan Fiscal Disparities," *Journal of Finance* (May 1968), 236.

act as alternatives or supplements to each other. Specifically, what is called into question is what David Minar has called the "zero sum outlook that elected officials tend to have about taxes," which results in "competition . . . [as] the predominant form of relationship."[16] This competition is presumed to exist on the state level and again on the local level. Two hypotheses suggest themselves. The first, which is apparently the implicit model relating educational and noneducational expenditures, is that the amount of resources is relatively fixed, and therefore, if noneducational expenditures are higher, educational expenditures are lower. The second is to repeat this in terms of local taxes. While this is true by definition in a proportionate sense—*i.e.,* the higher the proportion of noneducational expenditures, the lower the proportion of educational expenditures—the relationship is not nearly as evident when specific totals are examined. Thus, the hypothesis that there is a negative relationship between the levels of educational and noneducational expenditures is not borne out by the simple correlation. Based on the most recent data (1964–65), it appears that the correlations between the level of educational and noneducational expenditures are positive in the case of the large cities at +0.2784, and slightly higher for the suburbs at +0.3286. Thus, one does not find the expected trade-offs. A reversal does take place, however, in a more comprehensive multiple regression model in the case of the suburban areas, where it now appears that the basic relationship is inverse, if not of a zero-sum nature. In the cities, however, the relationship still appears to be an additive one. Or, in other words, the levels of educational and noneducational expenditures are more likely than not to move together.

These results point to the necessity of considering the relationship between educational and noneducational fiscal behavior in the large cities, and also of questioning some of the more traditional assumptions. Large cities have higher levels of expenditures and taxes than do their own outlying areas, due to the fact that the noneducational expenditures more than make up for any educational disparity in favor of the suburbs. The higher fiscal levels in central cities are a function of the differential assignment of functional responsibilities to governments in their areas as compared to their suburban areas. Further, past events and decisions often determine the relative level of expenditures. In many cases these are irreversible. The basic hypothesis, then, that higher noneducational expenditures and taxes lead to lower educational expenditures and taxes in the case of large cities, is highly dubious. While specific problems of

[16] "Interaction of School and Local Non-School Governments in Metropolitan Areas," *Metropolitanism: Its Challenge to Education* (Chicago: National Society for the Study of Education, 1968), 204.

individual cities must be analyzed in terms of their own detailed information and merits, the general picture is one which shows a higher over-all level of expenditures and taxes in the large cities. The recent increases in the large city educational fiscal requirements, accompanied by the failure of the large city to keep up with the national economic growth, have placed unparalleled burdens on the cities which cannot be seen without taking the noneducational sphere into account.

SUMMARY

The problems associated with noneducational expenditures in large city areas are important in themselves and they raise important issues insofar as educational finances are concerned. The traditional isolation and insulation of large-scale educational fiscal behavior from other aspects of city fiscal behavior have been in part responsible for the absence of noneducational fiscal direct consideration. Exceptions to the rule make the omission of this consideration more important.

The existing state of the art of analysis of large city expenditures indicates that most analyses fail to consider (1) the entire system of local governments providing services to large city areas, as well as (2) the differences occasioned by large variations in state-assigned functions, primarily in public welfare but including other functions as well. While there is still no agreement as to the precise effects of local conditions, apart from density, there is general agreement as to the much higher level of noneducational functions which are performed within large city areas. The precise effect of these factors on large city school finances will be considered individually and in conjunction with other factors in Chapter VII.

VI. The Political Context

Many areas of public policy that affect the fiscal and educational dimensions of large city school finances have been discussed in the previous chapters. At the local level, the large city school systems have a wide range of choice in their spending and taxing policies. This choice is constrained, however, by decisions of other public bodies at the local level. Especially important are the expenditure decisions by other school systems within the metropolitan area and decisions by the big city governments on the level of noneducational spending and taxing. The policies of state government, as discussed in detail in Chapter IV, are an exceedingly important influence on large city school finance. Many policies and decisions at the state level directly affect both the fiscal and educational dimensions of large city school finances in the local school system, including state aid to education, teacher salary mandates, retirement system requirements, certification requirements, class-size regulations, curriculum standards, mandates concerning the length of time a child must stay in school, and schemes to control the organization and size of school districts. States also exert indirect influence over the large city school system through a large number of policy areas that define state-local relationships. The differential impact of education aid and retirement system regulations between city and suburb is one example. Decisions involving noneducational aid, the assignment of responsibility to local governments for expenditures and taxation, property tax exemption policies, and tax and debt limitations are other policy areas through which the state indirectly influences large city school finances.

Since so many aspects of public policy affect school finance, it follows that a discussion of the political context of school finance in large city school systems is of critical importance. Professional educators have never stressed this context in their discussions of finance because of the persistent notion that "politics" and schools should be kept separate. Some observers have argued that the "no-politics" idea has helped to advance the political objectives of the education profession. The perpetuation of this myth has enabled educators to insulate themselves from the

114

rest of the political system. By so doing, they have been able to control information about the education function, thus obtaining a monopoly on policy initiation.[1] Since no one has found it politically advantageous to oppose education *per se,* the educators have maintained, until recently, a favored position in the public policy arena.

This favored position, however, is breaking down as the insulation around the education function is penetrated by a number of parties operating in the state-local political system. Meranto has argued that the breakdown of the educators' favored position is now under way in many major cities.[2] Bowles and Iannaccone have suggested that there is a breakdown of the "no politics" myth at the state level as well.[3] Bowles concludes:

> Significantly, the state politics of education is experiencing a shift from the consensus politics of the professional priesthood to the conflict politics of the public marketplace.

This conclusion is equally appropriate to the politics of education at the local level. One need only observe the spectacle of teacher strikes, school boycotts, and drives for local control of schools within the large city school systems to realize that the "professional priesthood" at the local level is being asked or told to make room for more participants in local educational policy-making.

These changes have great significance for large city school finance. If policy decisions that influence school expenditures and taxes are being made in a changing political context, we cannot assume that political variables are constant in our analysis of school finance. More groups are now making demands on public policy-makers, and the state and local political systems will have to accommodate them. These demands relate to many of the policy areas summarized above and discussed in detail in previous chapters. The remainder of the present chapter will assess the implications of the changing political context of the large city school system for the educational and fiscal dimensions of its finances.

LARGE CITY POLITICAL STRUCTURE

The political structure of large cities has been described as a diffused network of "core groups" which have the legal authority to make decisions in specific policy areas. Surrounding each of these core groups are

[1] B. Dean Bowles, "The Power Structure in State Educational Politics," *Phi Delta Kappan* (February 1968), 337–40.

[2] Philip Meranto, "Emerging Participation Patterns in School Politics," lecture presented at the University of Wisconsin, October 18, 1968.

[3] Laurence Iannaccone, *Politics in Education* (New York: Center for Applied Research in Education, 1967), 64–81, Bowles, *op. cit.* 337.

"satellite groups" which are attempting to influence the policy decisions of the core groups.[4] In local school systems, the core group for educational policy-making is generally the school board. In some cases the city council is also a part of this group. Until very recently, educational satellite groups have been dominated by a highly centralized school bureaucracy led by the superintendent of schools and including central office administrators, supervisory personnel, and the organizations representing them. The practical result of this situation is that certain powerful determinants of local educational policy—generation and flow of information, policy initiation, and accommodation of conflicting interests —have been largely controlled by the local educational bureaucracy. The perpetuation of the myth that politics and education have no relevance to one another has generated a habit in educational core groups of deferring to the professional educator on matters of educational policy, thus maintaining the strategic position of the professional bureaucracy in the educational policy-making process.

INDEPENDENCE FOR THE SCHOOLS?

It is not surprising, therefore, that the professional educators have fought hard to maintain their control over local educational policy decisions. One means of doing this has been to preach the "no-politics" ideology so diligently that educators have begun to believe it themselves. Another means has been to keep the education core group separate from all other policy core groups. This second approach to the maintenance of control over educational policy-making has been the source of a continuing debate. In this debate educators have championed the cause of independent school districts, politically separate from their overlying municipalities. Schoolmen have argued that without independence there would be undesirable political control over the schools, a removal of control over education from "the people" and a general downgrading in the quality of education. Many political scientists and economists have argued antithetically that education should be a part of municipal government. There is nothing so special about education, they argue, that warrants a special level of government. To the contrary, public resources cannot be efficiently allocated, and competing demands on the public sector cannot be effectively weighed without the existence of a central authority to consider all of the local demands on a given tax base. Those who argue against independence for the schools also contend that the presence of independent school systems fractures local governmental authority,

---

[4] Wallace S. Sayre and Herbert Kaufman, *Governing New York City* (New York: W. W. Norton, 1965).

makes financial planning at the local level impossible, and menaces municipal budgets.

The debate over the best administrative arrangement for the schools has raged for over a century, but over 95 percent of all local public school systems exist as separate governmental entities although no clear conclusions have been reached on the merits of the issues. Does the independent structure affect school finance? Most of the attempts to answer this question have tried to determine whether independent school systems are able to spend more for education than dependent systems.

Many of the studies of the fiscal implications of independence for schools have classified schools as either independent or dependent. Generally, school systems have been classified as independent when the school board has the authority to approve the budget and levy the necessary taxes. All other school systems are called dependent. The results of the studies using this definition have been unclear. They indicate that independent school systems may spend a little more than dependent systems, yet the slight relationship between independence and higher spending does not appear to be functional. Other variables such as the level of income, state aid, enrollment ratio, and the population of the school district seem to be largely responsible for the variations among school systems in tax and expenditure levels.[5]

Some recent studies have looked at the importance of independence relative to other variables, using such multivariate analyses as multiple regression.[6] None of these studies supports the notion that one kind of system has a great fiscal impact on the schools. The lack of any clear

[5] See, for example, William D. Firman, "Fiscal Independence of School Systems," paper presented to the Committee on Educational Finance of the National Educational Association, Chicago, Illinois, April 7, 1965; J. R. McGaughy, *The Fiscal Administration of City School Systems* (New York: The Macmillan Company, 1924). A similar study found that dependent systems spend more: Julius Margolis, "Metropolitan Finance Problems: Territories, Functions and Growth," in National Bureau of Economic Research, *Public Finances: Needs, Sources and Utilization* (Princeton: Princeton University Press, 1962), 261–64. These and other examples of similar studies are described and analyzed in: David C. Ranney, "School Government and the Determinants of Fiscal Support for Large City Education Systems," unpublished doctoral dissertation, Syracuse University, Syracuse, New York, 1966.

[6] Jerry Miner, *Social and Economic Factors in Spending for Public Education* (Syracuse: Syracuse University Press, 1963); H. Thomas James, J. Alan Thomas, and Harold J. Dyck, *Wealth, Expenditure and Decision Making for Education* (Stanford: Stanford University Press, 1963); Woo Sik Kee, "City Expenditures and Metropolitan Areas: An Analysis of Intergovernmental Fiscal Relations," unpublished doctoral dissertation, Syracuse University, Syracuse, New York, 1964; T. Edward Hollander, "Fiscal Independence and Large City School Systems," ed. Marilyn Gittell, *Educating an Urban Population* (Beverly Hills: Sage Publications, 1967), 108–13.

results in these studies has led a number of observers to conclude either that independence for schools does not make enough difference to concern us or that our classification of school systems does not take the right factors into account.

In view of the earlier discussion of the political position of the educational bureaucracy, it seems likely that the dichotomous classification of independent and dependent school systems is at best an oversimplification. In fact, several students of school government have argued that the narrow fiscal definition of independence should be broadened to include administrative and political independence. When the classification system takes this broader view, school governments tend to fall on points along a continuum with independence at one end and dependence at the other.[7]

The discussion by James *et al.* is particularly useful as a conceptual basis for the development of a more sensitive classification system. The key factor for determining the position of any given school system on the continuum was the nature of the authority over the operations of the public school system. Three major aspects of control over public education were considered. The first involved authority over the allocation of community resources to education. A second control concerned decisions on the administration and curriculum of the school itself. The third power determined the personnel who performed these responsibilities. From these three types, 10 control functions were developed. These were: budget approval authority, selection of budget approvers, budget review authority, selection of budget reviewers, curriculum decision power, selection of curriculum decision-makers, personnel decision power, selection of personnel decision-makers, taxing power, and the selection of the taxers. Each of these 10 control functions could theoretically be in the hands of either the electorate, the school board, the municipality, the county, a multifunction special district, or the state government.

Educators have traditionally argued that independence has placed education near the "people" and has freed the schools from direct association with other public functions. These arguments have been used as criteria for ordering school systems along a continuum. The six potential controlling groups were arranged ordinally, starting with those groups closest to "the people" and not directly responsible for performing other public functions. Only school boards and the electorate were thought to be free from other public responsibilities. The remaining four groups were therefore arranged according to their relative proximity to the local

---

[7] James *et al., op. cit.;* Firman, *op. cit.;* Eugene McLoone, "Advantages of Fiscal Independence for School Districts," paper presented at National Conferences on Educational Finance, St. Louis, Missouri, April 4, 1967.

school constituency. On this basis, the following order for the groups was devised:

1. Electorate
2. School board
3. Municipality
4. County
5. Multifunctional special district
6. State government or associated agency.[8]

The position of specific school systems on the independence-dependence continuum was based upon the distribution of formal control over education policy (as defined above), while the order of the groups themselves constituted the continuum. Thus, theoretically, the school system at the dependence end of the continuum would be one in which the state reviews and approves the local school budget, makes all decisions on curriculum and administration, and appoints all school personnel. The school system at the other end of the continuum would place control directly in the hands of the electorate.

Using this theoretical framework for classification, 37 school systems serving the largest cities in the United States were placed along the continuum. In reality, none of the school systems was at either end of the continuum. Furthermore, the various control functions were often spread among several of the 6 groups. Thus, the position of a particular school system on the continuum was determined by the ordinal position of the group which held the majority of the 10 control functions.

The 37 school systems fell almost evenly into 3 groups. In the analysis, the impact of a school system's size on fiscal levels was factored out by including only school systems serving the largest cities in the analysis. By using multiple regression analysis, the impact of other variables which could affect school finance was also held constant. These variables (as discussed in previous chapters) were income, the enrollment ratio, state aid, and the expenditures of suburban school systems. Two dependent variables were current educational expenditures per student and current educational expenditures per capita. In both cases, the position of the school systems along the continuum had very little impact on the level of school expenditures. Only the middle grouping along the continuum had a slight impact upon the expenditures.

One further regression model was analyzed in which educational expenditures as a percentage of all local expenditures was the dependent

---

[8] State controls such as educational aid, fiscal mandates, debt and tax limitations, and other statutory regulations that simply reflect the states' normal relationship to local school systems were not considered in the present classification. Only when state government was directly involved in fiscal, curriculum, and personnel decisions did the state's role influence the classification.

variable. In addition to the school system classification, the percentage of the population in owner-occupied homes, the enrollment ratio, per-capita noneducational expenditures, and state aid per capita were the independent variables. In this case, the classification of the school system was totally insignificant.[9]

The only statistically significant relationship between educational fiscal behavior and the classification of the school systems involved the middle category of the schools. Even this result proved to be ambiguous in terms of the theoretical positions of the advocates of independence or dependence. The history of ambiguous results such as these on the independence-dependence question is quite consistent. This does not mean that the position of the school in the large city political system is unimportant; rather, we can conclude that a school system's position along the independence-dependence continuum does not really measure the important aspects of its role in large city politics.

What the above results do indicate is that the position in the governmental structure of the educational core groups does not have such influence on large city school finances. Put another way, it does not appear to be critical as to where along the independence-dependence continuum the *authority* for making educational decisions lies. But this statement says very little about *influence*. Earlier we suggested that, at the local level, authority seems to be in the hands of the school system bureaucracy. In fact, a recent comparative study of school systems in Baltimore, Chicago, Detroit, New York, Philadelphia, and St. Louis concluded that in all cases educational policy-making is controlled by a small core of educators within the school system bureaucracy. The authors specifically pointed out that independence or dependence seemed to make no difference in the structure of influence over school-related decisions.[10] In our own classification system, Detroit and St. Louis were in the dependent category, New York and Baltimore were dependent, and Chicago and Philadelphia fell into the middle class of school systems; yet all had a very similar structure of influence.

The Gittell-Hollander study and other more intuitive evidence suggest two important points. First, in the case of education, those with the authority to make decisions do not necessarily have the primary influence over those decisions. Second, the structure of influence over educational policy-making appears to be fairly uniform, with most school systems being subject to the monolithic structure described above.

[9] For a complete presentation and discussion of the multiple regression analysis, see David C. Ranney, *op. cit.*

[10] Marilyn Gittell and T. Edward Hollander, *Six Urban School Districts: A Comparative Study of Institutional Response* (New York: Frederick A. Praeger, 1968).

THE CHANGING STRUCTURE OF INFLUENCE

At the beginning of the chapter, we noted that the structure of the satellite groups interested in educational policy is undergoing important changes. Basically, the change is to a more pluralistic system where information, policy initiation, and the accommodation of conflict are no longer the sole province of the local educational bureaucracy. On the basis of the above analysis, this change in the politics of education may be much more important to the financing of large city school systems than the independence issue was believed to be.

Increasing pluralism in the structure of influence over educational policy seems to be a result of two developments: one affects the structure of influence indirectly, while the other has its initial impact directly on that structure. The first development is suggested by a series of studies undertaken at Claremont Graduate School which conclude that school systems tend in the long run to be responsive to the demands of constituents.[11] These studies lend empirical support to the idea that social change in a community will lead to a turnover in school board membership. This in turn tends to result in involuntary turnover in the school system's superintendency and the selection of an outsider as the new superintendent. The new superintendent will select other outsiders to staff the local educational bureaucracy, and his selection will result in new policies which may be more in line with the wishes of the electorate. Based on this evidence, Iannaccone argues that critics of the school system are incorrect when they point to severe educational problems as evidence that schools are not responsive to citizens. In fact, he suggests, these critics are really saying that the citizens have not responded to these problems.[12]

Evidence that school systems are viable political instruments is convincing. The time period involved in the process of social change to policy change is quite long, however, and it is possible that by the time the school system responds through this evolutionary process further social changes may have dated the educational policy changes. Second, this type of change keeps the structure of influence intact. Only the personnel who control the educational satellite groups have changed. These points have two implications for large cities where, at the present time, social change is moving at a rapid pace.

First, those groups with an interest in educational policy will become impatient with the school's response to this social change. For this reason, they may seek a direct voice in policy-making to speed progress. Second, even if the pace of the school's response to change could be in-

[11] Laurence Iannaccone, *op. cit.,* 82–98.
[12] *Ibid.,* 82–83.

creased (as Iannaccone suggests it should), control over information and policy initiation would still be in the hands of educational bureaucrats who will be primarily concerned with keeping the existing school system running smoothly. As we will see later, many of the demands being made for change do not lend themselves to maintaining a smooth-running system. They call for sweeping redistribution of power, massive curriculum changes, and, in some cases, for the dissolution of the school system itself. Thus, a bureaucracy dedicated to the perpetuation of its own existence will not easily respond to demands for change in large city school systems. More important to the focus of this study, the demands, if met, will cost a great deal of money.

Therefore, dissatisfaction with the evolutionary process of change described by Iannaccone may lead to another method of change which may have profound implications for educational finance in the future. This method involves a fragmentation in the structure of influence over educational policy-making. Meranto has argued that this direct change in the influence structure is now taking place within the context of three developments: (1) the unionization and growing militancy of teachers; (2) the civil rights fight over school desegregation; and (3) the quest for black power as it relates to neighborhood control of schools.[13] The fiscal implications of this change will thus be determined by the demands being made by teachers, civil rights groups, and parents.

TEACHER-PARENT PARTICIPATION

The unionization and growing militancy of teachers reflect a bid to become more actively involved in educational policy decisions. In the past, the major teacher's organization, the National Education Association (NEA), was dominated and run by the representatives of the educational bureaucracy. The rise in the strength of the American Federation of Teachers (AFT) has provided teachers with the alternative of more direct representation in school policy-making. The AFT first gained wide notoriety when their New York affiliate, the United Federation of Teachers (UFT), became the bargaining representative for the teachers in the New York City School System. Their successes have strengthened other AFT affiliates, and have also forced the NEA to become more militant in behalf of teachers' interests.[14]

The teachers' drive for increased control over educational policy decisions could have an important impact on educational finance by generating pressure for greater expenditures. Not only are the militant

---

[13] Meranto, *op. cit.*

[14] Alan Rosenthal, *Pedagogues and Power* (Syracuse: Syracuse University Press, 1969).

teacher organizations demanding higher salaries, they are also seeking better working conditions which will cost more money. Proposals such as smaller class sizes, more special programs to handle the disadvantaged or difficult student, shorter working hours for some personnel, and better fringe benefits are all examples of the kinds of things which increasing teacher participation could mean. Implementation of these demands will be expensive.

As teacher participation breaks through the traditional power monopoly of the educational bureaucracy, a parallel development is in its infancy. This movement involves parents. For the most part, parents have participated in school affairs through their vote in the school board election (if there is one), an occasional visit to the teacher or principal, or a phone call to a school board member. In addition, there has been the vehicle of the Parent-Teacher Association (PTA). None of these contacts has involved any consistent or organized effort toward a parental voice in school policy. In the final analysis, most parents were convinced that the professional educators were best equipped to determine how to educate their children.

An important break with the traditional parent-school relationship developed when civil rights organizations began to oppose *de facto* segregation in the schools of large northern cities. Since the black population was living in concentrated areas, the civil rights activity amounted to a confrontation between the citizen and the educator over a fundamental educational principle—the neighborhood school concept. In some instances the desegregation fights have centered on busing programs and proposals for educational "parks" or campuses which would enable school systems to eliminate *de facto* segregation.

More often, however, and particularly in the largest cities, the drive for integrated schools never really materialized. In fact, segregation has become more pronounced since 1954 in all large city school systems.[15] But the civil rights movement did pierce the armour of the educational bureaucracy, thus paving the way for a much more fundamental kind of citizen involvement in the schools. Parent groups in black communities maintained the organization developed during the integration battles and are now beginning to push for more control over the policies of their children's schools. In fact, some black militant groups are advocating local control of schools in place of integration.

Many cities are in the process of some kind of decentralization. The local control concept was given a considerable boost when the Ford

[15] U.S. Commission on Civil Rights, *Racial Isolation in the Public Schools* (Washington, D.C.: Government Printing Office, 1967).

Foundation decided to finance "experimental school districts" in New York. These were designed to pave the way toward a decentralization of the New York School System into 31 semiautonomous units. The experimental districts were governed by locally elected boards of neighborhood people. What happened in New York is now well known. The interests of the school bureaucracy, the teachers union, and the parent groups clashed head-on when the Ocean Hill–Brownsville local community board tried to exercise its power by suspending 13 teachers and 6 supervisors "for the good of the community." The result was a teacher strike which was settled only by the intervention of state governmental officials. This clash represented a dramatic departure from the old system where policy initiation and the accommodation of conflicting interests were ironed out within the confines of the educational bureaucracy.[16]

It is not clear exactly what the entrance of local citizen groups into the educational decision-making process will do to the school finance picture. It is clear from looking at the kinds of issues with which parents are concerned that there will be additional pressures for higher expenditure levels. Parents are beginning to rebel against the physical conditions of inner-city schools. Broken windows, overcrowded classrooms, poor equipment, and obsolete textbooks are problems which citizen groups want resolved. Second, there is the matter of curriculum. Parents are questioning the subject matter of textbooks and the relevancy of the curriculum to the lives of their children. The ability of the present teachers to teach properly is also being questioned. Special personnel such as reading specialists, psychologists, and social workers are demanded. Greater effort on the part of school personnel to understand and relate to the community is being called for by the parents. Most of these demands are supported by a variety of outside critics and observers.

The magnitude of the problems that have generated these kinds of parental concerns can be illustrated by looking at some personally gathered data on an elementary school located in a black community in Chicago. The average sixth-grade student in this school is reading at a fourth-grade level. Only 16 percent of the entire student body is able to read at the appropriate grade level. Of the teachers, 75 percent are not certified by the State of Illinois. There are 33 students for every teacher. Of the students, 3 percent have been reported to have serious health problems; 32 percent are said to have serious adjustment problems. There is a 100-percent student turnover every year and a half. The

---

[16] There are numerous accounts of the Ocean Hill–Brownsville dispute and the decentralization of the New York School System. See, for example, Jason Epstein, "The Brooklyn Dodgers," *New York Review of Books* (October 10, 1968); Irving Kristol, "Decentralization for What?" *The Public Interest* (Spring 1968), 17–25.

school, which has 1,300 students, shares 2 psychologists, 1 socal worker, and 4 curriculum consultants with all of the other schools in the district —and there are 27,000 children attending schools in the district. Clearly, to bring just this one school up to a tolerable level of performance would be an extremely costly venture.

Another way of looking at the potential cost of meeting parental demands is to analyze the high school dropout situation. In 1962, it was estimated that roughly 20 percent of high school students in the 37 large city school systems dropped out of school between the tenth and twelfth grades.[17] In a study of the dropout situation in St. Louis, Burton Weisbrod estimated that the two-year cost for each dropout prevented was $8,200.[18]

These illustrations of the magnitude of the problems which are generating parental demands for participation in educational decision-making do not begin to enable us to estimate what the impact of these demands is likely to be on school finance. Nobody has been able to develop any hard-cost estimates, although the Weisbrod study is a step in this direction and does provide some indications. Second, we have no way of knowing what the impact of citizen participation is likely to be on education policy. There are some indications, however, that these issues will have to be faced by the large city school systems in some manner. The events in New York City provide one such indication. If the school systems cannot adapt to their demands, the critics threaten to move even further toward radical change in school policy-making. For example, proposals are being made to replace the public school systems with private schools. Under this plan, parents would be given public monies to enable their children to attend the school of their choice.[19] The growing strength of these and similar demands would suggest that the large city school systems are under considerable pressure to improve the quality of their education. While we cannot make any hard cost estimates of what this pressure will mean, we can safely conclude that demands for in-

[17] This estimate was made by the author on the basis of data in Daniel Scheiber, *Holding Power: Large City School Systems Project, School Dropouts* (Washington, D.C.: National Education Assocation, 1964).

[18] Burton A. Weisbrod, "Preventing High School Dropouts," in Robert Dorfman, ed., *Measuring Benefits of Government Investments* (Washington, D.C.: The Brookings Institution, 1963), 144–45. Weisbrod's estimate of $8,200 per dropout prevented includes expenses generated by dropouts who were in the program but who continued to be dropouts after the program was completed. These total expenses were divided by only the actual number of dropouts who returned to school.

[19] A number of private community schools have already been developed on an experimental basis. Some of these are being financed by the Ford Foundation. There are four of these schools presently in Boston, one of which has a budget of $200,000 for 117 students.

creased school expenditures generated by parental involvement in the changing structure of influence in local school politics are considerable.

BIG CITY POLITICS

All of the significant trends relative to the political context of school finance at the local level are not developing within the confines of the educational core group–satellite group relationships. There are some trends which directly affect other sectors of the big city political system, but which also indirectly influence educational finance. One of these continuing trends has been the decentralization of the metropolis and the subsequent development of multiple governments. A major point developed in the preceding chapters is that this structural characteristic of the metropolitan political system has an important influence on school finance. Big city school systems are influenced by the policies of the suburban school systems both because of the demonstration and labor-market effects of their close proximity. Second, we have pointed to the growing disparities between the city and its suburbs both with respect to social and economic characteristics and to certain state policies such as state aid and retirement system regulations.

The distribution of socioeconomic characteristics between the city and its suburbs, which has been generated by the continuing trend of decentralization, has a strong influence on the level of education expenditures and on the ability of the central city to pay for educational services. Second, the differential impact of state aid and retirement system policies also has a major influence on educational finance. Thus metropolitanization is producing a fragmented metropolitan governmental system which is, and will continue to be, an important political variable in explaining educational fiscal behavior.

Another trend in city politics pertinent to educational finance is the increasing militancy of public employees. This trend is recent, and its full impact on educational finance is yet to be felt. We do know that policemen, firemen, garbage collectors, and other city employees no longer consider the strike or the slowdown an inappropriate tool for achieving better working conditions. The results of these developments have already appeared in the form of massive salary increases. It seems likely that there will be further increases in salaries and in the level of fringe benefits and overtime pay, and perhaps decreases in the length of the working week. These developments will cause local public expenditures to rise even faster than experts were predicting just a few years ago.

The impact of growing public employee militancy should be clear from our discussion of the relationships between educational and noneducational expenditures in Chapter V. The pressures and conflicts over how the public pie should be cut will increase, and the large city school systems will be faced with a far greater "municipal overburden" than they now have. Thus, there will be an even larger constraint on the ability of local school systems to respond positively to the many expenditure demands that will be made upon them.

In summary, the changes in the large city political structure have great potential for influence on school finance. The changing structure of influence over education is leading to a more pluralistic system where administrators, teachers, and parents vie for control. This development seems to be much more significant than the traditional questions about the desirability of fiscal independence. The demands of both teachers and parents are generating pressures for greater expenditures. Simultaneously, the continuation of an old trend (metropolitanization) and the development of a new one (public employee militancy) are also generating expenditure pressures on the local political system as a whole.

While at the moment these trends seem to indicate that the traditional concern over fiscal independence is irrelevant, this too may be changing. Interestingly enough, the fragmentation of the structure of influence over educational policy may lead the contestants to work toward a formal authority structure which will benefit their point of view the most. To the educators, this structure may be a centralized independent school system. The teachers' unions may feel (as they do now) that their bargaining position will be enhanced by a centralized dependent school system. The parents' organizations have already indicated that they feel their influence will be maximized under a highly decentralized independent system. Thus the century-old debate over the "best" structure of authority relative to educational policy is likely to continue, but with very different parameters and fiscal implications. Whatever the outcome of all of these trends, the upward pressures on educational expenditures will be greater in the future than previously imagined.

STATE POLITICAL STRUCTURES

The previous chapters, particularly Chapter IV, have made it clear that the ability of local school systems to respond to these pressures is considerably influenced by public policy at the state level. Thus, discussion of the political context of large city school finance cannot ignore developments in state government. Two of these involvements which may have relevance to large city school finance will be considered here. One of these involves changes in the composition of the educational core group—the state legislature. The other is a shift in the structure of educational satellite groups at the state level. In our discussion of these trends, we must leave out a number of subjects which are critical to a thorough understanding of the politics of education at the state level. Our purpose here is to focus only on a few trends which are particularly important to the future of educational finance in large cities.[20]

LEGISLATIVE APPORTIONMENT

The core group for educational policy at the state level is the state legislature. It is the legislature which must make the final decisions on all state programs and appropriations that affect public elementary and secondary education. In some cases we could also consider the governor to be a part of the core group. He has a number of powers, particularly the veto, through which he can exercise formal authority over education.[21] But the governor's participation in legislative decisions is not a regular occurrence, so it is the legislature itself which constitutes the educational core group for most issues.

The major change which is now occurring in the structure of state legislatures involves reapportionment. In order to understand how this change is apt to influence the ability of local school systems to respond to the mounting pressures discussed above, we must say a few words about the role of the state legislatures in policy decisions that influence education.

State legislatures operate very differently in different states, which makes it difficult to generalize about their behavior. Based on data from several states, however, Dye has made some interesting observations about the role of state legislatures in policy formulations.[22] First, state legislators tend to represent the interests of their geographical constituency rather than large state-wide interest groups. Applying this generalization to education, a legislator would be more interested in the impact of a policy on the schools in his district than in the broader im-

---

[20] The general literature on state politics and the specific works on the state politics of education provide a comprehensive picture. See, for example, Herbert Jacob and Kenneth N. Vines, *Politics in American States* (Boston: Little, Brown and Company, 1965), especially Chapter IX, by Robert H. Salisbury, "State Politics and Education," 331–69. Also see the following specific books on the state politics of education: Nicholas A. Masters *et al.*, *State Politics and the Public Schools: An Exploraory Analysis* (New York: Alfred A. Knopf, 1964); Laurence Iannaccone, *op. cit.*; B. Dean Bowles, "Educational Pressure Groups and the Legislative Process in California, 1945–1966," unpublished doctoral dissertation, Claremont Graduate School, 1967.

[21] The governor's formal and informal influence over legislative decisions are discussed by Thomas Dye, "State Legislative Politics," in Jacob and Vines, *op. cit.*, 194–98. All but one state gives the governor veto power. In 35 states it takes a two-thirds vote to override the veto. Dye points out that in 1947 there were 1,253 vetoes cast by governors and only 22 of these were overridden.

[22] *Ibid.*, 151–206.

plications of that policy. A second point is that legislatures rarely initiate policy but rather act as arbiters among interests, either by supporting, delaying, or killing proposals presented to them. In the case of education, policy is generally initiated by state departments of education and submitted to the governor. The governor relies on the department and educational interest groups for the details of any policy proposals and concerns himself mainly with their cost. In considering an educational proposal from the governor, the legislators place great reliance on the judgment of a few highly regarded colleagues who have specialized in educational legislation.[23] So the major conflict over the details of educational policy proposals is not likely to occur within the state legislature if the legislators are asked to consider one unified set of proposals. They may clash over the allocation of funds to educational programs when their constituencies are directly affected, but not over the programs themselves.

Given this background on the role of state legislatures in policy formulation, we can now turn to the matter of apportionment and how it is likely to affect local school systems. It is a well-known fact that state legislative apportionment heavily favors rural areas. Until recently, at least one house and often both houses of legislatures based representation on geographical areas irrespective of population. As more people began to concentrate in urban areas, the value of the vote of urban legislators relative to the size of their constituencies began to decline.[24] In 1962 the historic U.S. Supreme Court decision in *Baker* v. *Carr* opened the door to the courts to decide whether state legislative apportionment was within the "equal protection of the law" provision in the Constitution.[25] Prior to this case, the courts had ruled that apportionment was strictly a legislative matter.

On June 15, 1964, the Supreme Court announced another decision on the apportionment of six states and established, among other things, that both houses of the legislature must be apportioned on the basis of population. The Court stated that even a state-wide referendum to the contrary could not alter this ruling. These cases have been named collectively after the first case in the series, *Reynolds* v. *Sims*.[26] Thus, all states have been forced to reapportion their legislatures to bring the value of the urban legislators' votes in line with the size of their constituency.

[23] Robert H. Salisbury, "State Politics and Education," *op. cit.*, 331–69.
[24] Paul T. David and Ralph Eisenberg, *Devaluation of the Urban and Suburban Vote* (Charlottesville: Bureau of Public Administration, The University of Virginia, 1961), cited in Thomas R. Dye, *op. cit.*, 157–59.
[25] *Baker* v. *Carr*, 369 U.S. 186 (1962).
[26] *Reynolds* v. *Sims*, 84. S. Ct. 1362 (1964).

No studies have been very successful in uncovering the policy manifestations of rurally dominated legislatures. For this reason, it is difficult to determine what reapportionment will do to policy that affects large city school systems. Some state policies which favor suburbs and rural areas have been cited in previous chapters. These policies provide some circumstantial evidence on the effects of malapportionment. State aid, for example, favors rural areas over metropolitan areas. The formulae for state aid to education and the choice of other functional areas to be aided by states also favor the suburbs over the city. The question is, will these policies change with reapportioned state legislatures? Will there be new legislative proposals which will help the problems of schooling the inner-city child? Will there be new state fiscal policies aimed at pulling the city out of its fiscal bind?

While it is not possible to give a clear answer to these questions, some informed guesses can be made. Earlier we noted that legislators tend to arbitrate conflicting interests based on their perception of how the outcome of the conflict will affect their individual constituencies. Much of the policy impact of reapportionment, therefore, should depend upon how the suburban legislators see their constituents' interests. To the extent that they see these interests more closely related to the central city than to the rural areas, the city may benefit, but in the near future this seems unlikely. In the case of state aid, for example, both suburbs and rural areas are benefiting from the present system. Thus, it is likely that reapportionment will result in suburban-rural coalitions which will do nothing to help the city. As more suburbs begin to age, however, and acquire many of the problems now faced by the city, the suburbs may cooperate with the central city. At the present time, many suburbs already have city-like problems. In fact, in the New York metropolitan area, the variation among suburbs with respect to socioeconomic characteristics and educational expenditures is greater than the variation among the 37 largest central cities.[27] As the number of suburbs with city-like characteristics grows, the policy implications of reapportionment will become more complex and unclear.

Assessment of the policy implications of reapportionment also runs into difficulties because we do not know how strong apportionment is or will be, relative to other factors that affect state policy. While studies have shown that urban and rural legislators tend to vote for their respective constituencies, how this phenomenon affects policy content has not been well established. Perhaps other intervening variables such as the

[27] Seymour Sacks and David C. Ranney, "Suburban Education: A Fiscal Analysis," *Educating an Urban Population,* ed. Marilyn Gittell (Beverly Hills: Sage Publications, 1967), 60–76.

industrialization of a given state, or social characteristics of individual legislators, explain state legislative voting behavior more than does the apportionment pattern. As far as policy content goes, moreover, there is much evidence to suggest that specific policies made by the state (especially in the case of education) are determined outside of the legislature by the satellite groups who are trying to influence legislative decisions. In the case of education, this means the educational interest groups and the state department of education.

THE CHANGING STRUCTURE OF STATE EDUCATIONAL SATELLITE GROUPS

Given the critical role of the satellite groups in determining the details of state education policy, it is important to examine some recent changes in the structure of these groups. There appear to be three key variables which help explain the importance of satellite groups in policy development. Their role is: (1) controlling the flow of information on which the policies are based; (2) the accommodation of conflict over the details of educational policy; and (3) the initiation of policy proposals.[28]

The Claremont study has produced a series of research efforts which suggest that the educational satellite group structures run through distinct developmental stages relative to the above three factors. These stages are responses to changes in the state legislatures.[29] Specifically in Stage I, there is no real structure to the satellite groups. Thus, control over information flows and the initiation of policy proposals is handled on an ad hoc basis and is not in the hands of any single organization other than the state educational bureaucracy. Accommodation of conflict during this phase is in the legislature.

During Stage II, the satellite groups become highly structured under the control of professional educators' organizations representing local school bureaucracies. Flows of information into and out of the state departments of education come basically from this highly organized alignment of satellite groups. In fact, the state educational bureaucracy itself is staffed with educators in sympathy with the administrative point of view. Thus, accommodation of conflict and initiation of policy comes from the monolithic satellite group.

In Stage III, this structure breaks apart as the organizations which make up the satellite groups begin to disagree with one another. Unlike Stage I, where there were few organized groups interested in educational

---

[28] Bowles, "Educational Pressure Groups and the Legislative Process," *op. cit.,* especially Chapter II.

[29] The description, analysis, and implications of the developmental stages are presented by Bowles, *ibid.,* and by Iannaccone, *op. cit.,* 37–81.

policy, there are many in Stage III and each tries to influence legislation. This stage is marked by multiple sources of information and policy initiation. It is also a stage of high conflict which is resolved in the state legislature. A final stage has appeared in at least one state where organizations making up the educational satellite groups develop an institution which attempts to smooth over conflict before it reaches the legislature.[30]

Iannaccone has argued that most states today are still in Stage II, but are evolving toward Stage III.[31] This would suggest that the structure of educational policy-making at the state level closely parallels the situation we described at the local level; that is, state educational policy has been controlled by the professional educator who is most closely associated with local school bureaucracies. This policy formulation process until recently has been heavily insulated from the potential participation of other groups having a stake in legislative decisions on educational matters.

The reasons for these changes and their implications for large city school finance are closely related. Preliminary results of a study currently being conducted by Bowles and Iannaccone indicate that state systems evolve somewhat naturally from one stage to another in response to changes in the state legislatures. The time period between initial changes in the legislature and stage shifts may be as long as 40 years. Their results also lend some empirical support to a further hypothesis being presented here: our hypothesis is that the present shift in many states from Stage II to Stage III is accelerated by the developments at the local level discussed earlier. Teacher and citizen groups, finding that their efforts to change educational policy at the local level are so constrained by state policies, are making an effort to break through the educational bureaucracy's hold on state educational policy development.

While this idea needs further testing through research, our earlier results—which demonstrated the critical role played by the state in local school finance—make the hypothesis a logical one. To the extent that it is correct, there is some reason to believe that the states today will be more responsive to the fiscal and educational needs of the large city than

---

[30] The School Problems Commission (SPC) in Illinois is such an institution. Masters *et al.* called the Illinois situation "structural consensus," and Iannaccone and his colleagues initially argued that Stage IV was one of "political consensus." In a forthcoming volume, however, Bowles and Iannaccone have concluded that there is not really consensus in the Illinois situation and that Stage IV actually represents an "institutionalization of conflict" outside the state legislature.

[31] Iannaccone, *op. cit.*, 14–81. Bowles has documented this specifically in California, *op. cit.* An article on New York State indicates that this may be happening there as well: Michael D. Usdan, "New York State's Educational Conference Board: A Coalition in Transition," *Phi Delta Kappan* (February 1968), 328–31.

in the past. Perhaps the cities will not have to shoulder the entire burden of the considerable demands being placed upon them. For the states to respond however, the structure of satellite groups will have to move from Stage II to Stage IV where the institutionalization of conflict will attempt to accommodate the interests of large city groups. It is not clear whether these conditions for policy change at the state level will be met. Nor do we know whether the conditions described above will be sufficient for a meaningful state response to local educational fiscal problems. It is clear, however, that the politics of education at the state level are changing and that the direction of change will have an important bearing on large city educational finance in years to come.

SUMMARY

This chapter has focused on the political variables in the analysis of educational finance in large city school systems. The political essence of the school finance picture is the structural change from a tight monolithic system with the professional administrator at the top to a more open, pluralistic system. In this sense, the traditional debate over independence versus dependence for local school systems was all for naught because, in either case, information flows, policy initiation, and conflict accommodation at the local level were controlled by the educational bureaucracy. Thus, it was the monolithic organization of the satellite groups, not the structure of the educational core group, which had the most important bearing on educational policy. At the state level, the educational satellite group (usually a professional educator-dominated coalition of the state education department and a variety of educational interest groups) also dominated the formulation of the details of educational policy.

These traditional structures are in a state of rapid change at this point in time. At the local level, the change to a more pluralistic decision-making structure indicates increasingly strong upward pressures on educational expenditures. As these pressures continue, the professional educators may continue to press for fiscal independence to exert greater influence over the educational core group. They may attempt to make up for the influence being lost as changes occur in the structure of the educational satellite groups. The changes at the local level seem to be filtering up to the state level and opening up the decision-making process there. The final disposition of changes at the state level is still not clear, but there does appear to be a good possibility that the changes in state educational policy formulation will make it easier for states to respond to the needs of the large city educational systems.

VII. The Empirical Model

In the earlier chapters, the major factors which influence and/or determine the resources devoted to large city school finances were considered individually from a variety of perspectives. In some cases the discussion was centered around the measures of resource allocation themselves, the dependent variables of this chapter; in others the discussion was in terms of what have generally been considered basic underlying factors which determine the allocation of resources to the large city school districts, the independent variables of this chapter. The discussion, which up to this point has been descriptive and explicitly partial, will be made more general and comparative through the use of multiple regression analysis. Further, the purpose here is to bring together, in as comprehensive a fashion as is possible, the findings of this study and those of other studies which have a bearing on our understanding of the financial problems of large city school systems, measured in both their educational and fiscal dimensions. The multiple regression framework of this analysis is designed to show both the combined and the individual importance of the several factors which are considered causally important from an *a priori* point of view.[1] The significance and relative importance of the factors affecting large city school finances will be considered in detail, using as consistent a framework as is possible throughout.

The statistical analysis will be almost exclusively from a national point of view, but with an integral recognition of the state and metropolitan contexts in which large city school districts operate.[2] The attempt will be to determine the common elements surrounding large city school problems when viewed across state boundaries in a nation where the basic influence of the state boundaries on both the dependent and in-

[1] See Hubert M. Blalock, Jr., *Causal Inferences in Nonexperimental Research* (Chapel Hill: University of North Carolina Press, 1964), Chapter II, for a discussion of the mathematical representations of causal models.

[2] Individual state and metropolitan contexts have provided the traditional focuses of school finances with only a limited focus on the national aspects of the problems involved.

dependent variables has been directly demonstrated throughout the study. However, some of the major findings concerning state- and metropolitan-bounded behavior patterns will be shown for purposes of comparison. In keeping with the general approach of this national study, the large cities will also be considered in terms of their suburban environments. This will be done using two alternate approaches. The first involves the direct incorporation of suburban school district financial behavior into the multiple regression analysis as an independent variable whose behavior can be isolated and interpreted. The second involves a multiple regression analysis of suburban school financial behavior directly parallel to that of the large cities. It is hoped that these two complementary approaches will provide a much better means of evaluating and understanding large city school finances than has previously been the case. Just as the suburban levels of school finances give meaning to the central city levels, so it is assumed that knowledge of the factors determining suburban behavior will give additional insight into the factors determining large city school finances.

Underlying the analysis of large city school finances is the clear indication and conviction that there is a multiplicity of factors which explain the observed behavior. Some of the factors appear to be unique to a particular area, either because of its past history or because of special circumstances, but there are other factors which appear to be operative in almost all areas of the country. The literature has explained in detail the variations of these independent variables, but the variations in the dependent variables have not been given equal attention. These variations in the dependent variables influence the meaning and explanatory power of the independent variables. At this stage it has not been possible to standardize the behavior, but certain important differences which were noted earlier in the study will be referred to again where appropriate.

The approach of this analysis will be more specifically spelled out than in most prior analyses. The reasons are twofold: first, in order to understand the operational importance of individual variables in a multiple regression analysis where there are strongly held hypotheses, it is necessary to be as consistent as possible throughout the analysis. If the structure of the model is changed in any way, it is not possible to draw inferences concerning individual parameter values, the major objective of the analysis. The second reason is that it is difficult to draw inferences concerning the determinants of the behavior patterns in different areas, *i.e.,* large cities and their suburbs, if the models vary. Not only are the models to be identical at each stage but, to understand the working of the system, the order in which the individual variables are introduced will also follow identical patterns.

The basic model of the analysis involves three independent variables:

1. Income, measured in this instance in per-capita terms (PCI);

2. The proportion of the total resident population attending public schools, *i.e.,* the enrollment ratio (ER);

3. The state aid received for local elementary and secondary schools (SA), where the dimension of aid will conform to the dependent variable.

Thus, when the dependent variable is in per-pupil terms, the aid will be in per-pupil terms (SAP) and, similarly, when the dependent variable is in per-capita terms, the aid variable will be so defined (SAC).

In addition to the basic model, two more variables will be introduced in a less systematic matter. The first is a per-capita measure of the alternative noneducational demands on the local government system of the large cities and their suburbs (TNC). This is viewed as a measure of budgetary alternatives. The final variable which is explicitly introduced is a metropolitan interaction variable which measures the effects of the expenditures on education in the outlying areas on those of the central city areas and vice versa. These are the appropriate dependent variables which are redesignated as independent variables.

To distinguish between central city and outside central city (suburban) areas the following subscripts will be used: [c] in the case of central cities and [o] in the case of outside central city areas. Thus, PCI[c] is per-capita central city income and PCI[o] is per-capita outside central city income. All variables in each question will have subscripts.

From a variety of prior analyses and from the evidence presented earlier in this study, it is assumed that the analysis is incomplete. This is not due only to unique circumstances surrounding many areas but also to the absence of two very important variables excluded because of lack of data and for conceptual reasons. The variable which is excluded for conceptual reasons is a measure of the property tax base.[3] Definitional differences are so enormous between states that only under the most trying circumstances is it possible to construct comparable measures. Even if such comparable measures are constructed, they cannot bear their operationally appropriate role to the dependent variables because of their varying relationships to state aid. This situation clearly does not apply to intrastate analyses. In addition to the conceptual drawbacks, a reasonable determination of property tax values becomes essential in

[3] See Chapter IV.

dealing with suburban areas, especially those which are in more than one county or more than one state.

The second important variable excluded from the main analysis is one which measures the influences of the "past" on contemporary school finances.[4] As has been demonstrated elsewhere in this study, even relatively crude, unedited data indicate that past decisions—often made under very different circumstances—are incorporated into present educational and fiscal practices. These are structural in nature (such as differential assumption of certain costs as, for example, those for retirement and/or a past history of relative affluence or poverty) but have considerable influence on contemporary educational finances. Data concerns and a desire to conform the central city and suburbs as models are the primary reasons for the exclusion of this variable from the main body of the analysis.

Using a step-wise approach, models applicable throughout this analysis will contain the following variables:

I. Income (PCI);

II. Income (PCI), Enrollment Ratio (ER);

III. Income (PCI), Enrollment Ratio (ER), State Aid, either per pupil (SAP) or per capita (SAC), depending on the dimension of the dependent variable (this is the "basic" model of the analysis);

IV. PCI, ER, SAP, or SAC plus noneducational expenditures per capita (TNC);

V. PCI, ER, SAP, or SAC, TNC plus the appropriate metropolitan school finance variable, the outside central city in the case of the city and the city in the case of the outside central city areas.

The principal dimensions of large city school finances to be considered, *i.e.,* the dependent variables are:

1. The educational dimension, as measured by per-pupil current expenditures (CEP);

2. The fiscal dimension, as measured by per-capita total local public elementary-secondary school expenditures (TEC);

3. The fiscal dimension, as measured by per-capita total local public elementary-secondary school expenditures financed out of their own sources, *i.e.,* nonaided education expenditures (NAEC).

This last is only a proxy for local school taxes because capital expenditures are generally financed out of borrowed funds and taxes must cover

[4] For more limited interpretations of the effects of the "past" on fiscal behavior, see Aaron Wildavsky, *The Politics of the Budgetary Process* (Boston: Little, Brown and Company, 1964), and the recent work of Ira Sharkansky, *Spending in the American States* (Chicago: Rand McNally, 1968), Ch. III.

not only current expenditures, but debt-service charges as well. On the other hand, "expenditures from own sources" is an important concept. ("Own sources" is an official designation of the Bureau of the Census.)

While each of these measures shows considerable variation for large cities and their suburbs, the relative variation, as measured by their coefficients of variation, indicates that they are neither excessively restricted nor excessively great and could be clearly drawn from a common universe. (See Table 30.)

These coefficients of variation are much lower than those found by Jerry Miner, who, with a much larger national sample, found coefficients of 72.1 percent for per-pupil current expenditures, and 82.8 percent for per-capita current expenditures.[5] These latter figures reflected the inclusion of a vast number of small rural districts as well as state differences. The analysis of large cities and their suburbs seems to be drawn from a far more common environment than the analysis of an undifferentiated national sample of districts. State-wide analyses generally show relative variability comparable to those of the 1962 sample.

DETERMINANTS OF SCHOOL FINANCES

The literature on the determinants of local school finances is relatively extensive; it is drawn not only from studies made by educators but by economists, sociologists, and others as well.[6] Because the statistical models are not comparable, it is difficult to draw conclusions concerning the nature, let alone the importance, of the individual factors. The differences emerge, as has been noted, from the nature of the variables as well as from the structural differences of the models. However, it is quite often possible to divide an analysis into its separate elements to deal with the problems at least partially, and to determine initially whether there are similarities or differences, depending on the level of aggregation and hence the relevance of these analyses to large city problems.

Historically, the most extensive literature of determinants of local school finances exists in the attempts to explain the level of current per-pupil expenditures in cross section, over time, or a combination of both. If one restricts the analysis to those which deal with the problem statistically, one can go back to the very origins of education administration in the works of Cubberly, Strayer, and Elliot, all of whom were directly influenced by the statistical innovations of E. L. Thorndike at the turn of

[5] Jerry Miner, *op. cit.,* 97.

[6] See Roy W. Bahl in *Functional Federalism: Grants-In-Aid and PPB Systems,* Selma J. Mushkin and John F. Cotton (Washington, D.C.: State-Local Finances Project of the George Washington University, 1968), 184–203, for a historical overview of the methodologies and the noneducational aspects of the literature.

TABLE 30

Sample Characteristics, Central City and Outside Central City Areas

	Central City			Outside Central City		
	Mean $	Standard Deviation $	Coefficient of Variation %	Mean $	Standard Deviation $	Coefficient of Variation %
CEP (1) Per-pupil current educational expenditures (1962)	376.33	83.61	22.2	438.38	106.77	24.4
TEC (2) Per-capita total educational expenditures (1962)	68.69	16.04	23.4	126.17	31.45	24.9
NAEC (3) Per-capita nonaided educational expenditures (1962)	47.23	14.94	31.6	89.60	26.34	29.4

the century,[7] or one can move to the more recent literature in the area of education and public finance.[8]

INCOME

A basic factor included in most analyses is income, measured in per-capita or median family terms. As shown in Table 31, which summarizes some of the more important relevant studies, this is perhaps the most common element of all studies. Regardless of the level of aggregation, some measure of income usually appears significant. The one very low value for local income, found by Jerry Miner, is nevertheless significant. The specific problems raised by the individual state analyses, carried on by Miner and others, pose special problems and will be considered briefly later, but they show the importance of income in a large number of individual states.[9]

The findings, as shown in Table 31, indicate that income appears to be most important in the case of the state-wide analyses and less so elsewhere. Income is presumed to be so powerful on the state level because it tends to measure both the demand for and supply of local school services. Most of the findings in the analysis of the relationship between family or per-capita income and per-pupil expenditures on a state level are of the same order as those found by Richard Welch and reported in Table 31.[10] For the even years, for which Office of Education data are available between 1950 and 1960, the highest correlation between these two variables was +0.867 in 1949–50 and the lowest was +0.821 in 1955–56.

The results of analyses of income and per-pupil expenditures on a school district or county average basis within a state or even among states are much more ambiguous than those found on a state-wide basis. As shown in Table 31, Jerry Miner, in the most comprehensive national analysis of school districts, found a simple correlation of only +0.25 between local income and per-pupil operating expenditures, although on an individual state basis he found several states in which the relationships between income and per-pupil expenditures were considerably higher. But Miner also found a number of states in which income was

[7] R. Callahan, op. cit., 189.

[8] See G. Alan Hickrod and Cesar M. Subulao, Increasing Social and Economic Inequality Among Suburban Schools (Downville: The Interstate Printers and Publishers, Inc., 1969), 45–55, for a comprehensive list of works in the field.

[9] See Miner, op. cit., 110–17.

[10] For a much more comprehensive analysis of the relationship between income and per-pupil expenditures see Richard Welch, Further Explorations with State Personal Income and State Education Expenditures, unpublished master's thesis: Syracuse University, 1968.

TABLE 31

SIMPLE CORRELATIONS, PER-PUPIL CURRENT EXPENDITURES AND SELECTED INDEPENDENT VARIABLES

Area Covered	U.S. (A)	New York State (B)	U.S. (C)	U.S. (D)	Metropolitan Areas			
					Central Cities (E)	Outside Central Cities (E)	Central Cities	Outside Central Cities
	State Aggre.	County Aggre.	School Dist.	Large-Scale Dist.	City Areas	Outside City Areas	School Systems	School Systems
Year	1960	1965	1960	1960	1957	1957	1962	1962
Sample Size	48	58	1,127	107	36	36	37	37
Variable								
Per-capita income (1959)	0.859	0.590	NA	NA	0.491	0.479	0.529	0.578
Median family income (1959)	NA	NA	0.25	0.554	0.448	NA	0.618	NA
Enrollment ratio	NA	−0.120	NA	NA	−0.717	−0.340	−0.528	−0.394
Percent in private school	NA	NA	0.25	0.577	NA	NA	0.439	NA
State aid as % total revenue	NA	NA	−0.28	NA	NA	NA	NA	NA
Aid per pupil	NA	−0.480	NA	0.430	0.319	0.204	0.361	0.447
Assessed value per pupil	NA	NA	NA	NA	NA	NA	NA	NA
Equalized value per pupil	NA	0.811	0.25	NA	NA	NA	NA	NA
Percent owner-occupied	NA	NA	NA	−0.249	−0.385	−0.312	−0.311	0.208
Percent nonwhite	NA	NA	−0.24	−0.411	−0.484	−0.537	−0.449	NA
Median years of education	NA	NA	0.17	0.170	NA	NA	0.007	NA

SOURCES: (A) R. Welch in S. Sacks, "Interstate Variations in Educational Expenditures." (B) New York State Department of Audit and Control; *Financial Data for School Districts, 1965.* (C) J. Miner, *Social and Economic Factors in Spending for Public Education.* (D) H.T. James, S.A. Kelly and W.I. Garms, *Determinants of Educational Expenditures in Large Cities in the United States.* (E) A.K. Campbell and S. Sacks, *Metropolitan America: Fiscal Patterns and Governmental Systems.*

either unrelated or negatively related to per-pupil expenditures.[11] Almost all intrastate and intrametropolitan studies show a more modest relationship between income and current expenditures than those found on a state-wide basis. The presumption is that income represents both the demand for and supply of public education at the state level; but the situation does not hold on the local level where other factors, notably the property tax base and its related state aid system, play a much more significant role.

Two recent studies illustrate these aspects of the income-expenditure relationship. The first study, that of Hickrod and Subulao, found income to be significant in a multiple regression analysis of suburban school systems in only one of five large metropolitan areas.[12] At the same time they found per-pupil valuation to be significant at the 0.01 level, and either first or second in importance in every one of their analyses. In the second study, a recent large-scale analysis of school systems in the metropolitan portions of five urban states, the mixed pattern noted earlier is found.[13] For two states, Massachusetts and New York, the correlations between income and per-pupil expenditures are positive and significant; in two, Michigan and Texas, they are almost zero; and in one, California, the result is comparable to that found by Miner for the United States.

In this study, income appears to be a significant factor in the 37 large central city and outlying areas under consideration, with simple correlations of $+0.529$ and $+0.578$, respectively. These are not quite the levels achieved in the state-wide analyses, but they are of considerable interest. As shown in Table 31, James and his colleagues found similar income-expenditure patterns for large school systems.[14]

In addition to measures of the level of income, some analysts have also included measures of income distribution. The inclusion of both income and income-distribution measures can create great difficulties because of the existence of multicollinearities. This is especially important when the level of association is much higher between the independent and dependent variables. The inclusion of these income-distribution variables may increase the unadjusted coefficient of multiple correlation (it cannot reduce it except by its effect on degrees of freedom), but it con-

---

[11] Miner, *op. cit.*, 110–17.

[12] Hickrod and Subulao, *op. cit.*, A–5. However, an "occupational index" was significant in four of the five areas.

[13] Policy Institute of the Syracuse University Research Corporation, *A Statistical Workbook: The Allocation of Federal Aid to Education* (Syracuse, 1970).

[14] H. Thomas James, James A. Kelly and Walter I. Garms, *Determinants of Educational Expenditures in Large Cities in the United States* (Stanford: Stanford University Press, 1966).

fuses the meaning that may be attributed to the separate variables. As will be indicated later, it is perhaps more important to know the relative importance of individual variables than to know something about a relatively complex model with strong but misleading interactions.

Since it is undesirable to make the analysis overly complex, the inclusion of separate variables which are significantly intercorrelated may then be justified only on very strong *a priori* grounds. This is certainly true of the relationship between educational aid and property values in many states where the one is often, but not invariably, the inverse measure of the other. If one looks at the total aid system, *i.e.,* noneducational as well as educational aid, the result may be very different than in the case of educational aid alone, as is true in Wisconsin. In this state the shared-tax system outside of education rewarded those areas with high property values and punished those areas with low values, although the educational aid system looked very good standing alone.[15]

THE ENROLLMENT RATIO

Another important problem area involves the extent to which the demand for education, as measured by the proportion of the total population enrolled in schools, affects the level of school finances. This has a quantitative as well as qualitative aspect. It is quite clear that the reason why the association between the income variables and the level of per-capita educational expenditures should be lower than that between per-pupil expenditures and income reflects variations in the proportions of the total population to be educated. This is true on the interstate as well as intrastate level of analysis. But the enrollment ratio encompasses a variety of factors especially relevant in the case of large cities. It shows the availability of nonpublic school education in the large cities and in the states with large cities. The question which emerges not only calls for analysis of the differential effects on the citizenry on voting for educational levies, but for the analysis of other interrelated factors as well. A low enrollment ratio introduces an upward bias on the amount of resources presumed to be available per pupil who attends school; as the ratio increases there is a bias in favor of a larger commitment of total resources in areas with higher enrollment ratios.

The enrollment ratio reflects the age distribution of the total population as well as the availability of nonpublic alternatives. Even if all children were attending public schools, the position of the large city school systems would be to have a relatively smaller proportion attending their schools as compared to those in the suburbs. Recent changes in

[15] For a detailed analysis, see John Riew in *Fiscal Balance in the American Federal System,* Vol. 2, *op. cit.,* 278–324.

the racial composition of almost all large cities has altered this to an extent, but a favorable age distribution has resulted in a smaller proportion of the population attending city public schools, particularly in the north central and northeastern United States.

Finally, the enrollment ratio is also clearly related to the number of persons attending secondary schools. As was indicated earlier, the proportion of the appropriate ages attending elementary and the first two years of secondary schools, apart from the attendance in nonpublic schools, is slightly less than 100 percent. Although they may not always be in attendance, they are almost universally enrolled. This is not true of the last two years of secondary school education; these are also the costliest years of education, and hence have a major effect on the level of school finances.

The general finding, as shown in Table 31, is that the enrollment ratio (or its counterpart, the proportion of school-age children attending private school adjusted for sign) is inversely related to the level of per-pupil expenditures, especially in the large cities but also in other areas included in this study. However, since it is assumed that the enrollment ratio increases with income due to the larger proportion attending secondary schools, that problem is especially difficult to deal with because the models contain different kinds of areas in a single national analysis. Similarly, a competition of forces emerges on the interstate level between the availability of nonpublic school education, and the increasing proportion of population attending schools as the income goes up; yet there is no conclusive data on this subject.

A variety of other local factors designed to distinguish among school districts have also been considered by previous analysts of the problems of school finance. Some of these are clearly related to income and enrollment, other variables have an independent existence. Of the other variables, some, such as the proportion living in owner-occupied housing, are measures of suburbanization and are of interest in distinguishing among cities.

In his detailed analysis of local school finances in large cities, David Ranney also included a variety of ethnic variables in addition to the nonwhite proportion.[16] The results, including those for nonwhite, are subject to very complex interpretation and are not as directly applicable to a comparative national analysis as are the other variables used in this analysis.

STATE AID

This next independent variable has been the subject of considerable debate. While this variable occupies a central role in this analysis, it is not al-

---

[16] D. Ranney, *op. cit.,* Chapter VI.

ways viewed as central.[17] Miner excludes it from direct consideration, although he notes its importance by inclusion of a state-wide proportionate share. Further, Miner implicitly recognizes aid by excluding it from his locally supported per-pupil current expenditures, one of his four dependent variables. That aid is a complex and potentially important variable is indicated by the fact that when aid is subtracted to arrive at unaided per-pupil current expenditures, the coefficient of variation rises from 0.721 to 1.057.[18]

The exclusion of aid has raised a set of problems which has resulted in a better statement of the nature of the dependent variables. Since the analysis deals with both the educational and fiscal dimensions of school finances, the aid variable should conform. A number of specific hypotheses emerge. While the determinants' literature has been ambivalent, the importance of aid has been clearly demonstrated, even when it is brought in by the back door (as a deduction, proportion, or as an amount). Rather than attempting to demonstrate its abstract significance, the emphasis in this study is on specified hypotheses concerning aid; both its direction and relative importance will be examined, but also, more specifically, the extent it adds to or replaces local effort. Results on a state basis have been presented by Renshaw and others,[19] but again their specific hypotheses have been too complex and generally unspecified. Miner, using a state average, found that as the proportion goes up the level falls.

The aid variable is significantly and positively related to large city and suburban school expenditures per pupil in this sample of large cities across state boundaries. These results contrast very sharply with the intrastate patterns, which are often negative. This is borne out by the data in Table 32, which show results for each state on a school system basis, consistent with the county-wide New York State findings of a negative correlation of −0.590 between per-pupil state aid and per-pupil current expenditures. It is quite clear that the assumption, often made, that because state money is included in the "expenditure variable that there should be some autocorrelation effect in the data,"[20] is directly challenged by the findings in Table 32 as well as elsewhere.

The difficulty is due to the existence of the property tax variable, which is of preeminent importance, as shown in Table 32; this factor, because of its relationship with per-pupil aid, also affects per-pupil expenditures both directly and indirectly.

For all five urban states shown in Table 32, the correlation between

[17] Hickrod and Subulao, *op. cit.*, 42.
[18] Miner, *op. cit.*, 97.
[19] *Ibid.*, 99.
[20] Hickrod and Subulao, *op. cit.*, 42.

TABLE 32

SIMPLE CORRELATIONS, PER-PUPIL CURRENT EXPENDITURES AND SELECTED
INDEPENDENT VARIABLES, SCHOOL SYSTEM BASIS, METROPOLITAN
PORTIONS OF STATES, 1967

	Calif.	N.Y.	Texas	Mich.	Mass.
Number of school systems	143	88	67	58	41
Median family income, 1959	+0.265	+0.612	+0.071	+0.091	+0.738
State aid per pupil, 1967	−0.334	−0.258	−0.177	−0.507	−0.346
State equalized valuation per pupil, 1967	+0.593	+0.461	+0.800	+0.715	+0.578
Aid/valuation	−0.402	−0.797	−0.264	−0.856	−0.559
Aid/income	−0.216	−0.283	−0.386	−0.113	−0.176
Income/ valuation	+0.260	+0.469	+0.152	+0.020	+0.439
0.01 Level of significance	±0.254	±0.283	±0.325	±0.354	±0.418

SOURCE: *A Statistical Workbook: The Allocation of Federal Aid to Education,*
Policy Institute of the Syracuse University Research Corporation, 1970.

per-pupil valuation and per-pupil aid is significantly negative, ranging from -0.264 in Texas to an $r = -0.856$ in Michigan. Hickrod and Subulao, dealing with suburbs, found this relation to be the case in four of the five metropolitan areas they studied. Only in the Chicago area, where they studied high schools, was this not the case.[21] Incidentally, if the valuation is partialed out, then the effect of aid is significantly positive in only two cases, Michigan and New York, and insignificant in the other three cases. This indicates a much more complex situation than the simple autocorrelation which is presumed to exist between per-pupil aid and per-pupil expenditures.

The role of the property tax base across state lines has been considered by Miner (using state-wide averages) and by James (using assessed valuations which he and his colleagues found to be no different from interstate equalized values). In both cases the results are significant, but not of the same order of the five states analyzed in Table 32 or New York State, using county units, where the result is highly signif-

[21] *Ibid.,* A–12.

icant at +0.811. Nevertheless, it was decided not to use the tax base in this analysis because of the conceptual and data difficulties involved in interstate comparisons.

METHODOLOGY

As already noted, the analysis is explicitly step-wise, not only in terms of statistical procedures but also in terms of an ordinally established set of strongly held hypotheses concerning the determinants of large city school finance.

The central city results at each stage are compared with those of a similarly constructed model of outlying suburban school behavior. The purpose is not only to determine the existence of significant relationships but, since the hypotheses are strongly held, to compare the parameter values of the hypothesized variables in the central city with those of the suburban areas.

The general approach throughout the rest of the statistical analysis is initially to determine how the "local" conditions, as measured by per-capita income and enrollment ratios, are related to variations in the level of behavior. And, at the risk of repetition, it should be noted that if meaningfully comparable data were available, the next step would have been to introduce the appropriate local property tax base which is con-sidered to be operative in each of the cities and suburban areas analyzed. However, due to the already noted severe data limitations, such informa-tion is not appropriate to interstate differences. The importance of appro-priate measures of tax base having been recognized, it is presumed that the findings will be limited by their exclusion. The next step is to intro-duce, specifically, the state aid variable. The precise interpretation of the "meaning" of the observed behavior is a function of the dependent vari-able to which it is being related as well as the independent variables. An attempt is made to distinguish between the extent to which aid replaces local effort, in whole or in part, or the extent to which aid is *expenditure* or *tax additive*. But, as is demonstrated, state aid is very important.

The next two steps are viewed as optional, but they also follow a pre-set routine. The first of these is designed to measure the effect of non-educational fiscal behavior on educational behavior. Because of the di-mensional differences, this step is not undertaken in the case of per-pupil expenditures, but it is undertaken in terms of the per-capita measures. The last variable introduced is designed to measure the interactions within metropolitan areas, *i.e.,* the effect of suburban educational finance levels on those of the central city and vice versa. As has already been indicated, it is presumed that there is a strong labor market–demonstra-tion effect operative within each area.

The step-wise analysis is designed not only to ascertain the effect of the introduction of the new variable on the ability to explain the total variability, but also to ascertain their effects on the observed values of the previously introduced variables.

In addition to the step-wise multiple regression analysis, the elasticities of the three-variable major model equations were computed, using their logarithmically transformed variables rather than the elasticities that are computed at their point of means. Here again, there have been earlier findings and specific hypotheses which will be tested and evaluated, using the large city and suburban data.

The elasticities are designed to measure the relative effect of a change in an independent variable on their dependent variable. When determined in their multiple regression context, this permits a measurement of the income, enrollment ratio, and state aid elasticities, holding other variables constant. Further, it permits the specific estimation and testing of the elasticities, as contrasted with the determination of the elasticity at the mean.

The specific hypotheses concerning regression coefficients for per-pupil current expenditures may be summarized at this point (Table 33). In

TABLE 33

EXPECTED VALUES, MODELS OF DETERMINANTS OF
PER-PUPIL CURRENT EXPENDITURES

	Per-Capita Income	Enrollment Ratio	State Aid Per Pupil	Metropolitan Interaction	$\bar{R}^2$
Large Central Cities					
Model I	+				
Model II	+	−			increase
Model III*	+	−	+(1)		increase
Model IV	0	0	0	+(CEP[o])	increase
Suburbs of Large Central Cities					
Model I	+				
Model II	+	−			increase
Model III*	+	−	+(1)		increase
Model IV	0	0	0	+(CEP[c])	increase

* Basic Model.

the case of the basic model explaining per-pupil current expenditures, the relationships are presumed to be positive and significant in the central city and suburban school districts for all variables except the enrollment ratio. Since the hypotheses are specified, it is possible and desirable to use single tailed tests of significance.[22] Further, the coefficients of multiple regression (R) and determination (R^2) are adjusted for degrees of freedom, and they are presumed to increase as additional variables are introduced.

In Model IV, it is further presumed that there are no differences in the relationships between the independent and dependent variables for the large cities and their suburban areas. However, because of expected multicollinearities, the behavior of the other independent variables is hypothesized as indeterminate.

The simple correlation matrix, Table 34, indicates that the low level of correlation which exists among the independent variables rises to a much higher level when the metropolitan interaction variable is introduced. The first three independent variables would be retained even if they were highly intercorrelated but, since they are not, their interpretation is accordingly simplified. The last variable shows the existence of a high degree of multicollinearity as expected.

The first set of models to be considered successively introduced income, the enrollment ratio, and state aid per pupil. This was done for both the central city and suburban areas. As already noted, the purpose was not only to determine the relationships, but to compare the observed parameter values of the central city and outlying areas. The first analysis indicates that per-pupil current expenditures in central city areas are positively and significantly related to per-capita incomes: for every $1 of income, per-pupil expenditures were $0.1618. This contrasts with a similar and even more significant positive relationship in the case of the areas surrounding these central cities. In the suburbs, expenditures were equal to $0.2150 of every $1 of income and, since the incomes were higher in the suburbs, the expenditures were thus appropriately higher. If the constant is taken into account, then the level of per-pupil expenditures in the suburbs was higher than in the central city areas for all except the very lowest levels of income.

The next step introduces the enrollment ratio as an explicit variable. This leads to a major increase in the "explained" proportion of the total variance in central city per-pupil expenditures; the increase is from an R^2 of 0.2591 to one of 0.5102, adjusted for degrees of freedom. Outside

[22] See Taro Yamane, *Statistics: An Introductory Analysis,* 2d ed. (New York: Harper & Row, 1967), 180–86.

TABLE 34

SIMPLE CORRELATION MATRIXES, PER-PUPIL EXPENDITURES

(A) LARGE CITY, SCHOOL SYSTEM BASIS, 1962 (PER PUPIL)

Variable	ER[c]	SAP[c]	CEP[o]	CEP[c]	Mean	Standard Deviation	Coefficient of Variation
Per-capita income (PCI[c])	−0.040	0.384*	0.452†	0.529†	$2,068.00	$273.00	13.2%
Enrollment ratio (ER[o])		−0.091	−0.488†	−0.528†	17.2%	3.2%	18.6%
State aid per pupil (SAP[c])			0.244	0.361*	$124.91	$52.54	42.1%
Current expenditure per pupil—outside (CEP[o])				0.605†	$438.38	$106.77	24.4%
Current expenditure per pupil—city (CEP[c])					$376.33	$83.61	22.2%

(B) OUTSIDE LARGE CITY, SCHOOL DISTRICT BASIS, 1962 (PER PUPIL)

Variable	ER[o]	SAP[o]	CEP[c]	CEP[o]	Mean	Standard Deviation	Coefficient of Variation
Per-capita income (PCI[o])	−0.368*	0.070	0.723†	0.678†	$2,182.00	$337.00	15.4%
Enrollment ratio (ER[o])		0.128	−0.201	−0.394	22.6%	3.0%	13.3%
State aid per pupil (SAP[o])			0.468†	0.447†	$165.48	$76.94	46.5%
Current expenditures per pupil—city (CEP[c])				0.605†	$376.33	$83.61	22.2%
Current expenditure per pupil—outside (CEP[o])					$438.38	$106.77	24.4%

* Significant at the 0.05 level of probability.   † Significant at the 0.01 level of probability.

central cities, the introduction of the enrollment ratio had virtually no effect on the relationship between income and per-pupil current expenditures, a relationship which changed just a fraction of a penny of every $1 of income. As expected, there is a clear indication that per-pupil current expenditures vary inversely with the enrollment ratios in the large central cities. Since the highest enrollment ratios are in the West and the South, the per-pupil expenditures are accordingly lower in the central cities in those sections of the country. While the direction of the effect of enrollment ratios is similar in the suburban areas to those of the central city areas, this variable itself is not significant at this stage of the analysis. Nevertheless, it improves the adjusted total explanatory power of the model from an R^2 of 0.4439 to one of 0.5972. The effect of the introduction of the enrollment ratio variable is minor insofar as income is concerned, with a nominal reduction in the level of expenditures for each $1 of income. As was noted earlier, enrollment ratios outside central city areas do not show the same regional patterns as they do in the case of the large cities. The result is somewhat surprising because the introduction of the enrollment variables raises the total explanatory power without itself being significant.

The introduction of state aid as the next variable is considered important for a number of reasons. It is especially important because of the already noted differential treatment accorded the central cities and their outlying areas within states and the desire to trace through the differential effects, if any, in aid patterns on expenditures. Furthermore, this situation is unlike the case of the federal or more recent educational aid programs, because the local governments are part of a state-local system where tax sharing and equalization are more important than the incentive motive which dominates federal aid. The problem is to see what the effect of aid is on per-pupil expenditures in the central city area and, finally, to see whether it alters the behavior of the other variables. The problem of the relationship between aid and local school behavior is more meaningfully interpreted in fiscal rather than educational terms. In this model it is assumed that the addition of state aid does not lead to a decrease in local effort, *i.e.,* that per-pupil aid is expenditure-additive. An alternative hypothesis would be that an increase in state aid would lead to a proportionate decrease in local effort, *i.e.,* that per-pupil aid is not expenditure-additive. In many states this was the announced objective of state aid policy.

The introduction of the per-pupil aid variable has virtually no effect on explaining, directly or indirectly, the variation in large city per-pupil expenditure levels. For every $1 of aid, expenditures are $0.2253 greater, but this is not statistically significant. And, as is evident, there is no relationship between enrollment ratios and state aid. However, there is a positive relationship between state aid and income, indicating that educational aid is higher in the states with wealthier central cities. In contrast, the introduction of state aid does have a major effect in explaining variations in the levels of per-pupil expenditures in suburban areas. The effect is an increase in per-pupil expenditures of $0.6095 for every $1 of education aid per pupil received. This raises the question as to why the aid does not operate to the same extent in the expenditure process of the large cities as it does in their suburbs. In the case of the suburban areas, the introduction of the aid variable not only improves the over-all explanatory power of the model, as distinguished from its failure to do so in the case of the large cities, but it improves the explanatory power of the enrollment ratio to a level which more closely approximates the situation in the large cities. There is a more significant and differentially higher level of expenditure per dollar of state aid in the case of the suburban areas as compared to their large city counterparts. This particular result is of interest, for it indicates that for every $1 of aid the amounts of expenditure were increased $0.2253 in the central city and $0.6095 in the suburbs, and on the average there were more dollars of aid in the suburbs than in the cities.

Comparing the results of Table 35, it appears that these three variables "explain" about half of the variation in large city per-pupil expenditures and almost two-thirds in the case of the suburbs. Further, for every $1 of income, per-pupil expenditures in the suburbs are higher on a per-pupil basis, after account is taken of the enrollment ratios and state aid, than they are in their large cities. This is surprising because the bias, if any, is in the direction of higher city costs due to the differential imposition of higher educational expenditure requirements on the school systems servicing large city areas.

On the other hand, the expenditure goes down by a greater amount in the central cities, as the enrollment ratio goes up, than it does in the outlying areas. For each percentage point of increase in the enrollment ratio, city expenditure per pupil is reduced by $12.92, while in the suburbs the decline is $8.63. Finally, aid shows a greater positive effect on the level of suburban school expenditures than on the level of the large city expenditures.

Measuring the results in terms of the standardized regression or beta coefficients, the relative importance of the variables may be considered and compared, particularly since identical models were used. In the central cities, income is important (+0.4545) and is offset by the enrollment ratio (−0.4972), with per-pupil aid for education (+0.1416) playing an insignificant role on the level of expenditures per pupil. This

TABLE 35

REGRESSION EQUATIONS, CENTRAL CITY AND OUTSIDE CENTRAL CITY PER-PUPIL EXPENDITURES

Dependent Variable	Income	Enrollment Ratio	State Aid Per Pupil	Constant	$\overline{R}$	$\overline{R}^2$
DEPENDENT VARIABLE						
(A) Per-pupil expenditures in central city	+0.1618† (0.0439)			41.72	0.5090	0.2591
	+0.1556† (0.0357)	−13.1967† (3.0332)		281.50	0.7142	0.5102
	+0.1319† (0.0385)	−12.9172† (3.0321)	+0.2253 (0.2009)	282.63	0.7167	0.5137
Standardized regression coefficient	0.4545†	−0.4972†	+0.1416			
Elasticity (Log transformations)	0.9703† (0.2089)	0.6313† (0.1408)	0.0325 (0.0568)		0.7476	0.5620
(B) Per-pupil expenditures in outside central city, CEP[o]	+0.2150† (0.0394)			−30.66	0.6662	0.4439
	+0.1954† (0.0425)	−5.8849 (4.6640)		144.78	0.7727	0.5972
	+0.1766† (0.0348)	−8.6275* (3.8360)	+0.6095† (0.1410)	146.87	0.8801	0.6403
Standardized regression coefficient	0.5569	−0.2452	+0.4392			
Elasticity (Log transformations)	1.0994 (0.1996)	−0.3708 (0.2364)	0.1574† (0.0555)		0.7592	0.5764

NOTE: Values in parentheses are standard errors.

* Significant at the 0.05 level of probability.   † Significant at the 0.01 level of probability.

$\overline{R}$ Coefficient of multiple correlation adjusted for degrees of freedom.

contrasts with the more important roles played by income (+0.5569) and state aid (+0.4392) and the lesser role played by the enrollment ratios (−0.2425) in the suburban areas.

ELASTICITIES OF THE DETERMINANTS OF PER-PUPIL CURRENT EXPENDITURES

Before turning to the effects of the metropolitan environment, which explicitly raises the problems of multicollinearity, the question of the elasticities of the individual variables will be considered. While it is possible to compute the elasticities of each of the variables at their means, neither their statistical significance nor alternative hypotheses, such as unit elasticity, can be tested. In particular, it is presumed that, in some cases the values might be hypothesized as unit elasticity (1), or they might be of a particular sign, plus or minus, or merely a sharing of tax burden (0). In this analysis, the data are transformed into their logarithmic values and a number of specific hypotheses are introduced: (1) educational expenditures are expected to show positive unit elasticity with respect to income; (2) they are expected to be negatively elastic with respect to enrollment ratios; and (3) they are expected to be positively elastic with respect to state aid. These are the counterpart hypotheses to the original multiple regression analysis, but with the assumption that per-pupil expenditures are unit-elastic with respect to income.

At +0.9703 the income elasticity of per-pupil current expenditures in large cities is significantly greater than zero, but is not statistically different from unity. The income elasticity of suburban per-pupil expenditure, at +1.0994, is significantly higher than that of central cities, but again it is not significantly different from unity. What is statistically significant is the high negative elasticity of enrollment ratios on city per-pupil expenditures. For every 1-percent increase in the enrollment ratios, expenditures decrease by 0.6313 percent, while the decrease in suburbia at 0.3708 percent is not significantly different from zero. Finally, the elasticity of per-pupil expenditures with respect to variations in aid is positive but not significant in the case of the cities, and positive and significant in the case of the suburbs.

The findings show a much higher responsiveness of per-pupil educational expenditures to local income than do those of Miner.[23] The major interpretation of the expenditure elasticity of aid appears to be associated with its fiscal, rather than educational, dimension.

The last step of this analysis of per-pupil expenditures consists in the placing of the large central cities in their interacting suburban environ-

---

[23] Miner, *op. cit.*, 107, found an income elasticity of 0.06 in the case of local income.

ments, and the converse in the case of the suburbs. At this point, strong intercorrelations emerge due, it is assumed, to their common metropolitan base, similar state characteristics, and, perhaps most importantly, because of labor market–demonstration effects. The introduction of the interaction variable clouds the meaning which may be attributable to the other variables. The introduction of the level of expenditures in the outside areas as an explicit variable raises the adjusted coefficient of determination, R^2, from 0.5137 to 0.6984 in the case of the large central city areas. In the case of the outside areas, the increase is from 0.6403 to 0.7065. It is thus clear that the introduction of the metropolitan interaction variable does add something over and above that contributed by the specific model variables themselves. This is designed to determine the net additional contribution of the labor market–demonstration effect on the level of expenditures. The effect is both absolutely and relatively greater in the case of the large central cities than it is in their outside areas. Or perhaps more meaningfully phrased, it appears that the position of the suburban areas today is determined to a much greater extent by the state aid which they receive than is the case of the large central city areas. The net results are not automatically determined by the size of the intercorrelation between the city and the suburban per-pupil expenditures of +0.605, which is equivalent to a simple coefficient of determination of 0.3660. No attempt was made to analyze the elasticities of the several variables after the introduction of the metropolitan interaction variable, because of the complex nature of the multicollinearities involved.

THE FISCAL DIMENSION

As already noted, the level of per-pupil expenditures tells us very little directly about the level of fiscal activity generated by the educational sector. It is quite clear that the level is reduced, other things being equal, by the enrollment ratio; but to what extent the other things are fiscally equal cannot be seen directly. Thus, while it is possible to introduce noneducational expenditures in the context of per-pupil expenditures, it is more meaningful to introduce it in the analysis of the per-capita fiscal activity where it is directly comparable.

The differences in per-pupil current expenditures only partly explain the differences in the total amount of resources devoted to education in the central cities as compared to the suburbs. The much higher enrollment ratios in the suburbs mean that per-capita total resources outside central cities devoted to education are much greater than the comparable amounts in central cities. Furthermore, there are differences between the central cities and their suburbs in per-capita amounts devoted to education, whether measured as own resources or as total resources. The literature of public finance is replete with a number of direct and indirect attempts to measure the effects of aid on the level of expenditure and taxes. The purpose of this section is to analyze the fiscal dimensions of large city school finances as directly as is possible, using the same step-wise approach used in the analysis of the educational division. Once again it is important to note the omission of the tax base as an explicit explanatory variable, and once again it is presumed that the analysis will be incomplete because of its exclusion.

The analysis of the fiscal dimension of local school finances has a far more restricted history than that of the educational dimension. The most comprehensive analysis of the problems is that of Jerry Miner. A summary of his and other findings is shown in Table 36. Curiously, state-wide variables are more important than local variables and, in the nonaided portions, the average level of state aid as a proportion of total revenue for schools stands out.[24] State-wide analysis of per-capita education expenditures does not show the same dominating importance of income as does the comparable analysis of per-pupil current expenditures.

There are some state-wide analyses of school taxes and school tax rates, but these are not immediately transferable to the fiscal dimensions of large city and suburban school districts herein considered.

As in the prior section, the first step will be to specify the hypotheses being tested. This will be done first for per-capita total expenditures devoted to public elementary and secondary schools, then for the per-capita expenditures for the same purposes financed out of own sources. While this is presumed to be a good proxy for local taxes, it has some limitations, but, at the same time, has its own independent importance and permits comparability between city and suburban behavior. The major limitations of nonaided expenditures as a direct measure of taxation emerge because taxes are raised for interest and debt-retirement purposes, as well as for current expenditures. On the other hand, non-aided educational expenditures, including those financed out of borrowing, is a meaningful category.

As already noted, suburbs spend considerably more per capita on education than do the cities. Similarly, they spend much more out of their own sources than do the cities. The analysis up to this point has been directed toward explaining per-pupil current expenditures; at this point the analysis is converted to a per-capita basis. In addition, the effects of alternative expenditure demands on the local governments, which were considered in isolation in Chapter V, now will be considered

---

[24] *Ibid.,* 98–99.

TABLE 36

SIMPLE CORRELATIONS, PER-CAPITA LOCAL SCHOOL EXPENDITURES AND SELECTED INDEPENDENT VARIABLES

Area Covered	U.S. (A) State Aggre.	U.S. (B) School Dist.	U.S. (B) School Dist.	Metropolitan Areas			
				Central Cities School Systems	Outside Central City School Systems	Central Cities School Systems	Outside Central Cities School Systems
Year	1962	1960	1960	1962	1962	1962	1962
Sample Size	48	884	880	37	37	37	37
	Total	Current	Nonaided Current	Total	Total	Nonaided Total	Nonaided Total
Median family income	NA	0.21	0.43	0.628	NA	0.592	NA
Per-capita local income	NA	NA	NA	0.548	0.425	0.438	0.535
Percent over $10,000	NA	0.29	0.55	NA	NA	NA	NA
Per-capita state income	0.625	0.42	0.57	NA	NA	NA	NA
Per-capita state-wide property	NA	0.32	0.42	NA	NA	NA	NA
Percent children under 18	NA	0.00	−0.25	−0.173	NA	−0.218	NA
Percent in nonpublic schools	NA	0.09	0.41	0.304	NA	0.082	NA
Percent nonwhite	NA	−0.22	−0.41	−0.313	NA	−0.306	NA
Percent moved last 5 years	NA	0.05	0.06	−0.154	NA	−0.151	NA
Salary entering teachers	NA	0.39	0.54	0.610	0.227	0.667	NA
Enrollment ratio	−0.060	NA	NA	0.270	NA	0.054	0.088
System size in ADA	NA	−0.05	0.00	0.267	NA	0.133	NA
Percent in secondary schools	NA	0.16	0.17	NA	NA	NA	NA
Per-capita school aid	0.389	NA	NA	0.428	0.557	−0.145	0.011
State average aid as % school revenue	NA	−0.26	−0.60	NA	NA	NA	NA

SOURCES: (A) S. Sacks and Robert Harris, "The Determinants of State and Local Government Expenditures and Intergovernmental Flow of Funds." (B) J. Miner, *Social and Economic Factors in Spending For Public Education.*

in conjunction with other factors. Again, not only will the determinants of the observed behavior be considered in step-wise fashion, but their elasticities will be analyzed in a manner similar to that of the previous section. This will have the advantage of isolating what may be called the expenditure elasticity of aid, as well as what may be called the tax-proxy elasticity of aid, and the other variables. The specific hypotheses, following the pattern laid down earlier, are shown in Table 37.

TABLE 37

EXPECTED VALUES, PER-CAPITA TOTAL EDUCATIONAL EXPENDITURES

	Per-Capita Income	Enrollment Ratio	Per-Capita Educational State Aid	Budgetary (Noneducational)	Metropolitan
Model I	+				
Model II	+	+			
Model III*	+	+	0		
Model IV	0	0	0	−	+

* Basic Model.

The hypotheses for income should be divided into two parts: first, that it is positive; second, that the levels, as measured by their regression coefficients, should be higher in the suburbs than the central city. This should be true even after the introduction of the enrollment variable. In the case of per-capita expenditure, it is presumed that the greater the proportion of the total population attending schools, the higher the level of expenditures. The aid variable is converted into fiscal terms, *i.e.,* as per-capita aid for local public elementary and secondary schools. Insofar as the enrollment variable is included, it is presumed that the local community is indifferent as to whether it raises money locally or whether it receives revenues from the state or the federal government. Furthermore, it is presumed that when other claims are higher, the level of educational expenditures would be lower, *i.e.,* the relationship between the noneducational expenditures and those for education would be inverse. Finally, it is presumed that the metropolitan or labor market–demonstration effect for education would be positive and again would cloud the relationships of the other independent variables with per-capita educational expenditures.

The simple correlations are generally in accord with the hypotheses (See Table 38). In one case the result is slightly surprising; central city income is more clearly related to suburban expenditures than to its own

TABLE 38

SIMPLE CORRELATION MATRIXES, PER-CAPITA EXPENDITURES

(A) LARGE CITY, SCHOOL SYSTEM BASIS, 1962 (PER CAPITA)

Variable	ER[c]	SAC[c]	TNC[c]	TEC[o]	TEC[c]	NAE[c]	Mean	Standard Deviation	Coefficient of Variation
Per-capita income (PCI[c])	0.040	0.363*	0.382*	0.695†	0.548†	0.428	$2,068.00	$273.00	13.2%
Enrollment ratio (ER[c])		0.355*	-0.439†	-0.142	0.270	0.051	17.2%	3.2%	18.6%
State aid per capita (SAC[c])			0.023	0.232	0.425†	-0.145	$20.72	$9.22	44.5%
Noneducation per capita (TNC[c])				0.396*	0.318	0.357*	$155.79	$44.54	28.6%
Education per capita-outside (TEC[c])					0.535†	NA	$126.17	$31.45	24.9%
Education per capita (TEC[c])						NA	$68.69	$16.04	23.3%
Nonaided education per capita (NAE[c])							$47.23	$14.94	31.6%

(B) OUTSIDE LARGE CITY, SCHOOL SYSTEM BASIS, 1962 (PER CAPITA)

Variable	ER[o]	SAC[o]	TNC[o]	TEC[o]	TEC[c]	NAE[o]	Mean	Standard Deviation	Coefficient of Variation
Per-capita income (PCI[o])	-0.368	-0.011	0.574†	NA	0.425*	0.461†	$2,182.00	$337.00	15.4%
Enrollment ratio (ER[o])		0.356*	-0.094	NA	0.227	-0.190	22.6%	3.0%	13.3%
State aid per capita (SAC[o])			0.414*	NA	0.557†	-0.045	$37.61	$18.49	49.2%
Noneducation per capita (TNC[c])				NA	0.573*	0.453*	$126.91	$38.56	30.3%
Education per capita-city (TEC[c])						NA	$68.69	$16.04	23.3%
Education per capita (TEC[o])						NA	$126.17	$31.45	24.9%
Nonaided education per capita (NAE[o])							$89.59	$26.34	25.8%

* Significant of the 0.05 level of probability.   † Significant of the 0.01 level of probability.

expenditures. But the simple correlations are merely indicative of some more difficult problems. The introduction of the enrollment ratios as explicit variables clarifies the importance of the income variables where they are clearly important in their own right. Once this variable is introduced, the expenditure per dollar of income clearly appears higher in the suburbs than in the large cities. Both instances show each variable to be significant. As in the case of per-pupil expenditures, the introduction of aid does not help explain variations in large city expenditures on education. Furthermore, the introduction of aid reduces the importance of the enrollment variable, for the two interact in determining the total amount of aid. This can be seen more clearly in the suburban than in the large city case.

The picture, as it emerges from the "basic model" which includes aid, indicates that for every dollar of income a distinctly higher proportion of income is devoted to education in the suburbs than in the central city. Furthermore, an increase of 1 percent in the enrollment ratio is associated with a greater increase in per-capita expenditures in the suburbs than in the cities. And finally, aid is not only greater but, for every dollar of aid, the level is increased by a greater amount in the suburbs than in the cities.

The problem of aid has also been approached in terms of the proportion of total expenditures financed out of aid. This particular formulation of the problem was the creation of Edward F. Renshaw.[25] The general presumption in this analysis is that, unlike the amount of aid, the aid as a proportion is inversely related to the level of expenditures. The results for the cities are in accordance with expectations. The results are interesting because aid, as a proportion of total expenditures, is slightly more significant than the level of aid in the central city case, although there is no over-all superiority of the proportional model over the per-capita model.

III (A)

$$TEC[c] = 0.0325 \text{ PCI} + 1.7012 \text{ ER}[c]$$
$$(0.0077) \quad\quad (0.6713)$$

$$- 25.5994 \text{ SA%}[c] - 18.95 \quad\quad \bar{R} = 0.6166 \quad \bar{R}^2 = 0.3802$$
$$(15.6610)$$

$$TEC[c] = 0.0293 \text{ PCI}[c] + 1.161 \text{ ER} \quad\quad \bar{R} = 0.5917 \quad \bar{R}^2 = 0.3502$$
$$(0.0086) \quad\quad\quad (0.7300)$$

$$+ 0.2804 \text{ SAC} - 17.65$$
$$(0.2734)$$

[25] Edward F. Renshaw. "A Note on the Expenditure Effect of State Aid to Education," *Journal of Political Economy* (April 1960), 170–74.

The relationship between aid and expenditures which exists in the cities is not indicative of suburban behavior, although the patterns are consistent. Aid, as proportion of expenditures, adds little to an understanding of the variations in the behavior pattern of the suburbs, either individually or in conjunction with other variables. In the suburbs, the level of aid is far more important than is aid as a proportion of total revenue. The finding that the lower the proportionate share, the higher the level of per-capita educational expenditures, is not at all consistent with the current trend of thinking concerning increased state responsibilities and warrants further analysis.

III (A)

$$TEC[o] = \underset{(0.0146)}{0.0546} \ PCI[o] + \underset{(1.5943)}{4.6243} \ ER[o]$$

$$- \underset{(35.2491)}{31.662} \ SA\%_o - 96.49 \qquad \bar{R} = 0.5401 \quad \bar{R}^2 = 0.2918$$

III

$$TEC[o] = \underset{(0.0139)}{0.0479} \ PCI[o] + \underset{(1.440)}{2.604} \ ER[o]$$

$$+ \underset{(0.220)}{0.786} \ SAC[o] - 66.64 \qquad \bar{R} = 0.6994 \quad \bar{R}^2 = 0.4893$$

In looking at the relative importance of the variables in Model III, as measured by the standardized regression coefficients, it appears that the levels of income and enrollment operate with the same degree of importance in the central cities and their suburbs; the basic difference between the central city and suburbs in this model is the importance of aid (Table 39). And once again it is clear that the differences among large cities are not a function of aid as are the differences among the suburbs.

As in the case of per-pupil expenditures, the next step is to analyze the elasticities of the individual variables. The logarithmically transformed variables are used. Again, the elasticities are almost identical to those observed in the case of per-pupil expenditures, with the sign of the enrollment ratio variable changing to conform to its hypothesized relationship to per-capita expenditures. First, the income elasticity of per-capita total educational expenditures shows a value of almost exactly unity in both city and suburbs. These elasticities are considerably higher than those found by observers Hirsch and Miner on a school system basis,[26] but are consistent with the *a priori* assumptions of this and other

[26] Miner, *op. cit.*, in his national sample found elasticity at the mean of +0.23 for all income measures and +0.00 for local income.

TABLE 39

Regression Equations, Central City and Outside Central City Per-Capita Expenditures

	Income	Enrollment Ratio	State Aid Per Capita	Constant	$\bar{R}$	$\bar{R}^2$
Dependent Variable						
(A) Per-capita expenditures, central city	+0.0322† (0.0083)			12.16	0.5242	0.2800
	+0.0329† (0.0079)	1.4582* (0.6706)		−24.33	0.5909	0.3492
	+0.0293 (0.0086)	+1.1610 (0.7300)	+0.2804 (0.2734)	−17.65	0.5917	0.3502
Standardized regression coefficient	0.4993	0.2329	0.1611			
Elasticity (Log transformations)	+0.9913† (0.2458)	+0.3475* (0.1741)	+0.0555 (0.0654)		0.6190	0.3832
(B) Per-capita expenditures, outside central city	+0.0398† (0.0139)			+39.54	0.4250	0.1806
	+0.0549† (0.0139)	+4.5962† (1.5431)		−97.48	0.5589	0.3124
	+0.0479† (0.0121)	+2.6040 (1.4400)	+0.7867† (0.0203)	−66.64	0.6993	0.4893
Standardized regression coefficient	0.5124	0.2513	0.4617			
Elasticity (Log transformations)	+0.9895† (0.2230)	+0.5708* (0.2812)	+0.1548* (0.0668)		0.6579	0.4329

Note: Values in parentheses are standard errors.

* Significant at the 0.05 level of probability. † Significant at the 0.01 level of probability.

$\bar{R}$ = Coefficient of multiple correlation adjusted for degrees of freedom.

analyses. Both cities and suburbs show significant positive enrollment elasticities of total educational expenditures, but in neither case is the increase in expenditure proportionate (*i.e.,* of unitary elasticity) to the increase in enrollment ratios. The relative responsiveness of education expenditures to enrollment ratios is higher in the suburbs than in the large cities. Finally, the much mooted question of state aid also can be analyzed in terms of the elasticities. Surprisingly, in the first instance the results are almost identical with the findings in the case of per-pupil expenditures. In both cases, the state aid elasticities are positive but not very large. By specifically including the enrollment ratio, these results provide a purer measure of aid elasticity. Nevertheless, this tells us very little about the impact on local effort.

Before turning to the question of the determinants of local effort, two additional variables are considered in the analysis of per-capita total educational expenditures in Models IV and IV(A). The first is the effect of explicitly taking into account noneducational expenditures; the second, which is introduced only in the large cities case, is the effect of the suburban environment, as measured by its level of educational expenditures, on the central cities own level. Due to the existence of extensive multicollinearities, the only results to be reported are the significance of the added variables and the adjusted coefficients of multiple determination. The addition of noneducational expenditures added some explanatory power to the central city model, but not to the suburban model. In both instances the effects are positive and contrary to the expectations that higher noneducational expenditures are associated with lower educational expenditures. Finally, the introduction of a metropolitan interaction term was significant in the large city areas, but not to the extent that it was in the case of per-pupil expenditures.

NONAIDED EDUCATION EXPENDITURES

The last step of this analysis is devoted to nonaided education expenditures. This measures the expenditures financed out of local sources and thus comes closer to answering the specific questions on the relationship between aid and the level of taxation. The approach is direct and deals with the income and aid elasticity of locally raised revenue.

Using the same step-wise analysis, it is clear that once again, for every dollar of income, locally financed expenditures are higher in the suburbs than in the central cities. The enrollment ratio adds nothing to the understanding of the variations in nonaided expenditures in the cities, but it does aid in the understanding of the level in the suburbs. The introduction of aid adds to our understanding of city nonaided expenditures, but is independent of the level of nonaided educational expenditures in the outside areas. The magnitude of the negative effect of per-capita aid is unusually high in the large cities, and it is not possible to reject the hypothesis that state aid is replacive of local efforts, *i.e.,* that the elasticity of aid is equal to -1. This is not true of the suburban areas.

The elasticities provide the closest answer to the questions of the responsiveness of locally raised expenditures to aid and other variables. These are summarized below in the text because of their importance. Again, Model III is used. Here the specific hypothesis is that a 1-percent increase in state aid is associated with a 1-percent decrease in locally financed educational expenditures, *i.e.,* that aid replaces local effort.

Cities

$$1.8995 \text{ PCI[c]} + 0.4168 \text{ ER[c]} - 0.3307 \text{ SAC[c]} \qquad \bar{R} = 0.6534$$
$$(0.3905) \qquad\qquad (0.2767) \qquad\qquad (0.1039) \qquad\qquad \bar{R}^2 = 0.4038$$

Suburbs

$$1.2463 \text{ PCI[o]} + 0.5966 \text{ ER[o]} - 0.1777 \text{ SAC[o]} \qquad \bar{R} = 0.5009$$
$$(0.3563) \qquad\qquad (0.4494) \qquad\qquad (0.0982) \qquad\qquad \bar{R}^2 = 0.2510$$

As expected, the income elasticity of locally financed expenditures is considerably higher than in either of the prior analyses, although surprisingly it is not statistically in excess of unity in the case of the suburbs. Enrollment ratio elasticities are positive, but not significant. Most interesting are the results concerning the aid elasticities of locally financed expenditures; both are negative as expected, but they are considerably less than the -1 hypothesized by the replacive hypothesis. Aid clearly does not increase local taxes, but neither does it reduce taxes by the proportionate change in educational aid. The specific figures are that for every 1-percent increase in aid, locally financed expenditures are reduced by 0.3307 percent (standard error of 0.1039 percent) in the case of the cities, and only by 0.1777 percent (standard error of 0.0932 percent) in the suburbs. This means that expenditures increase as aid is increased, but not by as much. Incidentally, the simple aid elasticity of locally financed expenditures in the large cities is only -0.1600 and is not significantly different from zero. However, the introduction of income and enrollment increases the negative elasticity to -0.3307, which is significantly different from zero but in no sense completely replacive of local effort.

SUMMARY AND CONCLUSIONS

The purpose of the analysis was to analyze the factors influencing large city school financial behavior across state lines. By systematically analyzing the educational behavior of large cities in their metropolitan context, and by comparing large cities to their own suburban patterns, it appears that there are factors sufficiently powerful that must be considered in the construction of national policy. As in the earlier chapters, large city school finances were viewed in both educational and fiscal dimensions.

Several factors explain a considerable portion of the variation in per-pupil expenditures. Due to the greater importance of aid as a determinant, a larger proportion of the variation in per-pupil expenditures is explained in the suburbs than in the cities; in addition, the effect of a dollar of aid is greater in the suburbs than in the cities. The inclusion of a metropolitan interaction variable (not included in the summary table) improves our understanding of city behavior to a greater extent than it does in the case of the suburbs. It is assumed that the reason for this is the greater importance of current considerations which are operative in the case of the suburbs but are not as strongly operative in the case of the cities. It is presumed that cities, in turn, bear a much greater built-in burden of history, part of which is reflected in the character of their suburbs.

This analysis also indicates that per-pupil expenditures have an income elasticity considerably higher than those found in prior cross-sectional analyses. In both the cities and their suburbs the income elasticities are approximately unity, and the hypothesis that they are significantly different from that value would have to be rejected. Variations in per-pupil expenditures are significantly and negatively related to the proportion of the population attending public schools. In particular, the enrollment elasticity is significantly negative in the case of the cities, but the value is still less than the proportionate increase in enrollment, which would be -1. As the enrollment ratio increases, the response is a reduction of expenditures, but not in proportion to the increase in enrollment. Finally, it appears that if income and enrollment ratio elasticities are held constant, the aid elasticity of per-pupil expenditures, while positive, is not significant in the large cities; in the suburbs, aid is significant.

The findings concerning total educational expenditures are consistent in both the regression and elasticity models with those of the current per-pupil expenditures. The changes are nominal, even though the former measures total expenditures—including those for capital outlays—on a per-capita basis.

The major set of findings are derived from the regression of each of the variables on the nonaided portion of per-capita total educational expenditures. While the model is generally not as powerful as when total expenditures are analyzed, the results are of interest because they measure the effects of aid on locally raised revenues more accurately than had been the case with per-pupil expenditures. The income elasticity of non-aided expenditures is significantly in excess of unity in the cities, while this is not the case in the suburbs. Locally financed expenditures show a negative elasticity with respect to aid, but the elasticity is not even close to -1, as is postulated by the replacive hypothesis. Thus, while the general aim of state aid for education is to reduce local taxes, on the average, a 1-percent increase in aid only led to a 0.33-percent reduction in locally financed expenditures in cities, and the reduction in the suburbs was only -0.18 percent. Thus, state aid is presumed to lead to higher expenditures rather than to a displacement of local effort by state effort.

The major implications of the statistical analysis for national policy are, first, that the widening disparities in income are reflected in even larger disparities in per-pupil current expenditures. Second, increases in enrollment ratios have a negative effect on per-pupil expenditures, especially in the large cities. Third, on the basis of the model of locally financed expenditures, it appears that aid leads to only a minor reduction in locally financed city educational expenditures, measured by their elasticities. This clearly means that the aid is expenditure-additive but does reduce the local effort somewhat. Finally, a major factor in the suburban level of educational expenditures, and presumably in the difference between city and suburban areas, is the level of state aid.

VIII. A Concluding Statement

The failure to recognize the complex fiscal plight of large city school systems has resulted in an outmoded fiscal policy and inaccurate analysis. It can also be stated that the financial problems of large city school systems have not been the result of a generalized failure to raise or spend money, although in some instances this is an accurate description. The fact is that there is hardly a large city school system that does not spend considerably more per pupil today than it did a decade ago, both in current and "real" dollars. The financial problems emerge instead from the complex interrelationships and deteriorating position of the large cities relative to their own suburbs and states, and, from the standpoint of school finance, these changes in the position of large city school systems have not been recognized and incorporated into effective policy. In addition to the usual difficulties associated with changes in policy, the basic analytical perspective of school finances continues to be phrased in terms of rural and suburban problems to the detriment of the cities. Until the basic approach to school finances is broadened to include the problems of large cities on at least a coequal basis with rural and suburban areas, the solutions will continue to be partial and inadequate.

Large city educational problems are undoubtedly greater than those contained under the general rubric of school finances, but financial problems tend to magnify them and make them more difficult to solve. Further, there are a variety of forces which do not enter the educational process directly but which, because they have an effect on the ability to mobilize resources for education in large cities, must also be considered in a study of large city educational finances.

The purpose of this last chapter will be to place the statistical findings of Chapter VII in the broader historical and generalized analytical context developed earlier in this study, in order to determine the policy implications of a nationally focused analysis of large city school finances. In turn, this requires a recognition of the effects of state, metropolitan, and municipal behavior on school finances. Patterns of behavior derived from a bygone period when cities were relatively well-off compared to

167

their surrounding areas, but which no longer fit today's altered circumstances, remain important from the standpoint of current policy.

No set of findings concerning large city school finances today can be fully appreciated without a recognition of the long-term decline of large city school systems from a position of educational leadership and prestige—measured in financial and educational terms—to one in which they are clearly subordinate in both dimensions to their suburban schools. This is true even in the case of those large city school systems, such as New York City's, which have individually and in combination with their state governments poured enormous sums of money and resources into their public elementary and secondary educational systems.

The financial problems of large city school systems are largely a function of their declining relative economic health of large cities, since the basic economic pattern encompassing all large cities is one of declining central areas and reduced manufacturing and industrial bases. This is sometimes hidden where the effects of annexation and consolidation, which are pervasive outside of the Northeast and Midwest, are not explicitly taken into account. The only other exceptions are those few cities which have been relatively late in developing and have, at least temporarily, sufficient vacant land to contain suburban-type developments within their own borders. The contemporary position of the large American city contrasts sharply to its relative well-being in the past, and it is this context which today is of such importance to the large cities and their educational systems.

Although there was poverty in the large cities in the past, their financial resources could be contrasted favorably with the lesser means of the smaller villages and rural areas which surrounded them, and there was recognition of the cities' greater fiscal capacity, still further enhancing their advantageous position. Consequently, the various aid formulae in the first half of the twentieth century established a favored position for rural and suburban areas. During this period the cities were able to provide the most comprehensive range and greatest variety of public education available, with the exception of a very limited number of affluent suburban areas. These were able to provide an even more comprehensive range and variety of noneducational services at the same time without undue extra burden.

The virtual monopoly in the range and variety of public elementary and secondary education which large cities enjoyed was in part due to the inadequacy of the small school systems which, until very recently, were scattered throughout the rest of the nation. This was the result of a combination of the physical inability to assemble large enough groups of pupils and the related lack of fiscal resources sufficient to provide the scope of education provided in the large cities. Changes in state aid policy, designed to provide more financial aid to the hard-pressed rural areas, and the introduction of the school bus as the principal mode of student transportation and the automobile as the principal mode of teacher and staff transportation, fundamentally altered this balance. In addition, the remarkable suburban explosion, which received the benefits of enormous economic growth and a rurally oriented school finance policy, contributes to an understanding of the relative decline in the position of the large city educational systems.

The early history of American formal education, apart from the dissemination of literacy, is mainly the history of city school systems. However, even before the advent of the automobile and the consolidation of rural and suburban schools, the large city system began to be challenged by a number of suburban school systems such as Newton, Garden City, Shaker Heights, and Winnetka, which were the vanguard in the transition from city to suburban domination of public elementary and secondary education. But, with these exceptions, the expansion of school systems to include secondary as well as elementary education continued until World War II to give the large city school systems an advantage over their smaller counterparts. That large city school systems still had many problems which were not solved is also clear, but the cities retained a relative fiscal advantage over other educational systems of the nation, including most suburban systems, until the middle 1950s.

A series of events, which appeared to be independent at the time but which we now recognize to be very much cut out of the same cloth, greatly affected the relative position of the large city educational system. At the time of their development, however, these gave the illusion of an almost permanent fiscal superiority of the central cities and their school systems over those of other areas. The Great Depression had a very detrimental effect on large cities, but the data indicate that they were better able to weather the fiscal crises of the period than were the rural and smaller urban areas. Enormous fiscal and educational burdens were imposed on large cities during the 1930s, but they were solved by a series of temporary expedients. The large-scale "Americanizing" experience of large city school systems, which Cubberley noted so caustically, was drawing to an end. At the same time, there was a recognition of the rural problems. These were translated into state aid systems which gave impetus to a massive consolidation movement, wherein rural and suburban school districts were to take advantage of the improvements in transportation in order to provide educational systems which could finally match the comprehensive city systems. Initially, the changes were slow, but they were also inexorable.

World War II gave the cities a last respite. The fiscal position of the city school systems, which had been so severely strained during the decade of the thirties, was greatly relieved. This gave the illusion, but not the underlying reality, of strength. School enrollments fell sharply after 1940, and public assistance and debt charges, which played such havoc with city finances during the early 1930s, were also sharply reduced. Also, as a result of the Depression period, the cities were placed under more legal constraints than all other governmental units by a series of tax and debt limits.

Resumption of the arrested suburban boom of the late 1920s and the newer suburban boom caused by the returning World War II veterans and workers who sought better housing, were responsible for the tremendous growth during the late 1940s. The statistics showing the movement to suburbia from 1940 to 1950 understate the great changes which started in 1946 and have continued up to the present. The movement to suburbia was characterized by severe fiscal strains on the governments providing educational and noneducational services to these newer communities—strains which emerged even in some of the most potentially prosperous communities. When very rapid growth occurs in a short period of time, a variety of problems arise. Most of these new communities had to provide locally financed water and sewage disposal facilities and local highways, but almost universally they "felt" the necessity to provide an educational system consistent with their high personal income and aspirations. The fiscal position of the large cities appeared advantageous compared to these newer suburbs. In policy terms, this resulted in the conversion of the state aid system designed to aid hard-pressed rural communities into one which was designed to aid the hard-pressed suburban communities.

The consequences for city school finances, however, were notably different between this tooling up of suburban educational systems and those of prior periods. The new suburban systems were conceived to provide a level of excellence which had no previous counterpart in terms of the number of children involved. Elaborate new school plants were constructed and operated on a level consistent with the highest educational aspirations. With limited resources and massive numbers of pupils to be educated, the model of state intervention, which had been put into operation in rural areas, was applied to the suburban areas. From a static perspective, the problems seemed disarmingly similar. However, the consequences, insofar as the large city systems were concerned, were quite different.

In the late 1940s and early 1950s, the available fiscal resources for most suburban school systems were very limited in relation to the objectives that were to be achieved. Many suburban school systems were still small in size and incapable of providing a full range and variety of elementary and secondary education. In general, the similar state aid treatment of rural and suburban school systems was superficial, although the consequences for large city school system finances were major. Rural systems had been in a process of long-term decline in importance as their proportion of the population decreased. There was little direct competition between the wealthy urban and impoverished rural systems, despite the fact that the two contrasted sharply enough to warrant a redistribution of state funds toward the latter.

When suburban systems became sufficiently large, they competed, in contrast to the rural systems, directly with the large cities. The one-sided competition in favor of the large city school systems, which allowed them to hire the best teachers from the long Civil Service lists in the 1930s and support an immense educational edifice, changed completely by the middle 1950s. Suburban school systems in general, but not necessarily individual systems, emerged educationally equal to, or better than, their central city counterparts. While not equally true of every large city, the nature and intensity of the fiscal and educational problems which were to confront these communities remained obscured during the decade and a half from 1940 to 1956, although the underlying conditions changed fundamentally. The ease with which many of these cities were able to maintain their fiscal positions, and the fiscal difficulties encountered by many suburbs, introduced a basic dynamic to state policy and local attitudes which was difficult to reverse, even after cities were no longer capable of dealing with their local fiscal problems. Despite the fact that its position was now altered, the large city continued to be treated as if it still could solve its problems with relative ease.

The related changes in the ethnic composition of the central city population and declining economic fortunes of central cities were not generally reflected in state policy or improved local policy. The increased number of blacks in large cities, replacing ethnic groups which had made extensive use of parochial schools, led to a major increase in the number of students attending public elementary and secondary schools. As a result of housing patterns, minority groups attended either old schools or new schools at a considerable distance. The welfare burden, which had been moved to higher levels of government, reemerged as a major local financial problem during a period of economic growth. This exacerbated the cities' fiscal plight, particularly that of such large cities as New York and Boston which, at least during this period, had the direct responsibility for public assistance.

It is in this general context that the patterns of large city finances in the 1960s must be interpreted. The entrance of the federal government into the educational arena has not fundamentally altered the picture of large cities or suburbs during the period under analysis. It has had a major effect on the ancillary services provided by large city educational systems, but has had a minimal effect on the major area of this study—the provision of regular full-time elementary and secondary education.

The educational picture of large cities during the latter part of the 1950s and early 1960s indicated that something had gone awry, but comprehensive data were not available until the 1962 Census of Governments. The choice of 1957 as the year to resume full-scale Census of Governments seems especially fortuitous because it provided benchmark data at precisely the last period of fiscal equilibrium of the large cities and their suburbs. It also represented the end of the era in which large cities could be said to be economically dominant. The reasons involved both the relative decline of the large city and the absolute growth of the suburban communities.

One additional fiscal crisis was to plague the suburbs in this latest period, yet it also served to improve the relative standing of the suburban school systems. From 1957 to 1964, the physical facilities of the suburban school system were completed. Demographic considerations indicated that the postwar school population was to reach a peak in 1964–65, and new high schools were built to accommodate vastly increased enrollments in a relatively short period of time. This last link in the suburban elementary and secondary school systems was again completed with the help of state policy. Indeed, what has been called the "sputnik" crisis in American education may have been merely a contributory factor in the completion of a system more unambiguously dedicated to excellence than any prior set of systems. In turn, these suburban high schools were to emphasize the limitations of their counterparts in the large cities. The process did not take place all at once, but it was pervasive. Individual suburbs suffered in the same manner as did the large cities at the time. Again, the availability of a temporary solution was to be detrimental to large cities. The large city high schools, which had been built many years before, were still adequate in size. The extent to which the cities were able to escape this crisis gave credence to the state aid policy designed to help suburban and other types of "rapid growth" communities.

The "educational balance" between the large cities and their suburbs that existed in 1957 had vanished by 1962. A more careful and detailed analysis probably would have indicated that even in 1957, in terms of their instructional budgets alone, the suburbs had slightly surpassed their large city counterparts, although the picture still showed considerable variation. In total local fiscal terms, the suburbs were able to focus a much greater proportion of their total fiscal resources on education than were their large city counterparts. When greater state aid was added to the local effort, this meant a much larger per-capita expenditure on education than was possible in large cities.

The simultaneous increase in large city enrollments which accompanied the movement of large numbers of blacks into the large cities was not accompanied by the kind of educational concern which was characteristic of many suburbs; nor was state aid policy sufficiently sensitive to the changing nature of the problems facing the cities. The isolation of educational finances from noneducational finances—an isolation which existed in theoretical treatises on school finances as well as in operational form—undermined the position of the large cities even after they no longer represented the concentration of economic power characteristic of their earlier position. Neither the high tax rates of the suburban school systems nor the low tax rates of the city school systems represented the total rates in the absence of the municipal and other noneducational tax rates. The totals showed that large cities specialized in noneducational functions, whereas the suburbs specialized in education.

The effects of noneducational finances on educational finances are complex, as they are derived from very different formal relationships which exist among and within states. The problem is not only a "municipal" one but a total noneducational one, involving an enormous variety of local governmental subsystems providing services and raising revenues. These systems contain counties, special districts, and townships, as well as municipalities modified by very different state arrangements. The complexity of arrangements does not hide the basic fact of much higher total noneducational responsibility of the large cities, even after the municipal governments had begun to share financing and service responsibilities with other local governments, with their states, and with the federal government.

The pattern of large city school finances analyzed in Chapter VII assumes meaning in terms of these foregoing factors, some of which are explicitly included in the analysis but all of which are implicitly included in the interpretation of the results. The analysis covered both the large cities and the suburban areas surrounding them. It explicitly took into account the differential flows of educational aid from the respective states. Further, the noneducational demands on the public sector were also explicitly included. Similarly, the relative portions of the total population attending public elementary and secondary schools are also included explicitly in the analysis. As in most prior analyses, income is included as a specific variable. As noted earlier, two important variables

were excluded from the analysis. The first is the segment of the population that is commonly considered educationally disadvantaged, apart
from income considerations—the Spanish-speaking and nonwhite communities; a preliminary analysis indicates that the effect of region con-
founds the meaning that might be attached to that variable. Second, from
an analytical point of view, the exclusion of the property tax base represents a major deficiency. However, as of this time, it is impossible to get
meaningful property tax base data which cross state lines, although they
are the single most important determinants of fiscal behavior within
states. Certain aspects of the property tax were considered and they
appeared to be of great importance; but since the principal purpose of
the analysis was to indicate the differential effect of a limited number of
determinants on a national sample of large city school finances as compared to their suburbs, the major analysis of Chapter VII was restricted
to income, the enrollment ratio, state aid, noneducational expenditures,
and the interaction between the large cities and their own suburban districts.

On the educational side, school systems in large cities show lower
current expenditures per pupil than do the suburban school districts
surrounding them. This was true even though there was a bias based on
expenditures, which is uniquely imposed on the large cities but not on
suburbs or other school systems within several of the states.

The models used in this analysis were explicitly designed to bring out
the various trade-offs and interactions among the major determinants of
large city school finances from a national and metropolitan point of view.
The results, while not as powerful as various analyses using state units,
are much more operationally meaningful as far as the large cities are
concerned. The major models developed to explain variations in per-
pupil expenditures (the educational dimension of school finances), explain a larger proportion of the variation in per-pupil expenditures outside the large cities than they do in the central cities. The exclusion of
property tax variables is a good reason for presuming that the over-all
explanatory model would be limited in its total power for both cities and
schools.

The major determinants of large city school expenditures are per-
capita income and the offsetting effect of the enrollment ratio. State aid
per pupil is of relatively little importance in explaining variations in per-
pupil expenditures if both income and enrollment ratios are known. In
contrast, state aid is more important and the enrollment ratio is less
important in the case of the suburbs. Income is slightly more important
in the case of the suburbs than in the case of the cities. The relationship
between income and expenditures indicates that for any given level of

income the per-pupil expenditure in the suburbs would be larger than in the city and, since the average income level is higher in the suburbs, this increases expenditures. Similarly, the effect of a dollar of state aid is higher in the suburbs than in the large cities. And once again, because the levels are higher, the effects on per-pupil expenditures are greater. The last factor, the enrollment ratio, operates more powerfully in the large cities than in the suburbs. However, from a dynamic point of view the situation was not very encouraging because it was precisely during this period that most large cities began to have major increases in their enrollment ratios due to the changing racial mix. This probably explains some of the increased pressures on central city per-pupil expenditures in recent years.

Some of the findings of the analysis are important because they place some of the variables on a much more rational basis than was evidenced in some earlier analyses. Thus, it appears that the income elasticity of per-pupil expenditures is not significantly less than unity—a figure which is much higher than those given in many earlier analyses, but much more in accord with *a priori* considerations.

Finally, as noted at the very outset of this study, the fiscal dimensions of school finances are not a direct reflection of the educational dimension. The relationships are identical in terms of total per-capita educational expenditures if the enrollment ratios are similar, and the relationships are identical in terms of locally financed expenditures if state and other aids are equal. And since the major differences among cities involve enrollment ratios and state aid, the fiscal and educational dimensions of large city school finances show rather different patterns. On the fiscal side, it is also very important to take into account the effects of noneducational expenditures on educational expenditures.

The problem of analyzing the fiscal dimensions of local school finances, especially when the noneducational side is included, is much more complicated than the analysis of the educational dimension. This, in fact, has been a major reason for the limited literature in this area. The complexity emerges from the noncoterminality of school systems, for which population and other socioeconomic data are not available, with other levels of governments and from the great variety in the assignment of the revenue and expenditure responsibilities for local governmental areas.

The results of the fiscal analysis of large city school finances are less satisfying from a statistical point of view than the comparable analysis of the educational dimension. The indication is that, on a national basis, the factors used to explain per-capita total educational expenditures are consistent with the model of per-pupil expenditures with a reversal in the sign for enrollment, *i.e.,* the higher the enrollment, the higher the per-capita expenditure. However, unlike the per-pupil analysis, the effect of any given change in enrollment ratios is greater in the suburbs than in the central city. The analysis of locally financed educational expenditures is quite unsatisfying from a national perspective. Once again it is presumed that the absence of meaningful property tax data is the principal reason for this deficiency.

The introduction of noneducational expenditures as an independent variable adds slightly more to our understanding of the variations in large city educational expenditures than it does in the case of the suburbs. Surprisingly, however, the effects are positive rather than negative, as one would presume from a model based on trade-offs between educational and noneducational expenditures. It appears that when the level of the one type of expenditure is high, the level of the other is also high.

Large city school finances deserve much more careful study from a state and national perspective than they have previously been accorded. This would be true apart from the very pressing educational and fiscal problems now confronting the vast majority of large cities. New analytical breakthroughs are necessary if we are to deal with the complex set of intergovernmental relationships which now characterize school finances. Further, it is necessary to know the state and metropolitan factors which influence large city school finances. What has been called the labor market–demonstration effect must clearly be taken into account in future analyses.

The objectives of this study have been twofold. First, the analysis has been designed to document and explain the disparities which exist between large city and suburban school finances on a national level. This involves an understanding of the contemporary socioeconomic position of large cities *and* their past standing. The analysis has been specifically designed to view large city school finances from a national perspective, taking account of the underlying state, metropolitan, and noneducational considerations which jointly determine their behavior. Second, the variables and the analysis have been aimed toward making large city school finance policy relevant from a national perspective. The factors which cannot be meaningfully documented on a national basis, such as the property tax base, or which are not readily translatable into policy terms, have not been considered. The "explanatory" power of the model has been reduced, but its usefulness has been enhanced accordingly.

The analysis indicates that city school finances have not been integrated into the domain of educational finance. In the past this was due to the economic superiority of large cities and the preoccupation with first rural and then suburban school finances. In spite of an interest generated by their educational institutions and relative economic decline, there has been little organized improvement in our understanding of large city school finances. The ultimate objective of this study is to subject the financial problems of large city school systems to the level of analysis that characterizes rural and suburban areas. In turn, this will permit the analysis of school finances to complement those changes in educational technology, which it is hoped will be sufficient to attain the almost incredibly ambitious set of goals which have been imposed on large city and other school systems.

The current inferior financial position of large city school systems is a reflection of their past superiority. The policies which were designed to help the smaller rural systems, having been applied to the growing suburban systems, have operated to the detriment of the large cities. It is essential to find a method by which the historically determined degenerative cycle of public school finance can be broken. This probably cannot be attained by reducing the resources flowing into the suburban and rural school systems, for their need and political power are very great.

Improving the condition of large city school systems can best be attained by a pinpointed federal program that will deal with financial needs of the large cities and other areas containing the concentrations of poverty which are so costly to local governments, both in the educational and noneducational spheres. The financial requirements of suburban and rural school systems can be most adequately dealt with by the system of state and local finance which has been able to provide such large sums of money since the end of World War II. Large cities, on the other hand, present problems which are very different and probably can be dealt with only on a national scale with a national resource base.

Bibliography

BOOKS AND MONOGRAPHS

Adams, Robert F. "Determinants of Local Government Expenditures." Unpublished doctoral dissertation, University of Michigan, 1963.

Bahl, Roy W. *Metropolitan City Expenditures: A Comparative Analysis* (Lexington: University of Kentucky Press, 1969).

Bailey, Stephen K., *et al. Schoolmen and Politics: A Study of State Aid in the Northeast* (Syracuse: Syracuse University Press, 1962).

Banfield, Edward C. *Big City Politics* (New York: Random House, 1965).

————. *Urban Government: A Reader in Administration and Politics* (New York: The Free Press, 1963).

Benson, Charles S. *The Cheerful Prospect* (Boston: Houghton Mifflin, 1965).

————. *The Economics of Public Education* (Boston: Houghton Mifflin, 1961).

————. *Perspectives on the Economics of Education* (Boston: Houghton Mifflin Company, 1963).

Birkhead, Guthrie S., ed. *Metropolitan Issues: Social, Governmental, Fiscal.* Background Papers for the Third Annual Faculty Seminar on Metropolitan Research, August, 1961 (Syracuse University, 1962).

Blalock, Hubert M. *Causal Interences in Nonexperimental Research* (Chapel Hill: University of North Carolina Press, 1964).

Bloomberg, Warner, and Morris Sunshine. *Suburban Power Structures and Public Education: A Study of Values, Influence and Tax Effort* (Syracuse: Syracuse University Press, 1963).

Bollens, John C. *The State and the Metropolitan Problem* (Chicago: Public Administration Service, 1956).

Bollens, John C., ed. *Exploring the Metropolitan Community* (Berkeley: University of California Press, 1961).

Bollens, John C., with G. Ross Stephens *et al. Metropolitan Challenge* (Dayton, Ohio: Metropolitan Community Studies, November 1959).

Bollens, John C., and Henry J. Schmandt. *The Metropolis: Its People, Politics and Economic Life* (New York: Harper & Row, 1965).

Bowles, B. Dean. "Educational Pressure Groups and the Legislature Process in California." Unpublished doctoral dissertation, Claremont, Claremont Graduate School, 1967.

Brazer, Harvey E. *City Expenditures in the United States.* Occasional Paper No. 66 (New York: National Bureau of Economic Research, 1959).

179

Buchanan, James M., and Gordon Tullock. *The Calculus of Consent* (Ann Arbor: The University of Michigan Press, 1962).

Burkhead, Jesse V. *Public School Finance: Economics and Politics* (Syracuse: Syracuse University Press, 1964).

————. *State and Local Taxes for Public Education* (Syracuse: Syracuse University Press, 1963).

Burkhead, Jesse V., Thomas G. Fox, and John W. Holland. *Input and Output in Large City High Schools* (Syracuse: Syracuse University Press, 1967).

Callahan, Raymond E. *Education and the Cult of Efficiency* (Chicago: University of Chicago Press, 1962).

Campbell, Alan K., and Seymour Sacks. *Metropolitan America: Fiscal Patterns and Governmental Systems* (New York: The Free Press, 1967).

Chinitz, Benjamin. *City and Suburb* (Englewood Cliffs, N.J.: Prentice Hall, 1964).

Cohen, Leo. *Comparative Fiscal Capacity and Tax Effort and Units of Government in Madison and St. Clair Counties, Illinois, 1950–1960* (Carbondale, Ill.: Public Administration and Metropolitan Affairs Program, Southern Illinois University, 1963).

Coleman, James L. *Equality of Educational Opportunity* (Washington, D.C.: Government Printing Office, 1966).

Conant, James B. *The American High School Today* (New York: McGraw-Hill, 1959).

————. *Shaping Educational Policy* (New York: McGraw-Hill, 1964).

————. *Slums and Suburbs* (New York: Signet Books, 1964).

Cremin, Lawrence A. *The Transformation of the School: Progressivism in Democratic Education 1876–1957* (New York: Alfred A. Knopf, 1962).

Cubberley, Ellwood P. *Public Education in the United States,* rev. ed. (Boston: Houghton Mifflin, 1934).

————. *School Finances and Their Apportionment* (New York: Teachers College, Columbia University, 1905).

Dobriner, William M. *Class in Suburbia* (Englewood Cliffs.: Prentice-Hall, 1963).

————. *The Suburban Community* (New York: G.P. Putnam's Sons, 1958).

Downs, Anthony. *An Economic Theory of Democracy* (New York: Harper & Row, 1957).

Drucker, Peter F. *The Age of Discontinuity* (New York: Harper & Row, 1969).

Duesenberry, James S. *Income, Saving, and the Theory of Consumer Behavior* (Cambridge, Mass.: Harvard University Press, 1949).

Dye, Thomas R. *Politics, Economics, and the Public Policy Outcomes in the American States* (Chicago: Rand McNally, 1966).

Easton, David. *A Framework for Political Analysis* (Englewood Cliffs, N.J.: Prentice-Hall, 1965).

————. *The Political System* (New York: Alfred A. Knopf, 1953).

————. *A Systems Analysis of Political Life* (New York: John Wiley & Sons, 1965).

Elliot, Edward C. *Some Fiscal Aspects of Public Education* (New York: Teachers College, Columbia University, 1905).

Ezekiel, Mordecai, and Karl A. Fox. *Methods of Correlation and Regression Analysis* (New York: John Wiley & Sons, 1959).

Fabricant, Solomon. *The Trend of Government Activity in the United States Since 1900* (New York: National Bureau of Economic Research, 1952).

Fairbanks, Robert. "Property Tax Behavior in New York State, 1949–1961." Unpublished doctoral dissertation, Syracuse University, 1963.

Fels Institute of State and Local Government. *Special Education and Fiscal Requirements of Urban School Districts in Pennsylvania, A Research Inquiry: The Impact of Social and Economic Conditions on Urban Education and State Fiscal Policy* (Philadelphia: University of Pennsylvania, 1964).

Ferber, Robert. *Statistical Techniques in Market Research* (New York: McGraw-Hill, 1949).

Ferber, Robert, and P.J. Verdoorn. *Research Methods in Economics and Business* (New York: The Macmillan Company, 1962).

Frasier, G.W. *The Control of City School Finances* (Milwaukee: The Bruce Publication Co., 1922).

Freeman, Roger A. *School Needs in the Decade Ahead* (Washington: The Institute for Social Science Research, 1958).

Furno, Orlando F. "The Projection of School Quality from Expenditure Levels. Unpublished doctoral dissertation, Teachers College, Columbia University, 1956.

Galbraith, John Kenneth. *The Affluent Society* (New York: Mentor Books, 1953).

Gans, Herbert J. *The Urban Villagers* (New York: The Free Press, 1962).

Gibbs, Jack P. *Urban Research Methods* (Princeton: D. Van Nostrand Co., 1961).

Gittell, Marilyn. *Participants and Participation: A Study of School Policy in New York City* (New York: Center for Urban Education, 1967).

————, and T. Edward Hollander. *Six Urban Districts* (New York: Frederick A. Praeger, 1968).

————, and Alan G. Hevesi, eds. *The Politics of Urban Education* (New York: Frederick A. Praeger, 1969).

Glazer, Nathan, and Daniel P. Moynihan. *Beyond the Melting Pot* (Cambridge, Mass.: Massachusetts Institute of Technology Press, 1963).

Goldberger, Arthur S. *Econometric Theory* (New York: John Wiley & Sons, 1964).

Gosnell, C., and L. Holland. *State and Local Government in the United States* (Englewood Cliffs, N.J.: Prentice-Hall, 1951).

Government Affairs Foundation, Inc. *Metropolitan Communities: A Bibliography* (Chicago: Public Administration Service, 1956).

————. *Metropolitan Communities: A Bibliography,* Supplement 1955–57 (Chicago: Public Administration Service, 1960).

Greer, Scott. *The Emerging City, Myth and Reality* (New York: The Free Press, 1962).

————. *Governing the Metropolis* (New York: John Wiley & Sons, 1962).

Gulick, Luther H. *The Metropolitan Problem and American Ideas.* The Cook Foundation Lectures (New York: Alfred A. Knopf, 1962).

Haig, Robert M., and Roswell C. McCrae. *Regional Survey of New York and its Environs.* Vol. I. *Major Economic Factors in Metropolitan Growth and Arrangement: A Study of Trends and Tendencies in the Economic Activities Within the Region of New York and its Environs* (New York: Regional Plan Association, 1927).

Hansen, Alvin H., and Harvey S. Perloff. *State and Local Finance in the National Economy* (New York: W.W. Norton & Co., 1944).

Harris, Seymour E. *More Resources for Education* (New York: Harper & Row, 1960).

Harrison, Forrest W., and Eugene P. McLoone. *Profiles in School Support* (Washington, D.C.: U.S. Department of Health, Education, and Welfare, Office of Education, 1965).

Hatt, Paul K., and Albert J. Reiss, Jr., eds. *Cities and Society* (New York: The Free Press, 1959).

Havighurst, Robert. *Education in Metropolitan Areas* (Boston: Allyn & Bacon, 1966).

Henry, Nelson B., and Jerome G. Kerwin. *Schools and City Government. A Study of School and Municipal Relationships in Cities of 50,000 or More Population* (Chicago: University of Chicago Press, 1938).

Hickrod, G. Alan, and Cesar M. Subulao. *Increasing Social and Economic Inequality Among Suburban Schools* (Downville: The Interstate Printers and Publishers, Inc., 1969).

Hirsch, Werner Z. *Paths of Progress for St. Louis* (St. Louis: Metropolitan St. Louis Survey, 1957.

Hoover, Edgar M. *Region in Transition* (Pittsburgh: University of Pittsburgh Press, 1964).

Hoover, Edgar M., and Raymond Vernon. *The Anatomy of a Metropolis* (Garden City, N.Y.: Doubleday Book Co., 1962).

Iannacone, Laurence. *Politics in Education* (New York: Center for Research in Education, 1967).

International City Managers' Association. *The Municipal Year Book* (Chicago).

James, H. Thomas. *School Revenue Systems in Five States* (Stanford: Stanford University Press, 1961).

James, H. Thomas, J. Allen Thomas, and Harold J. Dyck. *Wealth, Expenditures and Decision-Making* (Palo Alto: Stanford University Press, 1964).

James, H. Thomas, James A. Kelly, and Walter I. Garms. *Determinants of Educational Expenditures in Large Cities in the United States* (Palo Alto: Stanford University, 1966).

Johns, R.L., and E.L. Morphet. *Problems and Issues in Public School Finances* (New York: Teachers College, Columbia University, 1952).

Johnson, Byron I. *The Principle of Equalization Applied to the Allocation of Grants-in-Aid*. Federal Security Agency, Social Security Administration (Washington: Government Printing Office, September, 1947).

Kaufman, Herbert. *Politics and Policies in State and Local Governments* (Englewood Cliffs, N.J.: Prentice-Hall, Inc., 1963).

Kee, Woo Sik. "City Expenditures in Metropolitan Areas An Analysis of Intergovernmental Relations." Unpublished doctoral dissertation, Syracuse University, 1964.

King, Gary W. *Conflict Over Schools: A Sociological Analysis of a School Bond Election* (East Lansing, Michigan: Institute for Community Development and Services, 1963).

Krug, Edward. *The Shaping of the American High Schools* (Madison: University of Wisconsin Press, 1969).

Lindman, Erick L. *State Support and Municipal Government Costs* (Los Angeles: University of California, Los Angeles, 1964).

Securing Greater Economy in Local Government (Chicago: Commerce Clearing House, 1933).

Maas, Arthur M. *Area and Power: A Theory of Local Government* (New York: The Free Press, 1959).

McClure, William P. *The Structure of Educational Costs in the Great Cities* (Chicago: Research Council of the Great Cities Program for School Improvement, August 7, 1964).

McGaughy, R.J. *The Fiscal Administration of City School Systems* (New York: The Macmillan Company, 1924).

McLaughlin, Frederick C. "Fiscal Administrative Control of City School Systems," in *Fiscal Policy for Public Education in the State of New York* (Albany, 1947).

McLoone, Eugene P. *Effects of Tax Elasticity on the Financial Support of Education*. Unpublished doctoral dissertation, Urbana, University of Illinois, 1961.

Mace, Ruth L. *Municipal Cost-Revenue Research in the United States* (Chapel Hill: Institute of Government, University of North Carolina, 1961).

Martin, Roscoe C. *Government and the Suburban School*. The Economics and Politics of Public Education Series, No. 2 (Syracuse: Syracuse University Press, 1963).

―――. *Metropolis in Transition: Local Government Adaptation to Changing Needs* (Washington: Housing and Home Finance Agency, 1963).

Martin, Roscoe C., and H. Douglas Price. *The Metropolis and Its Problems* (Syracuse: Syracuse University, 1959).

Masters, Nicholas A., *et al. State Politics and the Public Schools, An Exploratory Analysis* (New York: Alfred A. Knopf, 1964).

May, Samuel C., and Majes M. Fales, Jr., *The State's Interest in the Metropolitan Problem* (Berkeley: University of California Press, 1955).

Mills, Frederic C. *Statistical Methods* (New York: Holt, Rinehart & Winston, 1955).

Miner, Jerry. *Social and Economic Factors in Spending for Public Education.* The Economics and Politics of Public Education Series (Syracuse: Syracuse University Press, 1963).

Mort, Paul R. *A New Approach to School Finance: 1961 Review of Fiscal Policy for Public Education in New York State, Staff Studies* (Albany: New York State Educational Conference Board, 1961).

Mort, Paul R., Walter C. Reusser, and John W. Polley. *Public School Finance,* 3d ed. (New York: McGraw-Hill, 1960).

Mumford, Lewis. *The City in History* (New York: Harcourt, Brace and World, 1961).

Munse, Albert R., and Eugene P. McLoone. *Public School Finance Programs of the United States, 1957–58* (Washington, D.C.: Government Printing Office, 1960).

Musgrave, Richard A. *The Theory of Public Finance: A Study in Public Economy* (New York: McGraw-Hill, 1959).

Mushkin, Selma J., and Eugene P. McLoone. *Local School Expenditures: 1970 Projections* (Chicago: Council of State Government, 1965).

Netzer, Dick. *Economics of the Property Tax* (Washington, D.C.: The Brookings Institution, 1966).

Phares, Donald. "The Structure of State-Local Tax Burdens, 1962." Unpublished doctoral dissertation, Syracuse University, 1970.

Perloff, Harvey and Lowdon Wingo, Jr., eds. *Issues in Urban Economics* (Baltimore: Johns Hopkins Press, 1968).

Ranney, David C. "School Governments and the Determinants of Fiscal Support for Large City Educational Systems." Unpublished doctoral dissertation, Syracuse University, 1966.

Reeves, Charles E. *School Boards: Their Status, Functions and Activities* (Englewood Cliffs, N.J.: Prentice-Hall, 1954).

Rice, Joseph M. *The Public School System of the United States* (New York: The Century Company, 1893).

Rosenthal, Alan. *Pedagogues and Power* (Syracuse: Syracuse University Press, 1969).

———. *Governing Education* (Garden City, N.Y.: Anchor Books, 1969).

Sacks, Seymour. *Municipal Taxation and Regional Development* (East Hartford, Conn.: Capital Regional Planning Agency, March 1963).

Sacks, Seymour, Robert Harris, and John J. Carroll. *The State and Local Government . . . The Role of State Aid, Comptroller's Studies in Local Finance, No. 3* (Albany: New York State Department of Audit and Control, 1963).

Sacks, Seymour, and William F. Hellmuth, Jr. *Financing Government in a Metropolitan Area* (New York: The Free Press, 1961).

Sayre, Wallace S., and Herbert Kaufman. *Governing New York City: Politics in the Metropolis* (New York: W.W. Norton, Inc., 1965).

Schaller, Howard G., ed. *Public Expenditure Decisions in the Urban Community* (Washington, D.C.: Resources for the Future, Inc., 1963).

Schreiber, Daniel. *Holding Power: Large City School Systems, Project: School Dropouts* (Washington, D.C.: National Education Association, 1964).

Schwebel, Milton. *Who Can Be Educated?* (New York: Grove Press, 1968).

Scott, Stanley, and Edward L. Feder. *Factors Associated with Variations in Municipal Expenditure Levels.* Berkeley: Bureau of Public Administration, University of California, February, 1957.

Seeley, J.R., R.A. Sems, and E.W. Loosley. *Crestwood Heights* (New York: John Wiley & Sons, 1956).

Sexton, Patricia. *Education and Income: Inequalities in Our Public Schools* (New York: Viking Press, 1961).

Sharkensky, Ira. *Spending in the American States* (Chicago: Rand McNally, 1968).

Simon, Herbert A. *Fiscal Aspects of Metropolitan Consolidation.* (Berkeley: Bureau of Public Administration, University of California, 1943).

Strayer, George D. *City School Expenditures* (New York: Teachers College, Columbia University, 1905).

Strayer, George D., and Robert M. Haig. *The Financing of Education in the State of New York.* Vol. I (New York: The Macmillan Company, 1923).

Studenski, Paul, *et al. The Government of Metropolitan Areas in the United States* (New York: National Municipal League, Committee on Metropolitan Government, 1930).

Swanson, Bert E. *Current Trends in Comparative Community Studies* (Kansas City: Community Studies, Inc., 1962).

Sweeney, John B., and George S. Blair. *Metropolitan Analysis* (Philadelphia: University of Pennsylvania Press, 1958).

Tax Institute, Inc. *Financing Metropolitan Government* (Princeton: The Institute, 1955).

Temporary Commission on City Finances, City of New York. *Toward Fiscal Strength: Overcoming New York City's Financial Dilemma* (New York: Temporary Commission, November 1965).

Thompson, Wilbur R. *A Preface to Urban Economics: Toward a Conceptual Framework for Study and Research* (Washington, D.C.: Resources for the Future, Inc., 1963).

Tompkins, Clarence R. *Nature of the Burgeoning Municipal Government* (Albany: New York State Educational Conference Board, 1961).

Turvey, Ralph. *The Economics of Real Property* (London: George Allen & Unwin, Ltd., 1957).

Vernon, Raymond. *The Changing Economic Function of the Central City* (New York: Committee for Economic Development, 1959).

U.S. Bureau of the Census. *1970 Census of Population and Housing: General Demographic Trends for Metropolitan Areas, 1960 to 1970* (Washington, D.C., 1971).

———. *Metropolis 1985* (Garden City, N.Y.: Doubleday Book Co., 1962).

———. *Myth and Reality of our Urban Problems*. Stratford Little Lectures (Princeton: Princeton University, Spring, 1961).

Vieg, John A. *The Government of Education in Metropolitan Chicago* (Chicago, 1938).

Walker, Mabel L. *Municipal Expenditures* (Baltimore: Johns Hopkins Press, 1930).

Weber, Adna F. *The Growth of Cities in the Nineteenth Century* (New York: Columbia University Studies in History, Economics, and Public Law, XI, 1899).

Welch, Richard D. "Further Explorations in State Personnel Income and State Education Expenditures." Unpublished master's thesis, Syracuse University, 1968.

Wildavsky, Aaron. *The Politics of Budgetary Process* (Boston: Little, Brown and Company, 1964).

Willbern, York. *The Withering Away of the City* (Tuscaloosa: University of Alabama Press, 1964).

Williams, Oliver P., and Adrian R. Charles. *Four Cities: A Study in Comparative Policy Making* (Philadelphia: University of Pennsylvania Press, 1963).

Williams, Oliver P., et al. *Suburban Differences and Metropolitan Policies* (Philadelphia: University of Pennsylvania Press, 1965).

Wood, Robert C. *1400 Governments* (Cambridge, Mass.: Harvard University Press, 1961).

———. *Metropolis Against Itself* (New York: Committee for Economic Development, 1959).

Woodward, Henry B. "The Effect of Fiscal Control on Current School Expenditures." Doctoral dissertation, Teachers College, Columbia University, 1958.

Wright, Deil S. *Trends and Variations in Local Finance: The Case of Iowa* (Iowa City: Institute of Public Affairs, University of Iowa, 1965).

Wynn, D. Richard. *Organization of Public Schools* (Washington, D.C.: The Center for Applied Research in Education, Inc., 1964).

Yakel, Ralph. *The Legal Control of the Administration of Public School Expenditures* (New York: Teachers College, Columbia University, 1929).

Yamane, Tara. *Statistics: An Introductory Analysis, 2d ed.* (New York: Harper & Row, 1967).

Yong, Hyo Cho. "State-Local Governmental Systems: Their Determinants and Fiscal Implications." Unpublished doctoral dissertation, Syracuse University, 1965.

ARTICLES AND PERIODICALS

American Academy of Political and Social Science. "Metropolis in Ferment," *Annals* (November 1957).

Aronovici, Carol. "Education and Community Planning," *Journal of the American Institute of Planners*, XXI (Fall 1955), 133–37.

Bahl, Roy W., and Robert J. Saunders, "Determinants of Changes in State and Local Government Expenditures," *National Tax Journal*, XVIII (March 1965), 50–57.

Baumol, William J. "Urban Services: Interactions of Public and Private Decisions," *Public Expenditure Decisions in the Urban Community*, ed. Howard G. Schaller (Washington, D.C.: Resources for the Future, Inc., 1962).

Beck, Morris. "Determinants of the Property Tax Level: A Case Study of Northeastern New Jersey," *National Tax Journal*, XVIII (March 1965), 74–77.

Berolzheimer, Joseph. "Influences Shaping Expenditures for Operation of State and Local Governments," *Bulletin of the National Tax Association*, XXXII (March 1947).

Bishop, G.A., "Stimulative versus Substitutive Effects of State School Aid in New England," *National Tax Journal*, XVII (June 1964), 133–43.

Bollens, John C. "Metropolitan and Fringe Area Developments in 1961," *The Municipal Yearbook, 1962* (Chicago: International City Managers' Association, 1962).

Bowles, Dean P. "The Power Structure in State Educational Politics," *Phi Delta Kappan* XLIX (February 1968), 337–40.

Brazer, Harvey E. "The Role of Major Metropolitan Centers in State and Local Finance," *American Economic Review*, XLVII (No. 2), 305–16.

———. "Some Fiscal Implications of Metropolitanism," *Metropolitan Issues: Social, Governmental, Fiscal*, ed. Guthrie S. Birkhead. Background Papers for the Third Annual Faculty Seminar on Metropolitan Research, August 1961.

Burkhead, Jesse. "Metropolitan Area Budget Structures and Their Significance for Expenditures," *Proceedings of the National Tax Association, 1959*. Harrisburg, 1960.

———. "Uniformity in Governmental Expenditures and Resources in a Metropolitan Area: Cuyahoga County," *National Tax Journal*, XIV (December 1961), 337–48.

Callahan, John J. and Donna E. Shalala. "Some Fiscal Dimensions of Three Hypothetical Decentralization Plans," Education and Urban Society, II (November 1969), 40–53.

Campbell, Alan K. "The Most Dynamic Sector," *National Civic Review*, LIII (February 1964).

———. "National-State-Local Systems of Government and Intergovernmental Aid," *Annals of the American Academy of Political and Social Science*, CCCLIX (May 1965).

————. "Taxes and Industrial Location in the New York Metropolitan Region," *National Tax Journal*, XI (September 1958).

Campbell, Alan K., and Philip J. Meranto. "The Metropolitan Education Dilemma: Matching Resources to Needs," *Urban Affairs Quarterly*, I (September 1966).

Campbell, Alan K., and Seymour Sacks. "Administering the Spread City," *Public Administration Review*, XXIV (September 1964).

Campbell, Roald. "Process of Policy-Making Within Structures of Educational Government: As Viewed by an Educator," *Government of Public Education for Adequate Policy Making*, ed. William P. McClure and Van Miller (Urbana, Ill.: Bureau of Educational Research, College of Education, University of Illinois, 1959).

Carrol, John J., and Seymour Sacks. "Local Sources of Local Revenues," *1961 Proceedings of the National Tax Association*, Seattle, 294–311.

Carter, Richard F. "Voters and Their Schools," Cooperative Research Project No. 308 (William R. Odell, Director). Palo Alto, California: Institute for Communication Research, Stanford University, June 20, 1960. Mimeographed.

Carter, Richard F., and John Sutthoff. "Communities and Their Schools," Cooperative Research Project No. 308 (William R. Odell, Director). Palo Alto, California: School of Education, Stanford University, December 1, 1960.

Colm, Gerhard. "Public Expenditures and Economic Structure in the United States," *Social Research*, IV (February 1936).

Curran, Donald J. "Intra-Metropolitan Competition," *Land Economics*, XL (February 1964), 93–100.

————. "The Metropolitan Problem: Solution from Within?" *National Tax Journal*, XVI (September 1963), 213–23.

Davies, David. "Financing Urban Functions and Services," *Law and Contemporary Problems*, XXX (Winter, 1965).

Davis, Otto A. "Empirical Evidence of Political Influences Upon the Urban Expenditure Policies of Public Schools," *The Public Economy of Urban Communities*, ed. Julius Margolis (Washington: Resources for the Future, Inc., 1965).

Downs, Anthony. "Metropolitan Growth and Future Political Problems," *Land Economics* (November 1961), 311.

Ecker-Racz, L. Laszlo. "Foreign Scholar Ponders the 1957 Census of Governments," *National Tax Journal*, XII (June 1959), 97–115.

————. "Whither State and Local Finance," *Journal of Finance*. Papers and Proceedings of the Twenty-Second Annual Meeting of American Finance Association (December 1960).

Ecker-Racz, L. Laszlo, and Eugene P. McLoone. State School Finance Laws Workshop. National School Board Association, 1968.

Educational Policies Commission. "Educational Independence and Human Values," *Perspectives on the Economics of Public Education, Readings in School Finance and Business Management,* ed. Charles S. Benson (Boston: Houghton Mifflin Company, 1963).

Eliot, Thomas H. *"Toward An Understanding of Public School Politics," American Political Science Review,* LII (December 1959).

Erickson, Donald A., and Andrew M. Greeley. *"Non Public Schools and Metropolitanism"* in Education Yearbook, 1966 (Chicago: National Society for the Study of Education, 1968).

Feinberg, Mordecai S. "The Implications of Core-City Decline for the Fiscal Structure of the Core City," *National Tax Journal,* XVII (September 1964).

Firman, William D. "Fiscal Independence of School Systems," paper presented to the Committee on Educational Finance of the National Education Association, April, 1965.

Fisher, Glenn W. "Determinants of State and Local Government Expenditures: A Preliminary Analysis," *National Tax Journal,* XIV (December 1961), 349–55.

———. "Interstate Variation in State and Local Government Expenditures," *National Tax Journal,* XVII (March 1964), 71–73.

Fisher, Glenn W., and Robert P. Fairbanks. "The Politics of Property Taxation," *Administrative Science Quarterly* (June 1947).

Friedman, Milton. "The Role of Government in Education," *Perspectives on the Economics of Public Education, Readings in School Finance and Business Management,* ed. Charles S. Benson (Boston: Houghton Mifflin Company, 1963).

Glazer, Nathan. "The School as an Instrument in Planning," *Journal of the American Institute of Planners,* XXV (November 1959), 191–95.

Greer, Colin. "Immigrants, Negroes and the Public Schools," *Urban Review,* 3 (January 1969), 9–12.

Greer, Scott. "Social Change and the Metropolitan Problem," *Metropolitan Issues: Social, Governmental, Fiscal,* ed. Guthrie S. Birkhead. Background Papers for the Third Annual Faculty Seminar on Metropolitan Research, 1961 (Syracuse: Syracuse University, 1962).

Groves, Harold M., and C. Harry Kahn. "Stability of State and Local Tax Yields," *American Economic Review,* XLII (March 1952), 87–94.

Hansen, Niles M. "The Structure and Determinants of Local Public Investment Expenditures," *Review of Economics Statistics,* XLVII (May 1965), 150–62.

Havighurst, Robert J. "City-School Cooperation in Developing Educational Policy and Practice," paper presented at the meeting of International City Managers Association, September 21, 1965.

Hawley, Amos H. "The Incorporation Trend in Metropolitan Areas, 1900–1950," *Journal of American Institute of Planners,* XXV (February 1959).

———. "Metropolitan Population and Municipal Government Expenditures in Central Cities," *Cities and Society,* ed. Paul K. Hatt and Albert J. Reiss, Jr. (New York: The Free Press, 1959).

Henderson, Harold L. "State Aids as a Possible Revenue Source for Cities," *Bulletin of the National Tax Association* (November 1946), 43–48.

Herson, Lawrence J.R., Fr. "The Lost World of Municipal Government," *American Political Science Review* (June 1957), 330–45.

Hirsch, Werner Z. "The Costs of Public Education," *Perspectives on the Economics of Public Education, Readings in School Finance and Business Management,* ed. Charles S. Benson (Boston: Houghton Mifflin Company, 1963).

―――. "Determinants of Public Education Expenditures," *National Tax Journal,* XIII (March 1960), 29–40.

―――. "Expenditure Implications of Metropolitan Growth and Consolidation," *Review of Economics and Statistics,* XLI (August 1959), 232–41.

―――. "Fiscal Impact of Industrialization on Schools," *Review of Economics and Statistics,* XLVI (May 1964), 198–208.

―――. "Measuring Factors Affecting Expenditure Levels for Local Government Services," St. Louis: Metropolitan St. Louis Survey, 1957. Mimeographed.

―――. "Spillover of Public Education Costs and Benefits," Cooperative Research Project No. 1045. Mimeographed.

Holland, Lynwood M. "Atlanta Pioneers in Merger: City Area Tripled and Services are Divided with County in Award-winning Movement to Solve Metropolitan Problem," *National Municipal Review* (April 1952).

Hollander, T. Edward. "Fiscal Independence and Large City School Systems," *Educating an Urban Population,* (Beverly Hills: Sage Publications, 1967.)

Hoyt, Homer. "Economics Background of Cities," *Journal of Land and Public Utility Economics,* XVII (February 1941), 188–95.

Jones, Victor. "Local Governmental Organization in Metropolitan Area," *The Future of Cities and Urban Redevelopment,* ed. Coleman Woodbury (Chicago: University of Chicago Press, 1953).

Kee, Woo Sik. "City-Suburban Differentials in Local Government Fiscal Effort," *National Tax Journal,* XXI (June 1968), 183–89.

Kuh, Edwin, and John R. Meyer. "Correlation and Regression Estimates When the Data are Ratios," *Econometrica,* XXIII (October 1955), 400–16.

Kurnow, Ernest. "Determinants of State and Local Expenditures Reexamined," *National Tax Journal,* XVI (September 1963), 252–53.

Leonard, Lawrence A. "State and Local Governmental Revenue Structures: A National and Regional Analysis," *National Tax Journal* (March 1958).

Lindblom, Charles E. "Decision Making in Taxation and Expenditures," *Public Finances: Needs, Sources and Utilization,* National Bureau of Economic Research (Princeton: Princeton University Press, 1961).

Long, Norton E. "The Local Community As an Ecology of Games," *American Journal of Sociology,* LXIX (November 1958), 251–61.

Mann, Arthur. "A Historic Overview: The Lumpenproletariat, Education and Compensatory Action," *The Quality of Inequality: Urban and Suburban Schools* (University of Chicago Center of Policy Study, 1968), 9–26.

Margolis, Julius. "Metropolitan Finance Problems: Territories, Functions, and Growth," *Public Finances: Needs, Sources, and Utilization,* National Bureau of Economic Research (Princeton: Princeton University Press, 1961).

———. "Municipal Fiscal Structure in a Metropolitan Area," *Journal of Political Economy,* LXV (June 1957), 225–36.

———. "On Municipal Land Policy for Fiscal Gains," *National Tax Journal,* IX (September 1956).

Martin, Roscoe C. "Action in Metropolis: Local Government Adaptation to Changing Urban Needs Assumes a Variety of Forms," *National Civic Review* (June and July 1961).

McClure, William P. "Structures of Educational Government: As Viewed by the Educator," *Government of Public Education for Adequate Policy Making,* ed. William P. McClure and Van Miller (Urbana, Ill.: Bureau of Educational Research, College of Education, University of Illinois, 1959).

McLure, Charles. "Tax Exporting in the United States: Estimates for 1962," *National Tax Journal,* XX (March 1967), 49–67.

Minar, David W. "Interactions of School and Non-School Governments in Metropolitan Areas," *Educational Yearbook, 1966* (Chicago: National Society for the Study of Education, 1968).

Monypenny, Phillip. "A Political Analysis of Structures for Educational Policy Making," *Government of Public Education for Adequate Policy Making,* ed. William P. McClure and Van Miller (Urbana, Ill.: Bureau of Educational Research, College of Education, University of Illinois, 1959).

Moseley, Alfred A. "A British View of American Schools," *The World's Work,* VII, No. 4 (February 1904).

Mueller, Eva. "Public Attitudes Toward Fiscal Programs," *Quarterly Journal of Economics,* LXXVII (May 1963), 210–35.

Munse, Albert R. "Weighting Factors in State Foundation Programs," *Proceedings of Eighth National Conference on School Finance* (Washington, D.C.: National Education Association, 1965), 26–62.

Musgrave, Richard A. "Approaches to Fiscal Theory of Political Federalism," *Public Finances: Needs, Sources, and Utilization* (Princeton: Princeton University Press, 1961).

———. "The Classification of Public Goods," *Perspectives on the Economics of Public Education, Readings in School Finance and Business Management,* ed. Charles S. Benson (Boston: Houghton Mifflin Company, 1963).

Mushkin, Selma J. "Intergovernmental Aspects of Local Expenditure Decisions," *Public Expenditure Decisions in the Urban Community,* ed. Howard G. Schaller (Baltimore: Johns Hopkins Press, 1963).

Ostrom, Vincent, *et al.* "Organization of Government in Metropolitan Areas," *American Political Science Review,* LV (December 1961), 831.

Ostrom, Vincent, Charles M. Tiebout, and Robert Warren. "The Organization of Government in Metropolitan Areas: A Theoretical Inquiry," *American Political Science Review,* LV (December 1961).

Penniman, Clara. "The Politics of Taxation," *Politics in the American States: A Comparative Analysis,* ed. Herbert Jacob and Kenneth N. Vines (Boston: Little, Brown and Company, 1965).

Polley, John W. "Educational Expenditures in High Expenditure and Low Expenditure School Districts in New York State," New York: Teachers College, Columbia University, 1964. Mimeographed.

Ratliff, Charles E., Jr. "Centralization of Government Expenditures for Education and Highways in North Carolina," *National Tax Journal,* September 1956).

———. "Centralization, Ability, and Effort in School Finance," *National Tax Journal,* XIII (March 1960), 41–44.

Renshaw, Edward F. "A Note on the Expenditure Effect of State Aid to Education," *Journal of Political Economy,* LXVIII (April 1960), 170–74.

Rothenberg, Jerome. "A Model of Economic and Political Decision-Making," *The Public Economy of Urban Communities,* ed. Julius Margolis (Washington: Resources for the Future, Inc., 1965).

Sacks, Seymour. "Central City and Suburban Public Education: Fiscal Needs, Fiscal Resources and Fiscal Realities," *Educational Yearbook, 1966* (Chicago: National Society for the Study of Education, 1968).

———. "Metropolitan Fiscal Disparities," *Journal of Finance,* XXIII (May 1968) 229–50.

———. "Present Patterns and Historical Trends in Educational Expenditure: The Constraints on the Planning for Education in Developed Nations," *World Yearbook of Education, 1967* (London: Evans Bros., 1967).

Sacks, Seymour, and Alan K. Campbell. "Fiscal Zoning Game," *Municipal Finance,* XXXVI (1964), 140–49.

Sacks, Seymour, and Robert Harris. "The Determinants of State and Local Government Expenditures and Intergovernmental Flow of Funds," *National Tax Journal,* XVII (March 1964).

Sacks, Seymour, and David C. Ranney. "Suburban Education: A Fiscal Analysis," *Urban Affairs Quarterly,* I (September 1966).

Salisbury, Robert H. "State Politics and Education" *Politics and the American States* (Boston: Little, Brown and Company, 1965).

Samuelson, Paul A. "Diagramatic Exposition of a Theory of Public Expenditures," *Review of Economics and Statistics,* XXXVII (November 1955), 350–56.

———. "The Pure Theory of Public Expenditures," *Review of Economics and Statistics,* XXXVI (November 1954), 387–89.

Saville, Lloyd. "Regional Contrasts in the Development of Local Public Finance," *National Tax Journal* (June 1962).

Sayre, Wallace S. "Urbanism and Government, 1957–1977: A Rejoinder," *Annals of the American Academy of Political and Social Science,* CCCXIV (November 1957), 82–85.

Sazama, Gerald. "Equalization of Property Taxes for the Nation's Largest Central Cities," *National Tax Journal,* XVIII (June 1965), 51–61.

Schlesinger, Joseph A. "A Two-Dimensional Measure of Inter-Party Competition," *American Political Science Review* (December 1955).

Schmandt, Henry J. "The Area Council Approach to Metropolitan Government," *Public Management,* XLII (February 1960).

Schmandt, Henry J., and G. Ross Stephens. "Local Government Expenditures," *Land Economics,* XXXIX (November 1963).

———. "Measuring Municipal Output," *National Tax Journal,* XIII (December 1960), 369–75.

Schnore, Leo F. "The Growth of Metropolitan Suburbs," *American Sociological Review,* XXII (April 1957), 164–73.

Shapiro, Harvey. "Economics of State and Local Government Finance," *Land Economics,* XXXIX (May 1963).

———. "Measuring Local Government Output: A Comment," *National Tax Journal,* XIV (December 1961), 394–97.

Shapiro, Sherman. "Some Socio-Economic Determinants of Expenditures for Education; Southern and Other States Compared," *Comparative Education Review,* VI (October 1962), 160–66.

Simon, Herbert A. "The Incidence of A Tax on Urban Real Property," *Readings in the Economics of Taxation,* ed. Richard A. Musgrave and Carl S. Shoup (Homewood, Illinois: Richard D. Irwin, Inc., 1959).

Spangler, Richard. "The Effect of Population Growth Upon State and Local Government Expenditures," *National Tax Journal* (June 1963).

Stephens, G. Ross, and Henry J. Schmandt. "Revenue Patterns of Local Governments," *National Tax Journal,* XV (December 1962).

Suits, Daniel B. "Use of Dummy Variables in Regression Equations," *Journal of the American Statistical Association,* LII (December 1957), 548–81.

Tiebout, Charles M. "An Economic Theory of Fiscal Decentralization," *Public Finances: Needs, Sources, and Utilization* (Princeton: Princeton University Press, 1961).

———. "A Pure Theory of Local Expenditures," *The Journal of Political Economy,* LXIV (October 1956).

———. "Economics of Scale and Metropolitan Governments," *Review of Economics and Statistics,* XLIV (November 1960), 442–44.

Tiebout, Charles M., and David B. Houston. "Metropolitan Finance Reconsidered: Budget Functions and Multi-Level Governments," *Review of Economics and Statistics,* XLIV (November 1962), 412–17.

Usdan, Michael D. "New York State's Educational Conference Board: A Coalition in Transition," *Phi Delta Kappan,* XLIX (February 1968), 328–31.

Vernon, Raymond. "Production and Distribution in the Large Metropolis,"

Annals of the American Academy of Political and Social Science, CCCXIV (November 1957).

Weisbrod, Burton. "Geographic Spillover Effects and the Allocation of Resources to Education," *The Public Economy of Urban Communities,* ed. Julius Margolis (Washington, D.C.: Resources for the Future, Inc., 1965).

————. "Preventing High School Dropouts," *Measuring Benefits of Government Investments* (Washington, D.C.: Brookings Institution, 1963).

Wood, Robert C. "Metropolitan Government 1975: An Extrapolation of Trends," *American Political Science Review* (1958), 108–22.

Index